Tracing Genres through Organizations

Acting with Technology

Bonnie Nardi, Victor Kaptelinin, and Kirsten Foot, editors

Tracing Genres through Organizations: A Sociocultural Approach to Information Design, Clay Spinuzzi, 2003

Tracing Genres through Organizations
A Sociocultural Approach to Information Design

Clay Spinuzzi

The MIT Press
Cambridge, Massachusetts
London, England

This book was set in Sabon on 3B2 by Asco Typesetters, Hong Kong.
Printed and bound in the United States of America.

Library of Congress Cataloging-in-Publication Data

Spinuzzi, Clay.
  Tracing genres through organization : a sociocultural approach to information design / Clay Spinuzzi.
    p.   cm. — (Acting with technology)
  Includes bibliographical references and index.
  ISBN 0-262-19491-0 (hc. : alk. paper)
  1. Information technology—Case studies. 2. Organization—Case studies.
I. Title. II. Series.
HC79.I55S675   2003
303.48'33—dc21   2003046406

10 9 8 7 6 5 4 3 2 1

Contents

Series Foreword

The MIT Press *Acting with Technology* series is concerned with the study of meaningful human activity as it is mediated by tools and technologies. The goal of the series is to publish the best new books—both research monographs and textbooks—that contribute to an understanding of technology as a crucial facet of human activity enacted in rich social and physical contexts.

The focus of the series is on tool-mediated processes of working, playing, and learning in and across a wide variety of social settings. The series explores developments in postcognitivist theory and practice from the fields of sociology, communication, education, and organizational studies, as well as from science and technology studies, human-computer interaction and computer-supported collaborative work. It aims to encompass theoretical frameworks including cultural-historical activity theory, actor network theory, distributed cognition, and those developed through ethnomethodological and grounded theory approaches.

In the first book of the series, Clay Spinuzzi offers a new perspective on work mediated by information technologies. The book brings to the foreground the evolutionary development of work practices through the everyday, collaborative, creative efforts of the actual users of technology. This aspect of computer-mediated work is often neglected by researchers and practitioners. Typical user studies, even those conducted according to most versions of user-centered design, focus on user needs and problems that should be addressed by specially trained designers, but the studies often ignore the invisible innovations of various kinds made in the course of everyday work to address the same or similar needs and problems.

To analyze the evolution of mediated work practices, Spinuzzi proposes a new methodology called *genre tracing*. This methodology, which draws on both genre theory and activity theory, enables the identification of integral units of work—official and unofficial genres—and follows their transformations at several levels of analysis concurrently. By providing insight into developmental transformations of mediated work, genre tracing can help capture the "design solutions" emerging in daily work and integrate them into new, more useful and usable systems and applications. Therefore, this analytical tool, and the book as a whole, will be of interest to both researchers and practitioners involved in the design of information technologies.

Bonnie Nardi
Victor Kaptelinin
Kirsten Foot

Preface

Denise Schmandt-Besserat argued in 1986 that Sumerian writing, which was at that time considered the oldest example of writing, essentially started as a quirky Sumerian accounting system. According to her account, tax collectors began making clay tokens representing livestock, bushels of grain, and containers of oil to tally the actual goods they had collected. Since it became unwieldy to carry around these tokens, eventually Sumerian bureaucrats began making clay "envelopes" to hold them. And since it was not possible to see inside these envelopes, they would press each token into the side of the clay envelope to make an imprint before firing it. The resulting group of impressions functioned as a tally of the livestock. Eventually some clever accountant realized that once the impressions were made, the tokens were moot. Soon the envelopes became round tablets and scribes eventually began imitating the tokens' impressions with a stylus. The rest, as they say, is history.

If Schmandt-Besserat's origin tale is correct, writing—perhaps the most powerful and protean tool we have ever devised, the one so many ancients believed to be a gift from the gods—can be traced back to a series of slapdash innovations largely meant to ease the lives of clerical workers. In the short term, these innovations were more or less invisible. Schmandt-Besserat estimates that 4,700 years went by between the invention of tokens and the innovation of clay envelopes; another 50 years or so went by between that innovation and the next one, that of impressing the tokens onto the envelopes. Another 100 years went by before the envelopes became tablets.

Contemporary workplaces are arguably even more fertile places for such innovations than the Fertile Crescent turned out to be, and innovations ripple through these workplaces much more quickly. Yet workers' innovations often continue to be invisible. They generally do not fit the accepted, official ways of doing things, so they tend to be ephemeral and rarely spread beyond the individual or small group that originated them. Only a very few are officially adopted by an organization and spread to a wider audience.

Genre tracing is a methodology for studying these ephemeral, invisible, ubiquitous innovations. It is designed to help examine these innovations in sociocultural terms, to scrutinize their genealogies, explore the contingencies that inspire them, and plot their trajectories within the activities they mediate. Genre tracing draws on genre theory to provide a unit of analysis, genre, for studying particular types of innovations as they evolve to respond to recurrent problems. It draws on activity theory to provide a theory of mediation and an examination of the different levels of activity in a given organization. The result of this synthesis is a sociocultural approach to understanding information design, one that provides a quite different picture from many of the popular user-centered design approaches normally brought to bear on this sort of problem. Whereas many user-centered design approaches tend to bury or replace these innovations, genre tracing seeks to forefront them as organic and necessary ways that workers adapt information to support their own endeavors.

To illustrate this methodology, in this book I draw on four interrelated studies of Iowa traffic workers using a database of traffic accidents. These workers came from various fields, labored in a variety of workplaces across the state, and met a wide variety of institutional and disciplinary goals. Along the way, they developed a startling array of ad hoc innovations to better adapt the database to their activities. Taken as a whole, these innovations can tell us a great deal about the activities in which workers labor and how designed information supports or fails to support that labor. Beyond *evaluating* information design, furthermore, these insights have interesting repercussions for *guiding* information design. In the last chapter, I explore those repercussions.

This book would not have come about without the help of many, many people. The editors of the Acting with Technology series, Bonnie Nardi, Victor Kaptelinin, and Kirsten Foot, were kind enough to accept my manuscript and to provide me with excellent editorial comments. Robert Prior at MIT Press shepherded the project through, providing details, procedures, and all sorts of help for a first-time author. David R. Russell worked closely with me on chapters 1 through 5; his imprint on this book is exceedingly deep. Davida Charney, my generous mentor at the University of Texas, was instrumental in helping me to organize and polish the manuscript. Roger Baer, Rebecca Burnett, Daniel Douglas, Lee-Ann Kastman, Dorothy Winsor, and Mark Zachry provided illuminating comments on various chapters at various stages of the project. Chapter 2 benefited greatly from the comments of my spring 2001 graduate students at Texas Tech University.

At Iowa State University's Center for Transportation Research and Education, Reginald Soulreyette, Michael Pawlovich, and Bradley Estochen lent their time and software to me, arranged for me to meet traffic workers, and helped this project in many other ways. At the Iowa Department of Transportation, Joyce Emery and John Nervig provided advice, information, and contacts. Traffic workers all over Iowa graciously allowed me to survey, observe, videotape, and interview them, as did several students in Reg Soulreyette's community and regional planning class in spring 1999.

This book is dedicated to my wife, Gail, my daughter, Isabella, and "everyone else in the house."

1

Introduction: Tyrants, Heroes, and Victims in Information Design

At a police station in the Midwest, a police officer named Barbara starts up the DOS-based database that she will use for locating and analyzing traffic accidents in a particular area. According to the software's manual, she should first unroll a three-by-three-foot map of the area, which is overlaid with six-digit numerical coordinates called node numbers. Then she should look up the node number for each intersection she is investigating and type them, one by one, into a dialog box. The cumbersome map is rich in unnecessary detail, takes the entire space of a cleared desk, and must be held down by paperweights so that it will not roll back up; it's no surprise that Barbara avoids using it. Instead, she opens a folder and takes out a Post-It™ note on which she had written down a series of node numbers some months before. The unwieldy node map is replaced by a conveniently sized note that holds only the details that she needs.

A common trope in the literature of user-centered design is the worker-as-victim: the everyday Joe or Jane who is oppressed by an unjust tyranny and in need of rescue. The tyrannical system could be imposed by selfish, shortsighted employers (Bravo 1993[1]), an antidemocratic capitalist system (Ehn 1989; Bjerknes and Bratteteig 1995), managers who do not understand or are opposed to the needs of workers (Bødker 1991; Gronbæk et al. 1993), a flawed work structure (Coble et al. 1996; Holtzblatt and Beyer 1996; Ramey, Rowberg, and Robinson 1996), poorly designed tools that do not take into account how workers actually get things done (Dumas and Redish 1993; Gronbæk, Kyng, and Mogensen 1993; Rubin 1994), or even a theoretical stance (Johnson

1998). The worker-as-victim is portrayed as needing to be rescued by a heroic figure, an information designer. This heroic figure is enlightened, principled, and capable, and is able to employ user-centered design methods to defeat the tyrannical system and rescue the victims—sometimes through the invention of a benevolent work structure (Beyer and Holtz-blatt 1998), sometimes by providing a better tool for accomplishing work activity (Bødker and Gronbæk 1996), sometimes by emancipating workers through organizing labor in a class struggle with management (Ehn 1989, 1993; Bjerknes and Bratteteig 1995; see Spinuzzi 2002e for a review), and sometimes by providing a more sensible theoretical system (Johnson 1998). But in any case, the designer listens to the worker-victims, synthesizes their comments and feedback, and develops the means of their rescue. The resulting solutions, it is asserted, lead to sustainability (Hackos, Hammar, and Elser 1997; Hackos and Redish 1998), worker empowerment (Beyer and Holtzblatt 1998; Bravo 1993; Clement and Van den Besselaar 1993; Ehn 1993), and the examination of users and technology use from their perspective (Johnson 1998). Designers strive for a well-considered system that, if properly constructed, will liberate workers who desperately need to be rescued. Indeed, Geoff Cooper and John Bowers (1995) note that human-computer interaction research in general, and user-centered design in particular, often justifies and legitimizes itself through this sort of "compassionate discourse." "It is important to recognize the rhetorical functionality of these characterizations of the user for HCI," they tell us. They add that "it is not so much that users are angry, frightened, and different from designers, it is more that, for this way of legitimizing HCI, they *have to be*" (p. 51).

But in the quotation that opened this chapter, Barbara is not waiting around to be rescued. Although the software is not set up to facilitate the particular tasks in which she is engaged, she does not wring her hands and wait for an information designer to come slay the dragon. She picks up available tools, adapts them in idiosyncratic ways, and makes do. Through these "invisible" innovations (Nardi and Engeström 1999; Suchman 1995) she subverts the information system, inventing her own ways to turn it to her needs.

Workers like Barbara tend to create their own practices, tools, and texts constantly, sometimes in cooperation with the existing information systems, sometimes in competition with them. For instance, Mark Zachry (2001a; see also Spinuzzi and Zachry 2000) describes computer users who co-opted managerial genres such as administrative memos to customize computer documentation. Christian Heath and Paul Luff (2000) relate how medical practitioners, construction workers, and personnel working for the London Underground rejected the use of computer technology for keeping records, relying instead on older paper documents that were more mobile and accessible. And Barbara Mirel (1988) notes that workers in her study avoided relying on official documentation by developing unofficial ways of sharing information, such as via intraoffice cliques and residential experts. As Geoffrey Bowker and Susan Leigh Star (1999, 159; see also Star 1995) conclude, "Imposed standards will produce workarounds. Because imposed standards cannot account for every local contingency, users will tailor the standardized forms, information systems, schedules, and so forth to meet their needs."

The messiness of everyday work life—the unofficial, unpredictable ways workers assert their own agency, turn to their own problem-solving skills, and individually or cooperatively design practices, tools, and texts to deal with recurrent problems—is reflected in a considerable number of thoughtful studies (e.g., Kyng and Mathiassen 1997; Nardi 1996). But as Button and Dourish (1996) point out, the problem comes about when attempting to link naturalistic studies, which describe these local innovations, with design methods, which translate the findings into design work. As I argue later in this chapter, many of the most popular user-centered design methods assume that the goal of research is to inform *centralized solutions*; they assume that design solutions must spring from, or at least be ratified and promoted by, decision makers with specialized knowledge. Even when unofficial user innovations have been proven useful, researchers working within these approaches tend to take such innovations as rough solutions to common underlying problems, solutions that should be officially refined and consolidated by a trained designer if these underlying problems are to be truly solved. If individuals such as Barbara have developed an innovative way to get work done, these designers might examine that unofficial innovation primarily so that they can develop an official, approved, standardized version that everyone can use. The operating assumption is that if innovations are to be effective, the worker-victims' many coping strategies must be united and refined by the designer-hero.

This operating assumption is particularly troubling to me because it is gaining a foothold in my own discipline, rhetoric, particularly in the subfield of technical communication. User-centered design approaches have correctly been seen as promising new avenues for analyzing and understanding audiences, but as I argue later in this chapter, the user-centered design approaches that have most often been adopted are those that cast workers are victims and designers as heroes.

In this book I propose a new understanding of technologically mediated work, for information designers in general and particularly for rhetoricians and technical communicators. I turn away from the trope of the worker-as-victim and its tendency to minimize or officialize workers' innovations. Instead, I place these innovations at center stage: I examine the crucial subversive interactions in which workers routinely engage as they use information systems to accomplish their activities. I do this not to heroically rescue the workers from a patronizing and disempowering trope; as we will see, they often do a pretty good job of "rescuing" themselves. Instead my goal is to better understand why information design so often fails to catch on and become sustainable, why workers so often alter the designed artifacts (particularly textual artifacts) they are presented with, and how designers might approach design tasks as true partnerships that result in designs flexible enough to be adopted.

To pursue these issues, I outline an alternative field methodology for investigating designed artifacts in the context of work activity—*genre tracing*—and illustrate it through four studies of diverse workers in a loose network of governmental agencies. Genre tracing bears a strong resemblance to the activity theory–based approaches that have been gaining ground in human-computer interaction and computer-supported cooperative work (e.g., Nardi 1996). However, it is particularly suited to applications in rhetoric and technical communication because it draws from rhetorical theory and makes texts (in the broad sense) central to its investigations. Although I do not go the extra step of outlining a design methodology in this book, in the final chapter I discuss some implications that this book has for information design.

At the same time, I believe that trained information designers can contribute much to the emergent innovations of workers, not by replacing those innovations with centralized solutions, but by helping to design systems that workers can modify. This book should not be read as advocating quietism, the notion that systems can and should always repair themselves. In fact, workers' innovations are disparate and often of the chewing-gum-and-bailing-wire variety; without designers to periodically consolidate and rethink these solutions, any given activity can begin to disintegrate as disparate solutions lead groups of workers in different directions. Rather, this book offers a methodology that can ideally encourage trained information designers and innovative workers to enter into true partnerships.

In this opening chapter, I first describe the user-centered design discussion as it is making its way into technical communication. I am especially interested in how the victimhood trope is used to justify the adoption of user-centered design approaches in technical communication. I then examine how a subset of user-centered design methods, what I call *fieldwork-to-formalization* methods, positions users in its characterization of workers, fieldwork, and formalizations. Next, I draw on M. M. Bakhtin's discussion of official and unofficial discourse to frame an alternative methodology: genre tracing. Finally, I briefly describe the genre tracing methodology and how it positions users.

"WRITERS, WRITERS EVERYWHERE": POSITIONING THE USER IN TECHNICAL COMMUNICATION

Technical communication is based in rhetoric, but it also draws from psychology, anthropology, sociology, and related approaches. Lately, technical communicators have also sought to align their field more closely with information design (e.g., Geisler et al. 2001; Hart-Davidson 2001) and other interdisciplinary fields such as human-computer interaction and computer-supported cooperative work. This realignment has led technical communicators to adopt methods from the related disciplines. And user-centered design methods appear to be a strong match, since they combine a humanistic mission of advocating for the audience, new empirical approaches to the ancient art of audience analysis, and strong frameworks for translating audience insights into design suggestions. These themes come together, for instance, in Smart and Whiting's contextual design study of office software. "Frequently," they note, "technical communicators view themselves as users' advocates, with the mistaken notion that, as nondevelopers who also use an application designed by someone else, they know what users want and need." But Smart and Whiting's team found that "if they truly wanted to become user advocates, they needed direct contact with users" (2002, 159), contact that they translated into information design through a popular user-centered design approach.

The introduction of user-centered design to technical communication is instructive because of the ways it is positioned and justified. In introducing user-centered design to technical communication, scholars have sometimes characterized information design as dichotomized between *user-centered design* and its opposite, *system-centered design*. Although I discuss these two approaches in more detail below, it is important to keep two things in mind about how these approaches are characterized. First, they are characterized as totalizing: every design approach and every evaluation of designed information can be categorized as being on one side or the other of the system-centered/user-centered divide. Second, few if any technical communication scholars advocate a system-centered view; system-centered design functions almost exclusively as a straw person, a demonstrably poor choice in contrast with the more favored user-centered design. (See Mirel 1998a for a related argument.)

In technical communication, user-centered design has been examined most extensively by Robert Johnson in his book *User-Centered Technology* (1998; for other technical communication literature on user-centered design, see Dumas and Redish 1993; Hackos and Redish 1998; Rubin 1994; Schriver 1997; Wixon and Ramey 1996). In the discussion that follows, I use Johnson's book to explore the methodological assumptions that underlie user-centered design as it has been represented in technical communication.

Methodological Assumptions of User-Centered Design

As Patricia Sullivan and James Porter (1997, 11) point out, in research literature the terms *method* and *methodology* are often used interchangeably. Although these terms deal substantially with the same subject—the question of how to bring a coherent approach to research—they express quite different things. A *method* is a way of investigating phenomena; a *methodology* is the theory, philosophy, heuristics, aims, and values that underlie, motivate, and guide the method. The distinction is important to keep in mind as we explore the methodological assumptions underpinning user-centered design as it has been represented in technical communication. As we will see, these methodological assumptions include the trope of worker-as-victim, and that trope shapes the methods and the sorts of things one might expect to learn from them. Furthermore, user-centered design is implicitly portrayed as the sole alternative to system-centered design.

Johnson sets up the dichotomy between system-centered design and user-centered design quite clearly, arguing that "the user-centered view is philosophically and practically at the opposite end of the spectrum from the system-centered view" (p. 129; see also p. 30). (Johnson uses system-centered design as a straw person for providing a contrast with user-centered design; in fact, he admits that there are few advocates of system-centered design (p. 124).) He draws several comparisons between system-centered and user-centered design throughout the book, both explicitly and implicitly (see especially pp. 25–33). Three of these are listed below:

- Whereas system-centered design is formalist (p. 25), user-centered design is social constructionist (p. 93).
- Whereas system-centered design is rationalist, determinist, and modernist (pp. 25–27), user–centered design is postrationalist, nondeterminist, and postmodernist.
- Whereas system-centered design involves centrally controlled design (pp. 25–27), user-centered design involves collective, cooperative design (pp. 30–32).

Indeed, the methodological assumptions of the two design approaches appear to be just about as far apart as they can get—binary opposites. Perhaps the most important comparison is the first one. In Johnson's view, system-centered design is founded on formalist thought, "based upon models of technology that focus on the artifact or system as primary, and on the notion that the inventors or developers of the technology know best its design, dissemination, and intended use." It perceives technology, people, and context "as constituting one system that operates in a rational manner toward the achievement of pre-determined goals" (p. 25). Johnson asserts that user-centered design, on the other hand, is founded on social constructionist thought, which is "based on the concept that reality is mutable, that there are no certain truths, and that knowledge is constructed through communally created knowledge and action." In this view, technology "can be interpreted and reinterpreted depending on the people involved, the context or situation in which it is designed, developed, or deployed, and the historical moment it resides within" (p. 93).

Johnson's concern is with how people are empowered or disempowered by the design of texts and other technological artifacts. He wants to "examine users and the phenomena of technological use from their perspective" (p. 4). In short, Johnson sees users as sociopolitically empowered through the help of a designer (in this case, a writer), someone who identifies with the users and who has the authority and skill to transform the way they perform their goal-directed actions—authority and skill that the users themselves do not have. Indeed, the things that Johnson promises to do in the book include:

- Recognizing and understanding how "cogs" of society actually have valuable, detailed knowledge (p. 61)
- Revealing moments of human knowledge and the essence of human involvement with technology (p. 132)
- Determining which medium will best fit the user situation and tasks (p. 133)
- Providing audience analysis for underpinning design work (p. 145)

Johnson's goals are laudable, reflecting the humanist values that underpin technical communication and opposing the disempowering effects of system-centered, Taylorist approaches. Yet in the way they are framed, these goals assume the victimhood trope. They position users as unable or unqualified to undertake design work on their own. Users are not cast as agents who initiate and implement change themselves. Despite the assertion, often repeated in user-centered design circles, that the user is a codesigner (e.g., Beyer and Holtzblatt 1998; Salvo 2001; Wixon and Ramey 1996), *users do not actually control the design*, either in Johnson's book or in the wider technical communication literature on user-centered design. At most, they nominate ideas that the designer then might choose to ratify during the final design of the artifact. Although Johnson criticizes system-centered design for assuming that designers of technology "know best its design, dissemination, and intended use" (p. 25), his brand of user-centered design makes the same assumption. The difference is that whereas system-centered designers rely solely on their own knowledge of the system, user-centered designers also draw on their compassionate studies of the users.

For instance, in their book on contextual design—the user-centered design method that has gained the most solid foothold in technical communication (see, e.g., Beabes and Flanders 1995; Hackos, Hammar, and Elser 1997; Hackos et al. 1995; Raven and Flanders 1996; Smart and Whiting 2002; Smart, Whiting, and DeTienne 2002; Wixon and Ramey 1996)—Beyer and Holtzblatt (1998, 370) say that they want to "co-design the system with the users." But they make clear that this co-designer status is relegated to describing work and providing feedback. Users should emphatically not be expected to understand the designers' work models, which describe the users' activities (p. 369); "It's their job to do their job, not design systems" (p. 371). And their innovations and feedback are useful only when designers consolidate and shape them to support the work models that the users are not able to understand. While users give valuable ideas during the prototyping phase, for instance, the designer "is free to think up a better mechanism" (p. 400).

As we have seen, Johnson casts workers as needing rescue. His list of goals calls for designer/writers to understand, identify with, and analyze the users so they can bequeath empowerment to the worker-victims more effectively; reveal the knowledge that has remained hidden even from the users themselves; determine the optimal media for users' tasks; and analyze users as an audience, the more-or-less passive receivers of the designer/writer's information. The workers are positioned as victims unable to rescue themselves.

Methods

Johnson turns to the methods of participatory design to accomplish his list of goals (see pp. 82–83). Again, these goals are worthwhile and

compelling (as is Johnson's book itself), but they are based in methodological assumptions that position the user as a victim to be rescued.

For instance, Johnson advocates that writers empower users by local-
izing and redesigning one sort of tool—documentation—in such a way
as to codify and formally document the word-of-mouth knowledge
and practices in a company (p. 149). The writers—a great number of
"writers, writers everywhere," in fact—would thus rescue users by consolidating informal, unarticulated practices into official, formal, and
authoritative documents. This process would have to be undertaken
carefully, by trained[2] writers, since the traditionally inflexible genres
of computer documentation structure and constrain users' work in un-
desirable and disempowering ways (pp. 140–141).

An illustration is provided by Johnson's description of a study undertaken by his students, in which they observed and interviewed an individual secretary as she walked through various tasks with a software
manual. The study involved the writers examining the user's work, then
utilizing the results to help redesign the manual. But it did not involve
inviting the user to codesign the manual or examining how the user supplemented the documentation with other practices and artifacts.

To sum up, as technical communicators have adapted user-centered
design approaches to their own field, they have drawn heavily on the
aspects that emphasize the victimhood trope. The trope is a natural
match to technical communication's focus on humanistic ethics, but it
ultimately leads to a paternalistic relationship between designers and
workers. This relationship is particularly reflected in fieldwork-to-
formalization methods such as the user-centered design method most
popular with technical communicators, contextual design (Beyer and
Holtzblatt 1998).

FIELDWORK-TO-FORMALIZATION METHODS: OBSERVING WORKERS, MODELING BEHAVIOR

In much user-centered design work—particularly in a variety of coherent
methods developed in the United States and Britain to help organizations
rapidly design information—descriptive, naturalistic studies of actual
work have been paired with abstract work models. This pairing re-

flects the interdisciplinary nature of user-centered design. The descriptive studies, patterned after the ethnographies used in anthropology and sociology, are meant to unearth the workarounds, innovations, and tacit practices workers have developed. The models, often drawn from management or systems design approaches, are suitable for generalizing, standardizing, regularizing, idealizing, and managing work, as well as for providing brief descriptions to systems designers. It is an uneasy pairing, one that assumes that researchers can easily move from the particular to the general, from divergent local practices to a single ideal model of the work. This disconnect is particularly strong in methods that, in this book, I will call *fieldwork-to-formalization methods*. Examples of fieldwork-to-formalization methods include contextual design (Beyer and Holtzblatt 1998); the research stage of joint application design (JAD; see Wood and Silver 1995); client-led design (Stowell and West 1994); and user-centered information design (Henry 1998); and to a lesser extent coherence (Viller and Somerville 2000) and other applications of rapid ethnography (e.g., Millen 2000). They vary in detail on both the fieldwork and modeling ends. For instance, Millen's approach pairs rapid ethnographies with informal, innovated causal models; JAD turns informal interviews and observations into highly formalized models; and contextual design has a high degree of detail on both ends.

Fieldwork-to-formalization methods are "meant to guide system design through the stages of gathering data from customers, modeling and interpreting that information, and designing and implementing systems based on that information" (Bisantz and Ockerman 2002, 263). That is, they bridge field studies (including naturalistic work observations, unstructured interviews, and analysis of artifacts used in the work) and information design through models or through categorical and sequential descriptions of the work. In doing so, they span boundaries between *organizations* (organizations that need information systems and organizations that produce them; see Korpela, Mursu, and Soriyan 2002) and between *disciplines* (workplace researchers and information designers; see McCarthy 2000). Furthermore, since these methods involve working within short engineering cycles, the data gathering is typically compressed and the analysis is done primarily through the same models used to communicate the results to systems developers (Macaulay, Benyon, and Crerar 2000; for examples, see Beyer and Holtzblatt 1998; Wood and Silver 1995).

Many researchers have called into question the assumption that moving from fieldwork to formalization is unproblematic. For instance, in an issue of *Communications of the ACM* devoted in part to workplace investigations, Liam Bannon (1995, 66; see also Sachs 1995) objects that formalizations are too reductive to capture the nuances of the fieldwork:

> The argument is not whether some level of abstraction and formalization of work processes is possible or desirable, but rather, whether such techniques could in principle capture all that is required, and how to manage what is inevitably left outside the representation. While some simply argue for more powerful representational forms, there has been a growing awareness that the problem is not simply one of richer notations or more ample resources but, more fundamentally, of an inappropriate concept of what can, in principle, be captured in any model of the work process.

So what *does* get captured in these models of the work process? As Yrjö Engeström (1999b, 63, 64) notes in his critique of business process reengineering (BPR)—a movement that is aligned with fieldwork-to-formalization methods (Wood and Silver 1995) and that shares their tendency to optimize work—"Attempts at making everyday practices of work visible are driven by different motives. In various management techniques, the overriding motive of visibilization is control." That motive leads, in Engeström's words, to "a quest for complete rationality and elimination of unnecessary steps." Work-process models tend to represent just such a managerial or organizational view of the work, as Patricia Sachs (1995) points out in her own critique of BPR. This view emphasizes the overall workings of an organization in generalities suitable for regularizing and rationalizing work; it assumes that work has an underlying structure that, once described, can be made more efficient. That is, the goal of such models is not to value workers' innovations themselves but to take them as symptoms of an underlying problem that can then be solved by manipulating the model—to rescue the workers from an inefficient system and empower them to meet management's goals. Naturally, these models are rarely made accessible to the workers whose work they describe.

Below, I discuss in more detail how fieldwork-to-formalization methods position and portray workers; describe the conduct of fieldwork; and translate the results of fieldwork into formalizations such as models, categories, and sequences.

Positioning the User: The Victimhood Trope in Fieldwork-to-Formalization Methods

Like many other user-centered design approaches, fieldwork-to-formalization methods often justify themselves through the victimhood trope. In these methods, designers offer workers freedom from their victimhood, but *victimhood* is conceived as coming from barriers to doing their jobs efficiently, and freedom consequently comes through a process in which their work is increasingly managed, regularized, and rationalized. Their workarounds and innovations are examined, formalized, modeled, collapsed with similar innovations, and finally mandated by the new system—or supplanted by other practices that the designer has determined are better. In other words, this sort of freedom comes through compliance with an increasingly formalized and rationalized work process in which workers may have input, but little or no final say. Workers enjoy *functional empowerment*, in which they are empowered to perform their tasks in a prescribed manner, rather than *democratic empowerment*, in which they have a decision-making role in how their organization operates and how technology fits into their jobs (see Clement 1994; Blomberg, Suchman, and Trigg 1997).

For instance, the contextual design literature emphasizes understanding and empathy for workers (synonymously called "users" or "customers"). "When we participate in the users' world," Holtzblatt and Beyer (1993, 94) say, "we want it shown to us so well that we know it—we want our feet to be sore where their shoes pinch." In fact, contextual design texts frequently include stories and scenarios describing how designers should put themselves in the workers' shoes. But these stories and scenarios, and their solutions, tend to focus on functional empowerment: how to improve the workers' efficiency and productivity by redesigning artifacts and practices. For instance, in the introduction to *Contextual Design*, Beyer and Holtzblatt (1998, 6) describe "the true story of one user trying to do a simple task: A user of a standard office system needs to print a label." After describing the user's frustrating efforts and her eventual abandonment of the task, Beyer and Holtzblatt conclude that "this system supports work poorly. It is poor not because functions are missing but because the system imposes a work model that does not make the job more efficient and does not match the user's expectations" (p. 7). A properly designed system, they argue, "provides an optimal match between the users' current way of working and the work practice introduced by the new system; it changes the work enough to make it more efficient but not so much that people cannot make the transition" (p. 8, their emphasis). The words *efficient* and *optimal* make frequent appearances throughout the rest of the text, underscoring contextual design's commitment to functionally empowering the workers.

Other fieldwork-to-formalization methods similarly position workers as victims of inefficient systems. In his description of user-centered information design, Henry (1998) lists a variety of users' reactions to "unusable" software, such as confusion, frustration, panic, and boredom. The most telling negative reaction is *"misuse or modification*. Those who know the software well may change it to meet personal requirements that do not advance organizational interests" (p. 7). That is, workers' innovations are positioned as a dangerous symptom of workers' victimhood. Similarly, Stowell and West (1994, 22, 29) describe client-led design as a way to avoid "a feeling of insecurity in those most affected," which can be manifested in "lack of cooperation, refusal to use the new information system, sabotage, withdrawal of goodwill, and industrial action." With client-led design, the underlying management problems are "unraveled" and clients buy into the process, which results—at least in the case study that Stowell and West present—in a more efficient company that produces new, high-quality products (Stowell and West 1994, chaps. 6–7).

The victimhood trope, then, is often used to underpin fieldwork-to-formalization methods. Specifically, these methods position workers as sharing management's goals of efficiency and work intensification, but describe the workers' attempts to "do their jobs" as being frustrated by poorly designed work processes and the information artifacts that support them. Workers' innovations are portrayed at best as symptoms of the underlying problem, and sometimes, uncharitably, as wrongheaded and fumbling attempts to resist the system. These innovations are rarely depicted as valuable solutions in their own right and never as solutions that can be allowed to remain under the control of their originators, never as locally grounded practices that can be adopted or rejected at the individual worker's discretion. Design problems are portrayed as systemic and systemwide, meaning that solutions should be implemented at the same scope. Consequently, fieldwork-to-formalization methods typically seek to rectify problems through a compassionate, efficiency-focused investigation of workers' actual work practices and artifacts, followed by a reductive modeling of the fieldwork in management's terms so that designers can develop the most optimal work structure and artifacts.

Which is not to say these workers are being victimized by fieldwork-to-formalization methods. I am not going to appeal to the same trope that I am critiquing! What I want to drive home here is that these methods attempt to fit workers into their story of designerly heroism, while at the same time workers like Barbara are quietly "rescuing" themselves by tailoring workarounds to their local situations.

Gathering Field Data

Given their goal of investigating actual work practices, fieldwork-to-formalization methods draw on a range of fieldwork techniques. These range from extremely informal to somewhat formal methods.

On the informal end of the scale, the research stage of JAD involves JAD facilitators visiting sites, talking with individual workers or groups of workers, looking at artifacts at the interviewees' work location, and informally observing work (Wood and Silver 1995, chap. 5). Facilitators are encouraged to ask workers about their business objectives (such as increasing productivity, decreasing costs, and improving customer satisfaction; see p. 54) and to look out for "distractions" and other breakdowns in work flow (p. 57); they are not encouraged to examine workarounds. Facilitators are not trained in fieldwork.

In the middle of the scale, contextual design involves a highly developed set of techniques that represent the adaptation of "ethnographic research methods to fit the time and resource constraints of engineering" (Holtzblatt and Beyer 1993, 93), including unstructured and semistructured interviews, walkthroughs, and artifact analysis (Beyer and

Holtzblatt 1998, chaps. 2–4; Raven and Flanders 1996). Designers are advised to look for the work's underlying structure and for opportunities to build designs on that existing work structure. Innovations are cast as symptoms of problems and as starting points for global redesign efforts. In this case, investigators are trained in three-day sessions. Similarly, client-led design involves action research, which—as Stowell and West (1994) use the term—mainly consists of interviews in which investigators focus on how various workers construe their organization's problems.

On the more formal end of the scale, coherence and rapid ethnography both involve observational fieldwork by trained researchers, although the fieldwork takes far less time than in the case of standard ethnographies. As Viller and Somerville (2000, 171; see also Millen 2000) say about coherence, "The approach should not be construed as 'ethnography-lite', some cut down or simplified version of ethnography. Rather, the method is informed by cumulative experience of applying ethnographic approaches to the development of requirements for computer-based systems."

These fieldwork approaches have come under attack by trained ethnographers, who complain that fieldwork is a difficult and problematic exercise demanding long training. For instance, Diana Forsythe (1999, 136; see also Cooper et al. 1995; Nyce and Lowgren 1995) critiques how "do-it-yourself ethnography" has been used by investigators untrained in ethnographic methods, including systems designers and content experts:

> The problem is that in ethnography as in some other pursuits, a little knowledge can be a dangerous thing: superficial social research may confer the illusion of increased understanding when in fact no such understanding has been achieved. This problem is illustrated by the nature of recent do-it-yourself ethnography in medical informatics [specifically, a Contextual Design project], in which brief exercises in shadowing, observation, and interviewing have been undertaken from a common sense stance without engaging the questions that define ethnography as anthropologists understand it. Such an exercise can result in a cognitive hall of mirrors. Without addressing basic issues such as the problem of perspective, researchers have no way of knowing whether they have really understood anything of their informants' world view or have simply projected and then "discovered" their own assumptions in the data.

As we saw in the previous subsection, these assumptions are likely to include (1) an underlying work structure that can be reified for the purpose of redesigning work and (2) the presence of workarounds like Barbara's as symptoms of problems in this underlying work structure.

These fieldwork-to-formalization methods share an explicit focus on the actual practices of workers, but the focus tends to be in the service of the victimhood trope. It leads investigators to examine how workers' efficiency is compromised by work practices and artifacts, and views workarounds as symptoms of underlying problems or, at best, rough solutions for the designer to improve and standardize. The methods do not act to sustain, enable, or understand innovations as a vital part of the work.

Building Formalizations

After the fieldwork come the formalizations—the models, categorical descriptions, and sequential descriptions—that can be used to communicate findings to software developers and to describe and design future systems. The object is to zero in on the specific aspects of the work that will affect the redesign. (As Macaulay, Benyon, and Crerar (2000, 40) observe, "Ethnographers tend to report their findings in lengthy monographs. Systems designers are thought to like diagrams with as little text as possible, although our own experiences have not entirely supported this presumption.") Formalizations are used to consolidate the field data and find overall patterns that might shed light on the underlying work structure. That is, they serve to rationalize work.

The formalizations used by the different methods tend to differ widely. On one end, client-led design (Stowell and West 1994) uses ten different high-detail formalizations culled from soft system methodology, structured system analysis and design method, object-oriented analysis, and other sources; on the other, user-centered information design (Henry 1998) employs task description, information-use models, and other relatively low-detail formalizations. Despite their differences, these formalizations tend to consolidate the innovations noted in the fieldwork and construct unified models of the underlying work structure. In doing so, they provide the designers with that which makes them heroes: a special viewpoint on the work that is inaccessible to the workers themselves, one that qualifies them to detect, ratify, and improve the best innovations of the workers. This managerial viewpoint focuses on values such as efficiency and work intensification. Take for instance this passage, in which Holtzblatt and Beyer (1993, 97–98) describe how to fold workers' innovations into the redesigned system:

> Our best ideas for improving the work often come from seeing how a particularly thoughtful person or group has solved their own problems. We build this solution into our abstract work models and our system, so all customers can take advantage of it. Once we have this consolidated model, we study it for problems and inefficiencies. We bring together data from all customers, keeping good ideas, fixing problems, and using technology to combine steps. When done, we have a statement of how our users will work, if we can implement the system to support it.

The consolidated model is not accessible to the workers themselves. As Beyer and Holtzblatt (1998, 369) say, "In Contextual Design, we don't even try to talk to our customers with our work models" because doing so would involve training these workers in this "new language" that explicitly describes aspects of work that the workers have never been able to articulate on their own. The work of reading models and translating them into design cannot (and should not) be left to the workers, who do not (and should not) have the means to rescue themselves: "Customers aren't technologists—they don't know the range of possibilities that technology could support. They may be either unrealistic or excessively cautious as a result. And they don't know what it takes to make a design hang together. And why should they, after all? It's their job to do their job, not to design systems" (p. 371).

Since the workers are not qualified to rescue themselves, they must rely on the heroic design team, whose members are trained in reading these models and are capable and principled enough to turn them into humane design decisions. Workers are allowed to give input on the system, but the designers know best how to design "a coherent response that hangs together as a new work practice" (Beyer and Holtzblatt 1998, 305).

OFFICIAL AND UNOFFICIAL SOLUTIONS

I should make clear at this point that it is not a bad thing for information designers to study how people do their work and to design artifacts and practices that might facilitate that work. Information designers, including technical communicators, *should* be trained, principled, and capable user advocates, and they *should* understand how workers are often constrained and disempowered by existing tools and ways of doing work.

Fieldwork-to-formalization methods have gone a long way toward these goals, and they offer plenty of success stories describing how workers are happy with the results of projects based on them. But these methods leave little room for examining worker agency. They pass over or try to control the unofficial, idiosyncratic, ad hoc solutions such as Barbara's innovation described at the beginning of this chapter. These methods are guided by the managerial goal of a *normative solution*: a tool or set of work practices that, once codified and optimized, can functionally empower the worker-victims.

The trope of worker-as-victim, I contend, devalues the multiple and innovative solutions that workers like Barbara develop, tends to paper over the contingencies to which workers continually adjust, and leads researchers to develop and use analyses that minimize the role of such contingencies while maximizing the role of commonalities in work. As I argue in chapter 2, fieldwork-to-formalization methods tend to assume some sort of structure that underlies the work of a range of workers, a structure that can be investigated, modeled, and repaired in such a way as to solve the workers' general problems. That structure might take the form of contextual design's work models (Beyer and Holtzblatt 1998), the tasks employed in usability testing (Dumas and Redish 1993), and so forth. In these cases, the data collection and analysis methods are designed to shift attention away from local exigencies and toward common problems and common solutions. Workers' innovations are seen as symptoms of an underlying problem; the researcher's role is to pin down that problem and the designer's role is to develop an idealized solution, a solution that may incorporate, but ultimately obviates, workers' local innovations. Thus they tend to minimize the agency of those workers— and miss some of the important differences in how workers undertake and conceptualize their work.

On the other hand, trained designers can avoid common pitfalls of workers' homegrown solutions, which tend to be of the chewing-gum-and-bailing-wire variety. Workers produce solutions that are devious, wily, and cunning, but often these solutions do not involve a deep understanding of the system, and sometimes they even run to superstition. Workers produce solutions that work—but often they do not produce solutions that work well *by their own criteria*, and often those solutions are not promulgated so that other workers can take advantage of them. The drawbacks of these ad hoc solutions, of course, lead designers to attempt to formalize or officialize them. As Star (1995, 111) puts it,

> Organizations attempt strategies that will try to create organizational consistency in the face of strong tensions between formal representations and empirical experience. The tensions arise from the fact that ad hoc strategies, work-arounds, and local knowledge that keeps organizations going [i.e., unofficial solutions] are first deleted from formal representations [i.e., official solutions]. When the formalizations become recipes for action, then further ad hoc work-arounds are necessary to make the prescriptions fit the local circumstances."

Star warns that "this can be an infinitely recursive process" (p. 111). To examine this dynamic, ever-shifting balance between designers' contributions and workers' innovations, I turn to language philosopher M. M. Bakhtin and his distinction between the official and the unofficial (1981, 1986).

Bakhtin argues that two competing impulses shape how we communicate: the centripetal and the centrifugal. The *centripetal* impulse is toward formalization, normalization, regularity, convention, stability—and stasis. Things are metaphorically drawn to the center and become official. In contrast, the *centrifugal* impulse is that of resistance, idiosyncrasy, ad hoc innovation—and chaos. Things metaphorically fly away from the center and become unofficial (Bakhtin 1981, 270–273). As Morson and Emerson (1990, 30) put it, official forces "seek to impose order on an essentially heterogeneous and messy world" while unofficial forces "either purposefully or *for no particular reason* continually disrupt that order."

Note that we are not dealing with a simple two-dimensional continuum or binary opposition. In this metaphor, centripetal force draws things in from all sides. Centrifugal force, on the other hand, pulls things outward in all directions: "Centrifugal forces are a panoply of the most heterogeneous elements. They may have no relation to each other except their divergence of the 'official'" (Morson and Emerson 1990, 30).

In these terms, fieldwork-to-formalization methods tend to be centripetal: they tend to normalize behavior and tools to produce centrally controlled, official solutions. On the other hand, workers' innovations tend to be centrifugal in that they resist a centralized system inadequately adapted to their particular, situated needs. Such innovations start out as idiosyncratic and unofficial solutions, often involving unconventional genres or unconventional genre usage. For instance, Barbara's Post-It note (what Bakhtin (1981, 273) surely would call a "low genre") was an opportunistic use of a ready-to-hand artifact and a basic genre, the handwritten list.

Yet there is no sharp line between official and unofficial innovations (Morson and Emerson 1990, 30). Like designers, workers feel the centripetal impulse and officialize solutions. For instance, handwritten lists like Barbara's were used by other workers I observed, and we can imagine that over time such lists could become relatively standardized (though still handwritten) so that they could be more easily shared and interpreted by the community of workers. Without the centripetal impulse, unofficial solutions can lead to chaos: imagine a new worker who is asked to work with the private, idiosyncratic filing system of another worker. A system that has become too officialized can be inflexible and rule-bound, unable to adapt to change, and unwilling to grant agency to workers; a system that has become too unofficial can be too flexible and chaotic, resistant to conventional approaches, and deficient in organizational memory and coherence. Typically, though, organizations avoid these extremes (as they must, if they are to continue functioning) and maintain a dynamic tension between centripetal and centrifugal impulses.

Neither centripetal nor centrifugal impulses are inherently wrong-headed. Indeed, fieldwork-to-formalization methods have often yielded strong designs that work better than the systems they replace, as many cases attest. But these methods attempt to replace local, idiosyncratic, or contingent solutions with universal, standardized ones. In other words, officialization entails consolidating flexible, rapidly developing solutions with less flexible, slowly developing, more extensively codified ones. The result might be a system that is closed, static, unable to accommodate local contingencies or changes because its components shut off productive linkages with unofficial innovations. The computerized information system described by Heath and Luff (2000), for instance, was so closed that workers could not find ways to link it with their own innovations, and they ended up abandoning it altogether. And even if workers find a closed system to be initially useful, their activities constantly change and diverge. A closed information system, like a perfectly tailored suit, "fits" only as long as its subject does not change.

Elsewhere Mark Zachry and I have discussed an open-systems design approach that attempts to balance official and unofficial solutions (Spinuzzi and Zachry 2000). In this book, I use the official-unofficial distinction to guide workplace research. I return to the question of design in the final chapter.

CONCLUSION

As I have suggested above—and as I will discuss in more detail in chapter 2—since fieldwork-to-formalization methods assume that workers are unable to empower themselves, the goal of research is to inform the development of idealized artifacts, work practices, and work structures meant to standardize work in ways that functionally empower workers. Certainly these methods sometimes entail examining user innovations, collecting feedback, and even collaborating with users to redesign artifacts. But in the end, the goal is to transform a messy set of ad hoc, unofficial solutions into a single, neat, coherent, official—and static—generalized solution.

If we are to study the dynamic tension of centripetal and centrifugal impulses rather than papering over the idiosyncrasies of users' unofficial solutions, an appropriate research methodology is needed. I contend that this methodology should be based in sociocultural theory, yet be connected solidly to existing research methods. *Genre tracing* is one such approach. Based in activity theory and genre theory, genre tracing draws on established methods that have been used with those theories. Genre tracing provides a way to highlight users' experiences with official and unofficial genres and to compare them across communities or workplaces.

Genre tracing is *dialogic* (Bakhtin 1981)—it draws on the metaphor of dialogue to examine how people interact with complex institutions, disciplines, and communities; how they solve problems and disseminate solutions; and how their conversations and problem solving are instantiated in artifacts. Genre tracing is concerned with examining the ways that workers rescue themselves—if that is indeed an appropriate metaphor—by developing unofficial, frequently unarticulated work practices and genres, by adapting old genres to new uses, and by linking their innovations to established, official genres.

Genre tracing draws on existing research methods, including many employed in user-centered design approaches, but repurposes them under different methodological assumptions. Genre tracing's methods are thus accessible to information designers. And since genre tracing draws on established methods, studies based on genre tracing can be held to similar standards of repeatability, reliability, and validity.

Genre tracing can be time consuming and labor intensive—just as ethnographic research, ethnomethodological research, and fieldwork-to-formalization methods can be. Like these other research approaches, genre tracing is best used at a major turning point, such as the beginning of a major design or redesign project (see chapter 2), and conceivably could be conducted in concert with these other research approaches. For instance, a genre tracing project could conceivably share the data collected in a contextual design project, although it would analyze those data in considerably different ways.

In the next chapter, I argue that the assumption of an underlying work structure, the methodological assumption that is so central to the attempts designers make to consolidate and officialize users' innovations, is deeply embedded in field-to-formalization methods. This assumption is problematic for multiple reasons. I then outline genre tracing as an alternative methodology for conducting workplace investigations.

2

Integrating Research Scope

Ellen, a worker at the Iowa Department of Public Safety, is examining traffic accident data in a database. She does so by using her mouse to select search options in a dialog box. She is focusing on the contributing circumstances to traffic accidents that she would like to study. Which traffic accidents involved teenagers? How many involved alcohol? Then she tries to check a checkbox and her choice doesn't register. Something has gone wrong. She stops thinking about specifying contributing circumstances and concentrates on the operation of clicking her mouse. *It turns out that she has to shift focus like this quite frequently, since she has a hard time precisely clicking on the small database fields with the oversized mouse pointer. So do many other users of this database across the state.*

But Rod, a worker at the Governor's Traffic Safety Board in Des Moines, never encounters such breakdowns—even though he is using the same database, performing similar searches, and using similar computer equipment. Rod has learned that he can click on field labels *rather than the fields themselves, and that makes it easier to select items because the labels are much bigger targets than the fields. For Rod, the mouse pointer is not oversized at all. Now that he habitually clicks on labels rather than fields, Rod thinks about what circumstances he wants to specify rather than on how to specify them.*

The designer-as-hero trope we encountered in chapter 1 is based on an unstated assumption: if workers are victimized by usability problems, it takes a principled, capable, Solomonic information designer to discern the crux of the problem and devise a solution that changes the course of the activity. Once the crux of the problem is treated via a formal solution, the symptoms of the problem dissolve.

But if we question the designer-as-hero trope, we may start to doubt that things are so simple. What if the problem has no crux? What if usability problems cannot be neatly divided into cause and symptoms? If so, it is difficult for designers to be heroes (or for workers to be victims, for that matter) because there is no tyrant to overthrow, no dragon to slay. It is difficult to come up with an overarching design decision, such as a new interface, a revised manual, or even a reorganized work structure, that can solve all of the problems that crop up in work activity. And that means that workers' innovations and the destabilizations[1] they encounter become more important for designers to examine as they attempt to find ways to contribute—as partners.

In the epigraph, for instance, Ellen is having trouble using a database. An interface designer might argue that the crux of her problem is the mouse pointer: it is simply too big to be used with precision. Shrink the pointer and the effects of the problem should disappear. But Rod has figured out a completely different way to make the problem disappear, by bypassing the mouse pointer in favor of the keyboard, and he has learned this trick so well that it has become automatic for him. So, then, is the crux of the problem the size of pointer, or the training that workers receive, or something else?

Individual mouse clicks are rarely the focus of user-centered design research. User-centered design approaches tend to use field methods and design techniques that work at different levels. For instance, researchers using one of the fieldwork-to-formalization approaches discussed in chapter 1 might take the work structure or work culture to be the crux of the problem: they might examine how Ellen's and Rod's workflow and office cultures differ, how their interpretations of the data reflect the activities in which they are involved, and how different artifacts in their work environments contribute to the work going on at the Department of Public Safety and the Governor's Traffic Safety Board. These investigators work on the scope of entire organizations. Researchers using approaches such as usability testing, on the other hand, might take the database's interface to be the crux of the problem; they might investigate ways designers could modify the interface's design to better serve users.

They work on the scope of individuals and small groups. Both types of approaches might lead researchers to notice the differences in the operations that Ellen and Rod have learned, but both will take those operations as merely symptoms reflecting the disease, the "real" design problem. And each approach identifies a different "real" crux of the problem.

However, given the central concern of this book—examining the crucial subversive interactions in which workers engage as they use designed information—it becomes necessary to view operations such as mouse clicks as more than just symptoms of a deeper problem. As Rod's example shows us, workers can innovate at the level of operations as well (a point I will explore more fully later in this chapter). Workers' operations must be examined in their own right, as interactions—often centrifugal, subversive interactions—that coconstitute (reciprocally make up, shape, sustain) the cultural activities and goal-directed actions in which workers engage. At the same time, we must also examine work activities and goal-directed actions, where workers may also innovate. In short, to examine the centrifugal aspects of workers' labor, it becomes important for us to *integrate research scope*: to examine the three levels of activity, actions, and operations so that we can discern how they interact, how they coconstitute each other, and how innovations at any given level affect the other levels.

In this chapter, I discuss reasons for abandoning the causal assumption described above in favor of research that integrates the three levels of scope. First I describe what I call the *problem of unintegrated scope*: an undesirably limited focus on a particular level of scope. I discuss how others have dealt with integrated scope in both technical communication and human-computer interaction. Next, I use the sociocultural[2] understanding of *artifact* as a starting point for developing the genre tracing methodology, which offers an integrated-scope unit of analysis and a set of heuristics for integrating research scope.

THE PROBLEM OF UNINTEGRATED SCOPE

Researchers turn to field methods because they seek contextualized data—that is, a broader understanding of how workers do things. Unfortunately, in practice, *context* has often been a limiting term simply encompassing the *circumstances* that surround a given worker—the worker's cultural-historical surroundings and the goals the worker has taken up (see Spinuzzi 2000). These circumstances "contextualize" the worker's observed behavior. In this view, macroscopic and mesoscopic context is separate from workers' microscopic operations. For instance, when Ellen clicks a mouse, a researcher might contextualize that operation through an understanding of her work activity and goal-directed actions. Context becomes an underlying structure at either the macroscopic or mesoscopic level, a structure that causally affects the other two levels. For example, in Contextual Design, once researchers have modeled the underlying work structure, they can manipulate that macroscopic structure to yield (presumably) fundamental changes in workers' mesoscopic actions and microscopic operations (although Beyer and Holtzblatt (1998) do not use these terms; see pp. 38, 44). By changing the contextual foundation, the designer changes the work activity across all levels of scope.

In fieldwork-to-formalization methods, the researcher attempts to discover such an underlying structure so that design work can focus on changing that structure (that is, to find and treat the crux of the design problem). Single-scope field methods thus tend to produce design solutions oriented to that level of scope. Contextual design develops new underlying work structures at the macroscopic level, for instance (Beyer and Holtzblatt 1998, 215–228; Holtzblatt and Beyer 1993, 96–99).

But what if no one level of scope takes a foundational role—what if there *is* no crux to the design problem? If we rely on the crux assumption and it is actually unwarranted, we may miss opportunities to meet goals crucial to our work as information designers: to "examine users and the phenomena of technological use from their perspective" (Johnson 1998, 4), to design texts that empower workers (Geisler et al. 2001; Johnson-Eilola 1997; Selfe and Selfe 1994), and to provide sustainable solutions (Hackos, Hammar, and Elser 1997; Hackos and Redish 1998; see also Engeström 1999a, 36).

Sociocultural theory points to an integrated-scope approach that draws no such lines between the observed person or thing and the context, or between operations on one side and activities and actions on the other. Rather, sociocultural theorists and researchers argue that the relationships among activities, actions, and operations coconstitute each other (Hovde 2000, 400; Russell 1997a; see also Cole's (1996) discussion of two levels of context; R. Engeström 1995; Y. Engeström 1990, 1992). That is, work activities constitute goal-directed actions, which in turn constitute habitual operations—but operations can reciprocally structure goals and actions and shape activities. Along these lines, Barbara Mirel (1998a, 10, 13) criticizes task-oriented documentation for attempting to "break tasks and knowledge into finer and finer levels of detail until, at a fine enough grain, component parts are rule driven and generic." In contrast, Mirel argues that no matter how fine the grain, "knowing and learning take place in a dynamic system of people, practices, artifacts, communities, and institutional structures," and that such dynamic systems always coconstitute even the finest grain of human activity. Similarly, Christina Haas (1996, 37) argues that "studies of technology tend to focus either on the fine-detailed, real-time processes of technology development, learning, or use; or they examine the broad sweep of change at the cultural and historical level"—but they do not examine how to relate these macroscopic and microscopic levels. And without a more thoroughgoing examination of how the levels of scope coconstitute each other, information designers who look for a crux can easily develop solutions that inadvertently destabilize or damage such coconstitutive relationships.

These relationships are not typically examined—and are inherently difficult to examine—through single-scope approaches, which by definition privilege one level of scope over another and which take that level of scope as foundational to the other levels. They lend little attention to how that level is constituted and made meaningful through what occurs at the other levels.

Below, I examine the three levels in more detail. Drawing on the work of Kari Kuutti and Liam Bannon in particular (Kuutti and Bannon 1991, 1993; Kuutti 1995, 1996; see also Bødker 1996, 1997; Kaptelinin, Nardi, and Macaulay 1999; Muller et al. 1995; Turner, Turner, and Horton 1999), I define the three levels of scope (table 2.1) and draw from activity theory to analyze each level.

Table 2.1 is based in large part on a perceptive article by Kuutti and Bannon. In "Searching for Unity among Diversity: Exploring the

Table 2.1
Three levels of scope with corresponding HCI domains and activity theory terms (based on Spinuzzi 2002e, 8, and Kuutti and Bannon 1993, 266)

Level	HCI research/ design object area	HCI background theory	Activity theory term
Macroscopic	Contextual (organizational) interaction	Social contexts, enriched information processing, cognitive psychology	Activity (cultural-historical, unconscious)
Mesoscopic	Conceptual interaction	Cognitive psychology, mental models	Action (goal-directed, conscious)
Microscopic	Physical/technical interaction	Psychophysiology	Operation (habitual, unconscious)

'Interface' Concept," Kuutti and Bannon (1993) draw on the work of Juhani Iivari to argue that human-computer interaction researchers have traditionally studied information systems in terms of different "layers" or "subdomains" or "abstraction levels" (what I term *levels of scope*). These perspectives are typically discussed as organizational (or contextual), conceptual, and technical layers (p. 265). Furthermore, these layers are not typically integrated in human-computer interaction research: each is studied separately, with its own theoretical assumptions, methodologies, and methods. For instance, an approach that focuses on the organizational layer, such as contextual design or the other fieldwork-to-formalization methods discussed in chapter 1, generally does not also deal with conceptual or technical issues. If it does, it deals with them as aspects or symptoms of issues at the organizational layer. Similarly, an approach that deals with the conceptual layer, as usability testing often does, treats the organizational layer as context at best.

In other words—although Kuutti and Bannon do not explicitly argue this—when researchers and designers focus on a particular layer, they seek design problems at that layer and they tend to see that layer as the one in which workers' problems originate. Whatever problems the workers encounter are assumed to emanate from the layer under con-

sideration. As I have argued elsewhere (Spinuzzi 2002c), researchers
and designers seek a single crux to workers' problems, a foundational
problem at the layer under consideration that is manifested in symptom-
atic problems at the other layers. A researcher focusing on the organizational (macroscopic) layer, for instance, might take Ellen's problems with
mouse clicking to be a symptom of organizational problems, while a
researcher focusing on the conceptual (mesoscopic) layer may see these
problems as symptoms of an inadequate mental model.

Kuutti and Bannon (1993), however, argue that single-level or single-
scope approaches are barking up the wrong tree because the three levels
need to be integrated to gain a fuller understanding of workers' problems. They argue for an "integrative perspectives" approach (p. 263) in
which the different layers of information systems design are studied and
elaborated in a "coherent theoretical framework" (p. 267). Like others
arguing for an integrated approach to human activity (Bødker 1996,
1997; Spinuzzi 2002c), Kuutti and Bannon turn to activity theory for
this integrated approach: "What makes the Activity Theory approach of
special interest is that it explicitly attempts to manage the relationships
between the different levels, rather than simply labeling them" (p. 267).

These levels have been discussed in various terms: as *why, what,* and
how levels (Bødker 1996, 1997) and as macroscopic, mesoscopic, and
microscopic levels of scope (Spinuzzi 2002c). Below, I discuss the three
layers and how activity theory integrates them.

The Macroscopic Level: Cultural-Historical Activity

The fieldwork-to-formalization methods I discussed in chapter 1 tend to
focus on the macroscopic (organizational or contextual) layer. Anyone
who is familiar with contextual design, for instance, should recognize it
in Kuutti and Bannon's (1991, 9) description of this layer:

> *The organizational domain* ... consists of a description or model which
> tries to provide a "rich picture" of actual organizational practice, including
> the inconsistencies and contradictions that are inevitably part of the situa-
> tion. This model is used as the basis for initiating change in the current
> situation. Some particular areas are selected to be supported by the IS [in-
> formation system] and this support is defined using organizational rather
> than computer terminology. This includes a fuller understanding of the

users' work and descriptions of the ways that IS should support the work and the overall functioning of the organization.... Sometimes the development of this definition is called defining the *requirements* of the system.

Kuutti and Bannon prefer to call this layer the "contextual" layer because it reaches beyond organizations to the cultural-historical activity in which those organizations are involved. It involves ways workers, work communities, cultures, and societies understand, structure, collaborate on, and execute their evolving cooperative enterprises (Leont'ev 1978, 1981; Engeström 1990, 1992; Nardi 1996; Russell 1997a; Winsor 1999). Such activities are undertaken to fulfill the *motives* around which these relatively stable activities have developed. An activity's motive involves transforming a certain *object*, a material or social concern. Activities are typically undertaken by interrelated groups of workers and are usually unconscious. They tend to take place over extended periods of time—days, months, years.

For instance, in a contextual design project, Coble et al. (1996) studied physicians' work to generate requirements for a physicians' workstation. They selected ten participants from six area hospitals and a medical school, then performed one- to six-hour inquiries that involved observations and interviews. The results were analyzed in an *affinity diagram*, a treelike structure that helped the researchers organize similar observations from different participants. The diagram allowed the researchers to find and consolidate similarities across users so that they could construct an overall model of the work structure. The results were also analyzed in *consolidated work models* representing task sequence, workflow, and context across all users.

Although Coble et al. do not describe it this way, the physicians' work can be seen as an *activity system* in which doctors, nurses, technicians, and others work together to cyclically, continuously perform an activity: transforming patients, the activity's object, from the sick into the well. Since the activity of running a hospital is cyclical, medical workers have developed and honed localized ways of doing things. The doctors that Coble et al. describe have developed a complex set of genres (such as office charts) and practices (such as procedures, ways of contacting other workers, and ways of distributing work). Yet these activities are not static. Indeed, Coble et al. believe that the newly designed workstation will positively transform the physicians' activity. (Such transformations are not always positive, however. See Engeström 1995; Heath and Luff 1996; Luff and Heath 1998; Zuboff 1988).

A field study that focuses on the macroscopic level, such as Coble et al.'s, is typically longitudinal: a shorter, more targeted study would miss important aspects of the work. Macroscopic studies involve investigating the activity and its meaning. And, like Coble et al.'s study, such field studies often tend to take observations at other levels as *symptoms* of the work activity, useful primarily in constructing models of the underlying work structure that causes these symptoms.

The Mesoscopic Level: Goal-Directed Action

In contrast, the mesoscopic level is that of goal-directed *action*—the tasks in which people are consciously engaged. Actions fulfill certain *goals* or localized objects as part of the general activity. Leont'ev (1978, 63) provides the illustration of the man who, being hungry, prepares fishing equipment. The man's macroscopic motive is hunger, a motive he shares with others in his community. His immediate, mesoscopic goal—properly prepared fishing equipment—does not in itself satisfy that motive; he may not even be thinking about his hunger as he performs actions directed toward his goal, such as weaving a net or tying a fly. He may even give the equipment to others in exchange for their catch, rather than obtaining the fish himself. Leont'ev concludes that these actions constitute human activity—"human activity does not exist except in the form of action or a chain of actions" (p. 64)—but at the same time these individual actions are not explicable except in the context of the activity.

Field studies that focus on the mesoscopic level of action tend to examine how individuals or small groups execute routine tasks with specific tools. For instance, Michael Muller (1993) describes how he brought a mesoscopic technique, PICTIVE, to bear on various design problems. (Muller et al. (1995) describe PICTIVE as a *microscopic* method, but they use the term more or less the way I use the term *mesoscopic*, as a way to focus on the detailed tool-mediated structure of work.) In each case, Muller and his colleagues identified a specific problem that users had noticed or anticipated as they utilized an artifact to meet specific goals (for instance, difficulties interpreting a report), then redesigned the artifact to avoid those difficulties. In these studies, Muller focused on the mesoscopic level of the tool-in-use and its design problem. The actions involved in using these tools are necessary links in the network of actions that makes up an organization's activity. Such actions take minutes or hours to accomplish.

A field study that functions at the mesoscopic level, such as Muller's, focuses not on the work activity but on the local goals that users set for themselves and the tools and actions they use to accomplish those goals within a cultural-historical context. These goals, tools, and actions are often seen as the crux of the usability problem. In this case, Muller and his colleagues believed that in reforming the goal-directed actions, they would cause changes in the overall work activity.

The Microscopic Level: Minute Practice

Finally, the microscopic level is that of moment-by-moment *operations* (Leont'ev 1978; Bødker 1991; R. Engeström 1995; Y. Engeström 1990, 1992; Russell, 1997a), which are the minute practices, reflexes, and habits on which workers draw as they carry out their labor. These operations respond to *conditions*—that is, specific configurations of the work environment. An operation is the mode of performing an act (Leont'ev 1978): an unconscious step in carrying out an action within certain conditions. Operations are studied moment by moment.

Operations are also called *operationalized actions* since they begin as conscious, goal-directed actions that are then operationalized or made automatic. Leont'ev (1978, 66) provides the classic example of a driver learning to shift gears:

> Initially every operation, such as shifting gears, is formed as an action subordinated specifically to this goal and has its own conscious "orientational basis" (P. Ya. Gal'perin). Subsequently this action is included in another action, which has a complex operational composition in the action, for example, changing the speed of the car. Now shifting gears becomes one of the methods of attaining the goal, the operation that effects the change in speed, and shifting gears now ceases to be accomplished as a specific goal-oriented process: Its goal is not isolated. For the consciousness of the driver, shifting gears in normal circumstances is as if it did not exist.

He does something else: He moves the car from a place, climbs steep grades, drives the car fast, stops at a given place, etc. Actually this operation may, as is known, be removed entirely from the activity of the driver and be carried out automatically.

Operations can surface once again as actions, though, if the driver encounters a "breakdown" (Bødker 1991), a kind of focus shift in which unexpected conditions cause him to focus on the tool, making it his object. For instance, if the driver accidentally puts the car in third gear instead of first, it lurches and stalls rather than driving the way he expected. At that point, he must shift the car back to first gear. The shifting is performed as a conscious, goal-directed action rather than an unconscious operation.

New operations, then, do not spontaneously come into being: they always begin as conscious actions that become automatic. However, operations can still be considered innovations. For example, in this chapter's epigraph, Rod has learned an operation (or if you prefer, operationalized an action) that others have not, one that makes his work easier by ensuring much more success in clicking fields. It is impossible to tell from the data available whether Rod initially operationalized the action of clicking on labels when working with the accident database or whether he learned the operation when working with another piece of software and unconsciously applied it to this database. In both cases, this operation represents an unusual and successful (that is, innovative) variation of mouse use. In the second case, the operation certainly represents an innovation, a solution originating in one activity that is applied to another.

Ethnomethodological field studies often focus on microscopic operations. For instance, Greatbatch et al. (1995) used Conversation Analysis to investigate how doctors' work changed when they began using a computerized system in sessions with patients. The researchers videotaped 250 consultations and transcribed both conversations and keystrokes to examine how the two were coordinated. They found many such coordinations. For example, they found that when doctors were done typing, they would signal that they were ready to talk to patients by repositioning their hands, striking the final key with more force than usual, or shifting their gaze away from the monitor. These unconscious operations helped the doctors to communicate with patients and structure their work.

A field study that functions at the microscopic level, such as Greatbatch et al.'s, focuses on the operations on which users draw in their moment-by-moment interactions. Few field studies function at the microscopic level, though; this level is more often studied through experimental methods and goals-operations-methods-selector rules (GOMS) (Card, Moran, and Newell 1983).

Integrating the Three Levels of Scope

The three levels of scope provide quite different pictures of the work being studied—different in terms of time spent during a study, events being studied, and range of users being studied. According to sociocultural theory, the three levels of scope complement each other. For instance, insights into work activity collected at the macroscopic level can shed light on operations at the microscopic level and vice versa. But as Kuutti and Bannon argue, most human-computer interaction approaches—particularly the fieldwork-to-formalization approaches I discussed in chapter 1—tend to be single-scope. Thus they tend to overlook how work is coconstituted at the different levels of scope.

By *coconstitution,* I mean that even though we can analytically separate the three levels and even though we need to use different methods and theoretical constructs to study each one (see Raeithel and Velichkovsky 1996, 288), they are ultimately intertwined. They do not share a cause-and-effect relationship in which (for example) cultural-historical activity *determines* actions and operations, or actions are simply *contextualized* by activity, or operations simply *make up* actions and activities. Changes in an activity can be initiated at any level of scope.[3]

To integrate the levels of scope, I turn to the same theoretical framework that Kuutti and Bannon do: activity theory. We have seen how activity theory provides a coherent framework for discussing macroscopic activity, mesoscopic actions, and microscopic operations. In the next section I discuss mediation and how genre theory offers an integrated-scope unit of analysis for examining mediated activity.

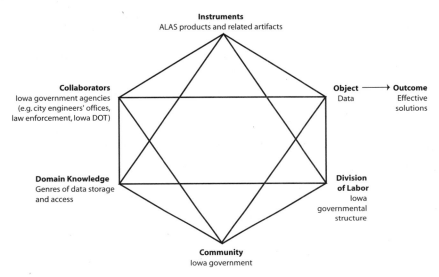

Figure 2.1
An activity system, in which one or more collaborators accomplish objectives in joint labor. The labor is mediated by instruments, the collaborators' domain knowledge, the community in which the labor is accomplished, and the division of labor within that community.

FROM ARTIFACTS TO GENRES

Activity theory posits that in every sphere of activity, *collaborators* use *instruments* to transform a particular *object* with a particular outcome in mind (figure 2.1). For instance, in chapter 5, we will see how traffic safety workers used maps, a database, reports, manuals, and other instruments to regularly, cyclically transform raw traffic accident data into recommendations. They performed these transformations to meet outcomes such as safer roads and reduced expenses. Indeed, these traffic safety workers—like all workers—found themselves involved in multiple interpenetrating activities, and sometimes these activities contradicted each other in ways that caused tensions. For instance, the traffic safety workers found that to conduct their work properly, they had to acquire various computer literacies, interact with workers involved in other activities such as city engineering and law enforcement, and learn genres that originated in other activities.

Mediation

Activities are shaped in part through what figure 2.1 calls *instruments* but are sometimes labeled *tools, mediational means,* or simply *mediating artifacts*: material artifacts that an individual or group uses to accomplish an action with a particular outcome in mind (see, e.g., Miettinen 1999). In the example above, when workers turned accident data into recommendations, they mediated this work with maps, reports, and other mediating artifacts.

In activity theory, mediation is based on the work of L. S. Vygotsky (1978, 40), who argues that human beings use "extrinsic stimuli," modified material objects or signs, to "control their behavior from the outside." As Michael Cole (1996, 108) describes it, people use these external instruments to reach some goal, and in the process, the people themselves are psychologically transformed: as they use these external means to regulate themselves, they begin to think and act differently. One of Vygotsky's favorite examples was the Russian custom of tying a knot in one's handkerchief to remind oneself of something (just as someone in the West might tie a string around her finger). Examples more germane to a work context include to-do lists, items stacked in the order to which they need to be attended, and even chairs and desks, which implicitly prescribe the position in which office work is done. In mediating workers' actions, these artifacts help the workers meet their goals by regulating or controlling their own actions—for instance, making sure they attend to all the tasks they have set for themselves. The artifacts thus transform the ways workers conceive of their work activity, solve problems, set new goals, and so forth. In fact, mediation has the broadest implications for human activity: in the Vygotskian account, mediation is what makes human consciousness possible (see also Cole 1996, 108; Lee 1985, 76).

These mediating artifacts, then, do not simply serve as a bridge between the workers and the object of their work. Mediated actions are not just a detour from unmediated actions, a different set of goal-directed steps leading to the same outcome. Rather, mediating artifacts qualitatively change the entire activity in which workers engage (Cole 1996, 119). Introducing computer technology into various North American companies, for example, has fundamentally changed the way work is done, the knowledge needed to do it, and even the criteria for its success (Zuboff 1988).

Artifacts

As we have seen, mediation is typically performed with physical artifacts made meaningful in human activity. According to Cole (1996, 117),

> An artifact is an aspect of the material world that has been modified over the history of its incorporation into goal-directed human action. By virtue of the changes wrought in the process of their creation and use, artifacts are simultaneously *ideal* (conceptual) and *material*. They are ideal in that their material form has been shaped by their participation in the inter-actions of which they were previously a part and which they mediate in the present.

Since they emerge from cultural-historical activity, in part to mediate it, artifacts bear the material traces of an ongoing activity, represent problem solving in that activity, and thus tend to stabilize the activity in which they are used. Marx Wartofsky sums up this general understanding of artifacts when he says that they play the same role in cultural evolution as genes play in biological evolution (quoted in Engeström 1999a, 29).

This understanding of artifacts as simultaneously representing and maintaining an activity is common in human-computer interaction. For instance, Carroll and Campbell (1989) consider artifacts to be concrete, implicit theories about how work should be done (see also Bisantz and Ockerman 2002). In a similar vein, distributed cognition sees artifacts as material links in chains of problem solving (Hutchins 1995).

There is some slippage in the term *artifact*, which is sometimes used to mean individual items and sometimes applied to classes of items such as timesheets (Brown 2001) and checklists (Hutchins 1997). Furthermore, in design circles, attention has increasingly been paid to customized arti-facts such as prescription labels—that is, templates that can be auto-mated to produce large numbers of similar but unique artifacts (Sless 1998).

In activity theory, artifacts are more specifically seen as a "crystalliza-tion" of aspects of historically developed activity (e.g., Leont'ev 1978,

65). In one discussion of computer-mediated activity, Susanne Bødker (1997, 150) explains that "artifacts crystallize knowledge so that operations which are developed in the use of one generation of technology may later be incorporated into the artifact itself in the next." She describes how computer-based artifacts are situated in history and thus shaped and defined by historical activity:

> The fact that artifacts are historical devices also means that artifacts-in-use are reconstructed more or less continuously: Replacing one generation of technology with another is perhaps the most dramatic example of such a change, but use also changes through the influence of other artifacts and through learning—that is, through the development of, and breakdowns in, the actions and operations in which the computer application is used.
>
> To sum up, human cognition is mediated not only by computer artifacts. Underneath this, the activity is historically crystallized in these artifacts. (p. 151)

Like objects, tools are not socially neutral. As Leont'ev (1981, 216) points out, "handling" a tool entails far more than merely holding it: "handling" implies knowing how to use it in specific ways for specific activities. A tool, Leont'ev says, carries within itself a certain socially developed mode of action; the hand wielding the tool is subordinated to the tool's mode and its socially developed system of operations is "fixed" in the tool (pp. 216–217). It *embodies* socially developed rules. The subject appropriates the tool's operations by developing his or her own abilities.

But this is not to say that tools deterministically affect the activities in which they are used. Activity theorists do not deal with universal affordances. Rather, a tool embodies modes of action when it is encountered within a specific cultural-historical milieu and used with a particular objective. Under these conditions it will tend to reproduce certain ways of acting in the user. In other words, it is unproductive to draw a clear distinction between the tool and the rules that govern it within a specific activity. Thus, Bødker (1997, 151) insists on discussing *artifacts-in-use-in-a-certain-praxis* rather than as things in themselves.

Genres

Like artifacts, genres are sometimes described as tools-in-use (Russell 1997a) and are usually studied in a mediatory role (e.g., Artemeva and Freedman 2001; Russell 1997a; Winsor 1999; but see Geisler 2001). At the same time, genres have some unique qualities that add to the socio-culturalist account of artifacts, qualities that make them valuable in conducting the integrated-scope analysis I have in mind.

In the tradition of the North American genre school (see Russell 1997b, 226), genres have been defined as a typified rhetorical response to a recurring social situation (Miller 1984); shared expectations for recognizing how certain tools in certain conditions can help people act purposefully in an activity (Russell 1997a); "socially recognized types of communicative actions used by organizational members for particular communicative and collaborative purposes" (Yates and Orlikowski 2002, 14); and in similar ways. These definitions and others are barking up pretty much the same tree. A quick reading might lead us to think that genres are merely artifact types (see Brown and Duguid 1994). But that is not quite accurate. What is too often underemphasized is genre's role as a sort of *tradition*.

When I characterize genre as a tradition, I draw from the work of Mikhail Bakhtin, whose work underpins the North American genre school's. Bakhtin and the members of his circle (P. N. Medvedev and V. N. Voloshinov) emphasized that genres are not simply text types; they are culturally and historically grounded ways of "seeing and conceptualizing reality" (Medvedev and Bakhtin 1978, 134). Genre, then, is more than a concrete psychological theory or a material embodiment of recurrent activity. Genres are not discrete artifacts, but traditions of producing, using, and interpreting artifacts, traditions that make their way into the artifact as a "form-shaping ideology" (Morson and Emerson 1990, 282–284). That is, they emerge from cultural-historical activity and represent, reflect, stabilize, and help constitute that activity (G. Smart 2002). In terms of cognition, they represent the "thinking out" of solutions just as artifacts do (see Bakhtin 1984, 270). But they also represent the development and stabilization of worldviews, including the values, ethics, and other humanistic concerns implied in them. As Morson and Emerson (1990, 291–292) argue,

> Each genre implies a set of values, a way of thinking about kinds of experience, and an intuition about the appropriateness of applying the genres in any given context. An enormous amount of unfinalized cognitive content is acquired each time we learn a new kind of social activity with its attendant genres, content whose very nature has remained largely unexamined.

Genres convey a worldview, not by laying out a set of explicit propositions, but by "developing concrete examples" that "allow the reader to view the world in a specific way" (Morson and Emerson 1990, 282). And not just the reader: "Each author who contributes to the genre learns to experience the world in the genre's way" (p. 282). Bakhtin develops this understanding of genre in his discussions of the novel and other literary genres, but we can easily see how nonliterary genres also convey worldviews. To pick two genres related to the studies in chapters 3 through 5: recommendation reports tend to conceive of the world in terms of problems that must be solved by applying clearly defined criteria to a particular set of data (Rude 1995), while maps view the world in ways that collapse space and ideology (Barton and Barton 1993).

With the tradition aspect of genre in mind, we can talk about genres mingling, merging, splitting, disintegrating, and being repurposed. Genre provides a way of lending dimension to the genetic aspects of given artifacts—to make connections among discrete artifacts that, on the surface, may bear little resemblance to each other (see Russell 1997b, 226). Genre is thus much more than a category of artifact. Yes, the dialog boxes encountered by Ellen and Rod in the epigraph can indeed be seen as an artifact category. But as we will see in chapter 3, these dialog boxes are also genetically related to the paper forms that workers once had to fill out. In a cultural-genetic sense, the dialog boxes continue the tradition of the forms that preceded them. They are not the same *artifact*, and indeed some might be inclined to see them as *metaphors* for the older paper forms (see Spinuzzi 2001b). But they are at least partially the same *genre* and imply the same worldview, the same understanding of the activity and what it values.

People develop genres so that they can accomplish activities. As those activities change, the genres also change (Bakhtin 1981, 1986). It is for that reason that genre is considered a *relatively stable* type of utterance. This is where the notion of genre memory becomes important: as cultural and literary traditions, genres convey and "remember" the past. Morson and Emerson (1990, 290) characterize genre as "the residue of past behavior, an accretion that shapes, guides, and constrains future behavior."

Genres are doubly oriented: they are oriented toward *history* and *addressivity*. In regard to history, genre represents ways that participants in a given social sphere have developed to deal with particular activities within that sphere. These strategies do not spring up ex nihilo for each speaker. Each speaker is in some degree a respondent, not the "first speaker" (Bakhtin 1981, 69). In other words, genres are the result of an ongoing dialogue among speakers in a particular sphere of activity, and the past dialogue of those speakers imposes itself on present speakers in ways they might not even recognize:

> A genre is always the same and yet not the same, always old and new simultaneously.... A genre lives in the present, but always *remembers* its past, its beginning. Genre is a representative of creative memory in the process of literary development. Precisely for this reason genre is capable of generating the *unity* and *uninterrupted continuity* of this development. (Bakhtin 1984, 87)

Genre is thus a sort of social memory that its practitioners accept without their explicit recognition that they are doing so. Such genre habits are extremely powerful because they provide us with ready-made strategies for interpreting not just discourse in a genre, but the world as seen through the "eyes" of that genre (Medvedev and Bakhtin 1978, 133–135). Bakhtin (1981, 249) clarifies this idea further:

> Cultural and literary traditions (including the most ancient) are preserved and continue to live not in the individual subjective memory of a single individual and not in some collective "psyche," but rather in the objective forms that culture itself assumes (including the forms of language and so-cial speech), and in this sense they are inter-subjective and inter-individual (and consequently social); from there they enter literary works, sometimes almost completely bypassing the subjective individual memory of their creators.

The genre embodies a galaxy of assumptions, strategies, and ideological orientations that the individual speaker may not recognize. It represents others' "thinking out" of problems whose dialogue has been preserved in the genre. (Examples can be found in Bazerman 1988; Berkenkotter and Huckin 1994; Yates 1989.)

Genres, although temporarily stabilized social constructs, are also dynamic and reshapable by any speaker for her or his specific utterance. Utterances are unique and unrepeatable as a function of the speech situation in which they are uttered; by the same token, genres are mutable in that they are made by their speakers to address specific speech situations.

This *addressivity* can manifest itself in something so minor as a change in tone or a use of irony, and as significant as the very selection of genre, a blurring among genres, or an introduction of new elements to an existing genre that help it to perform its functions better. One example of the latter is Charles Bazerman's (1988) study of the genre of the experimental article, in which he chronicles how this genre gradually crystallized, in part to substitute for the lack of eyewitnesses (who once were customarily present at experiments).

When I use the term *genre* in this book, as in most North American genre scholarship, there is some necessary slippage because a given artifact can be seen as an instantiation of a genre (or, as we will see in chapter 5, of multiple genres). For instance, in the headnote, Rod is working with a dialog box, an instance of the dialog-box genre. In the chapter 1 headnote, Barbara uses a map and a handwritten note, both of which are artifacts that are instances of genres. In both situations, the artifacts are connected—in their production, interpretation, use, and modification—to larger traditions of use, traditions that have developed in given sociocultural milieus to mediate activities within these milieus. In the studies in chapters 3 through 5, I depict this slippage in activity system diagrams by placing genre instances in the *instruments* slot and genre knowledge in the *domain knowledge* slot. The confluence of these two points is what Russell (1997a) and others refer to when they talk about genre as a "tool-in-use."

North American genre theorists are generally in agreement with the characterization of genre above. But they have focused on different aspects of genre in their theoretical and empirical work—significantly, aspects that occur at different levels of scope, although some overlapping occurs (see table 2.2). Below, I discuss how they have examined these aspects and how their work can be drawn together to understand genre as an integrated-scope unit of analysis.

Genre at the Macroscopic Level   At the level of *activity*, genre is seen as shaping and being shaped by its sociocultural milieu. As Bazerman (1988) argues, genres develop in a given activity and evolve as the activity evolves. Thus genre analysis has often been used to investigate the recurring organizational activities in which genres are used. We have

Table 2.2
Three levels of scope, their activity theory terms, and genre as a unit of analysis that encompasses them (based on Spinuzzi 2002e, 18)

Level	Activity theory term	Genre conception
Macroscopic	Activity (cultural-historical, unconscious)	Genre as social memory (Bakhtin 1984, 1986), genre as shaping and shaped by sustained disciplinary activity (Bazerman 1988; Yates 1989), genre as social action (Miller 1984)
Mesoscopic	Action (goal-directed, conscious)	Genre as tool-in-use (Russell 1995, 1997a), genre as constellations of strategies (Schryer 1993, 2000), genres as tactics (Hovde 2000)
Microscopic	Operation (habitual, unconscious)	Genre as coherent collection of habits (Spinuzzi 2001a), genre as operational rules (Engeström 1995; Russell 1997a), genre as structuring work (Bazerman 1997), genre as distributed cognition (Freedman and Smart 1997; Syverson 1999)

seen in the above discussion how genres "remember" their past (Bakhtin 1984, 106) and how they pull it into the present along with an entire worldview that is applied to the present activity—but also how, in addressing the present activity, genres continue to develop. A given genre may remember its past, but it "lives in the present" (p. 106). In examining genres, then, we can gain an overall understanding of the activities they have historically mediated. At the macroscopic level, genres are frequently examined and compared diachronically (Bazerman 1988; Berkenkotter and Huckin 1995; Yates 1989), and sometimes in terms of how they connect individuals' personal histories of writing with their assimilation into disciplines and organizations (Berkenkotter and Huckin 1995; Myers 1990; Prior and Shipka 2002; Schryer 1993; Winsor 1996), with the attendant changes in objectives, values, and ethics.

Genre at the Mesoscopic Level At the level of *action*, genre has variously been described as a tool-in-use (Russell 1997a), a stabilized-for-now site of social or ideological action (Schryer 1993), and a constellation of strategies or tactics (Schryer 2000; Hovde 2000). Researchers working with this concept of genre tend to examine written documents, interfaces, and even nontextual artifacts such as telephones (Brown and Duguid 1994) as genre instances that workers consciously select, interpret, produce, and use to mediate their goal-directed actions. Genre at this level of scope is typically taken to be instantiated in an artifact—usually a text—that is used to meet an actor's goals. When goals change, actors might choose to abandon the genre for another, more amenable one. For instance, in her ethnographic study of how faculty at a veterinary college taught students a system for keeping medical records, Catherine Schryer (1993, 228) found that students consciously chose to use the school-sanctioned records genre in class, but many planned to discontinue it in practice because it was too cumbersome.

Genre at the Microscopic Level   At the level of *operation*, genre is conceived as a coherent collection of habits (Spinuzzi 2001a), as operationalized rules (Engeström 1995; Russell 1997a), and as the typification of talk used to maintain regularity and structure of work (Bazerman 1997). Researchers working with this concept have tended to see genre as a set of operationalized actions that, once learned, serve as coherent sets of operations that can be unconsciously drawn on to perform familiar, repeated tasks. Russell (1997a, 515) describes it this way: "Put in simplest terms, a genre is the ongoing use of certain material tools (marks, in the case of written genres) in certain ways that worked once and might work again, a typified tool-mediated response to conditions recognized by participants as recurring." For those familiar with the genre, this typified response is an operationalized action: "The first time one takes the action of using a new tool (whether a clutch pedal or a semicolon), it requires a conscious decision to act, but with repeated use, it may become a routine operation, usually unconscious."

As Russell's article illustrates, theoretical studies in this vein tend to emphasize situated, condition-triggered uses of genres. Empirical studies in the same vein tend to examine workers' fine-grained, moment-by-moment operations—particularly those that contribute to interpretation

(Freedman and Smart, 1997)—and ways in which destabilizations of genre features can disrupt these operations (Engeström 1995).

Integrating Genre: Toward an Integrated-Scope Unit of Analysis   These conceptions of genre at the different levels of scope are different, yet reconcilable. That cross-scope flexibility has made genre a useful framework for guiding research, particularly in technical communication, a field that takes as a central focus the typified ways people communicate at work (Miller 1984). Indeed, the wealth of scholarship examining genres at different levels means that a genre-based methodology has plenty of established methods from which to draw as it identifies and analyzes genres. Thus, an integrated-scope understanding of genre yields a unit of analysis uniquely suited for integrated-scope research in information design. That unit of analysis allows us to tackle the problem of unintegrated scope, since we can trace a given genre or group of genres across the levels of scope, observing how they interact at each level.

FROM GENRES TO GENRE ECOLOGIES

The notion of genre provides a strong base for examining how workers use information systems to mediate their work. In this section, I build on that base by examining *compound mediation*, the use of several coordinated mediational means in an activity. I also discuss *systematic destabilizations*, the insight that if the levels of scope coconstitute each other, then destabilizations (usability problems) at one level of scope necessarily coconstitute destabilizations at the other levels of scope. As I discuss these two concepts, I draw examples from the studies in chapters 3 through 5.

Compound Mediation

In chapter 3 we will see that one central insight of genre tracing is that people's activities—at all three levels of scope—are mediated in multiple ways by dynamic, shifting collections of genres. *Compound mediation* can be defined broadly as "the ways that workers coordinate sets of artifacts to help them get their jobs done" (Spinuzzi 2001c, 58; see also Spinuzzi 2002a, 2002d; cf. Johnson-Eilola 2001 for a discussion in a somewhat different tradition). For instance, city engineers in Iowa tend to use a particular sort of map, a *node map*, to help them determine whether particular roads need traffic signals at a given intersection. Maps are mediational genres, representations that have developed through repeated use to help workers visualize the data in useful ways. The object of their work is the traffic data, which workers intend to transform in ways that will help them meet larger objects (such as making decisions that can lead to safer streets).

Mediational genres can be produced by information designers, but they are also frequently developed by the workers themselves. For instance, many workers that I observed (including workers in law enforcement, traffic safety, and city or county engineering) developed their own system of handwritten notes to help mediate their activity. These genres were identifiable because they were regularly used in certain ways to accomplish certain actions—for instance, to structure how workers interacted with a database of traffic accidents.

Communities, then, develop genres over time to mediate relatively stable, cyclical activities. As those activities change, the genres also change (Bakhtin 1981, 1986). Genre thus represents the community's history of problem solving; its solutions are preserved in its genres (e.g., Bazerman 1988; Berkenkotter and Huckin 1995; Yates 1989), making it possible for us to trace genres across historical eras as well as across levels of scope, as I demonstrate in chapter 3. Since they represent the distributed problem solving of a community, genres can be seen as examples of distributed cognition (Freedman and Smart 1997; see also Syverson 1999; Hutchins 1995).

Any given genre is used to mediate activities in one or more activity systems. But it does not and cannot do the work of mediation all by itself—genres are oriented to different sorts of problems and have developed relatively stable connections or coordinations with other genres. For example, in this chapter's epigraph, Ellen and Rod use the dialog box in coordination with other genres: maps, reports, node tables, and a host of others. Activities are mediated by an entire dynamic, shifting ecology of different genres (Spinuzzi and Zachry 2000), each with its own history, its own origin, and its own worldview and ideological orientation. Genre tracing provides us with insights into how such ecologies of genres jointly mediate the workers' operations, actions, and activities.

Systemic Destabilizations

Each genre in the ecology, as we saw in the previous section, can be traced across all levels of scope. So can systemic destabilizations involving those genres. User-centered design is preoccupied with such destabilizations, conceived as design or usability problems, and with good reason: destabilizations may cause workers to draw poor inferences, for instance, and in the case of traffic workers, the repercussions of such inferences may include traffic accidents, injuries, and deaths. Single-scope field methods can help to detect such destabilizations, but since they assume a crux or underlying problem at the chosen level of scope, they tend to see destabilizations as merely symptoms of this crux. They follow the destabilizations only so far, and thus they miss the reverberations that each destabilization triggers in the activity. So they offer solutions that address one level of scope, and since levels of scope are coconstitutive, their single-scope solutions may be unsuccessful. Genre tracing, on the other hand, recognizes that the levels are coconstitutive and that destabilizations at one level can coconstitute destabilizations at other levels.

For example, in the study of traffic workers in chapter 4, I found that destabilizations tended to cluster around one particular genre in the ecology, the node map. This genre is a hybrid (see chapter 5) of the genre of the road map, used in traditional accident location and analysis, and the genre of the node-link system, used in computerized work. These parent genres had developed separately to mediate different activities, and assume different problem-solving strategies, cultural assumptions, and ideologies. And since these activities are mediated by entire genre ecologies, when the genres of the map and the node-link system were hybridized, they each dragged in other genres in their separate ecologies: the map brought in report forms, colored pins, and writing implements, while the node-link system brought in punch cards, dialog boxes, and database queries. Each genre, its assumptions, and its linkages are preserved in the resulting hybrid.

By tracing connections among genres, we can gain insights into how the parent activities' differences manifest themselves through destabilizations at all levels. The macrolevel *contradiction* between the two representations (and the activities in which they evolved) engendered mesolevel *discoordinations* between specific genres originating in different activities. Since the genres retained their orientation to their originating activities, they conflicted in their problem-solving strategies, cultural assumptions, and ideologies. Workers thus encountered microlevel *breakdowns* as they attempted to use these discoordinated genres to mediate their work. These destabilizations reverberate: microlevel breakdowns reciprocally constitute mesolevel discoordinations, which in turn reciprocally constitute contradictions. This reciprocality means that the activity system is always in flux, always off balance, as systemic destabilizations at each level reverberate across the other levels.

Tracing genres and their destabilizations across the levels of scope can lead us to examine how genres support activities, how they mediate these activities and each other, and how they coconstitute their activities. Once a researcher builds a coherent (though always unfinalized) understanding of how genres do these things, the researcher should be able to trace destabilizations from any level to the other levels to see how (or whether) destabilizations constitute each other.

FROM GENRE ECOLOGIES TO GENRE TRACING

Information designers use design approaches to develop texts and deploy genres that accomplish crucial goals: to understand workers, to empower those workers, and to provide those workers with sustainable solutions. Yet these important goals may be thwarted by single-scope methods, which deny the coconstitutive nature of the different levels of activity. When Contextual Design takes the macroscopic work structure as its unit of analysis, for instance, it consolidates work models based on observations of a relatively small number of workers; its solutions can ignore or even conflict with the unofficial innovations that other workers have developed (Hackos, Hammar, and Elser 1997). I suggest that an alternative is needed, a field methodology[4] that presents an integrated-

In the studies in chapters 4 and 5, the videocoding database allowed me to find larger trends in how workers interacted with genres. For instance, as I illustrated at the beginning of this chapter, nine of the twelve workers I observed in the chapter 4 study repeatedly encountered breakdowns when trying to enter data into a dialog box. A tenth worker apparently did not use the database long enough to encounter such breakdowns. But two other workers used the database for considerable periods of time and never encountered these sorts of breakdowns because they used different, more successful operations for entering data— for example, entering data with the keyboard rather than the mouse. Breakdowns, I found, could be traced to larger issues of mesoscopic genre perception and macroscopic contradictions between interface paradigms.

CDB Tables   Once the researcher has collected and analyzed data at all levels of scope, she or he can integrate them, particularly in terms of the destabilizations identified through the other heuristics. CDB tables (table 2.3) help to trace how systemic destabilizations associated with given genres manifest themselves across levels. These tables guide the researcher in identifying a destabilization at one level, then looking

Table 2.3
Using a contradiction-discoordination-breakdown table to trace systemic destabilizations across three levels

Level	Destabilization	Example
Macroscopic (activity)	Contradiction (from activity system diagram)	Qualitative vs. quantitative representations of the roadway system (map vs. node-link system).
Mesoscopic (action)	Discoordination (from genre ecology diagrams, videocoding database)	Workers must perform difficult conversions between maps and numerical designations.
Microscopic (operation)	Breakdown (from videocoding database)	Typed wrong numerical information (county, city, node number).

Note: Using the table, a researcher can draw on other heuristics to identify destabilizations at each level, then explore ways the destabilizations might be connected. (Based on Spinuzzi 2002e, 27.)

for ways that destabilization coconstitutes destabilizations at the other levels.

For instance, when conducting the study of traffic workers described in chapter 4, I wrote into a table one of the classes of microscopic breakdowns I had observed—the typing of incorrect information into a dialog box. I then looked for ways that this particular destabilization connected to destabilizations I had observed at other levels, and entered those destabilizations into the table as well. The result is table 2.3, which traces a breakdown to a mesoscopic discoordination between tools-in-use and a macrolevel contradiction between two different representations of a roadway system. I had detected these destabilizations separately, but through the CDB table, I was led to speculate on how they might be connected. Understanding these connections can help researchers to see how the different levels of scope coconstitute each other and how destabilizations in particular are manifested at the different levels. The CDB table also can show how workers are dealing with destabilizations through their own unofficial innovations.

Limitations of Genre Tracing

Although genre tracing can be a powerful methodology for examining genre-mediated activity and generating design suggestions, it has several limitations. Since it is labor intensive, genre tracing cannot be quickly deployed the way usability testing and some forms of participatory design can. And since it involves careful, prolonged study of activities, unlike contextual design, it requires trained researchers. Also, since genre tracing requires significant time and resource commitments from researchers, participants, and organizations, it may not be suitable for all organizations. Finally, like many observational approaches, genre tracing can get bogged down in data. Yet for projects in which these commitments can be marshaled—commitments, I should point out, that are not unlike the commitments that must be marshaled for large-scale ethnographic, ethnomethodological, or contextual design studies—genre tracing can provide an integrated-scope understanding of work activity suitable to information design.

CONCLUSION

In this chapter, I have addressed the problem of unintegrated scope by outlining an appropriate field methodology in accordance with sociocultural theory. The methodology allows us to produce more complete and nuanced understandings of human activity. It leads us to avoid the single-scope assumptions that result from the trope of worker-as-victim, since it provides no totalizing level of scope that we might imagine we can control. It encourages us to facilitate workers' attempts to develop local innovations, since—unlike the single-scope approaches described here—it does not assume that such innovations must be replaced or approved by a designer-hero.

Furthermore, genre tracing is based solidly in rhetorical theory, tackles issues of evaluation and design that are central to technical communication's mission, and involves methods familiar to technical communication researchers. At the same time, the combination of theory, issues, and methods yields a unique approach to user-centered design in technical communication. By explicitly conceptualizing the problem of unintegrated scope and providing heuristics to integrate different levels of scope, genre tracing avoids separating text from context or privileging one aspect of activity over another.

In the remainder of this book, I lay out the research methodology of genre tracing, including theoretical apparatus and heuristics, but also examples of how the methodology can be realized in specific research methods. To illustrate, I draw on four interrelated research studies I conducted in 1998–1999.

The research studies all involve the activity of traffic accident[6] location and analysis in the state of Iowa: a vast, loose network devoted to cyclically transforming experiences with traffic accidents into coded data, and from data into arguments, behavior, and physical roadway changes. Like Barbara, the police officer I mentioned at the beginning of chapter 1, many people are interested in locating traffic accidents and analyzing their causes—and often for very different reasons. For example, Barbara and other police officers used the results of their searches to determine what sorts of violations to crack down on. City and county engineers investigated whether to erect stoplights and signs, what roads should be graded, and which bridges should be raised. Workers at the Governor's Traffic Safety Board investigated the relationships between traffic accidents and drunk driving. Legislators decided where they stood on issues such as road improvement and driving laws. And many of these people and organizations also used accident data in local, state, and federal grant proposals to argue for increased project funding.

The different workers and organizations engaged in this activity all used the same data, but for very different things. As we will see in the studies, workers customized the information system for their own uses by employing a wide array of unofficial innovations. By examining the innovations and how they supplemented (and sometimes resisted) the official information systems, I have produced accounts of work that resist the trope of worker-as-victim; those accounts might lead to very different sorts of information design.

3

Tracing Genres across Developmental Eras: The ALAS Activity System

1963 *A police officer in Ottumwa, Iowa, opens the drawer of a filing cabinet and pulls out a thick sheaf of traffic accident reports. Each has been filled out by hand or with a typewriter. Sometimes they're useful for keeping track of who in Ottumwa has been in accidents, where the accidents have tended to occur, and what conditions are most dangerous for drivers. When there are legal disputes, the officer might find himself looking through this file cabinet for the accident report, or he might need the reports to count how many other accidents have occurred in that same spot. But not today. Today, these reports all get sent to the Department of Transportation (DOT) offices in Ames, Iowa, where they will be counted, cataloged, and summarized in a report along with traffic accidents from all ninety-nine counties in the state. The report's data are typically about two years behind, and they tend to be pretty broadly defined—raw numbers of accidents involving fatalities, for instance, will be broken down by road system and accident type. The report will provide a nice overview, but it won't allow the officer to examine specific locations or combinations of factors.*

1975 *Another police officer in Ottumwa hears about a new service the DOT is providing. It turns out that those traffic accident reports are being fed into a computer system in Ames, called ALAS. Now if the officer has a complicated search to run—for instance, if he wants to search for all accidents at a particular intersection involving wet pavement and alcohol—he can fill out a form and mail it to the DOT. A reply will come in a matter of weeks. The officer sees the potential for zeroing in on accident causes as well as for providing evidence for grant proposals, so* *he sends off for some of these forms. But when he gets them, they seem overly complicated. He winds up calling the DOT directly and explaining his search needs over the phone.*

1990 *A third officer in Ottumwa has been using the DOT's service regularly. In fact, it's become an important part of her job: she is in charge of determining where to set speed traps and which traffic violations should be given special attention, and sifting through accident data helps her to make these determinations. She has become frustrated with the current system, though. It takes weeks, which means that it's hard to use for exploration. If running a search on one set of conditions gives her a certain result, she may want to follow up with a similar search—but that's just not practical with such a long turnaround. So when she finds out through the DOT newsletter that there's a new system that she can install on her office computer, called PC-ALAS, she gives the DOT a call. Soon a DOT circuit rider has delivered a floppy disk that holds the program and the data for her county. The interface isn't too hard, although it's sort of quirky, and she quickly begins conducting her own searches. Over the next few years, she comes up with suggestions for improving the system, including adding functionality; these suggestions are often incorporated by the developers.*

1997 *A fourth officer joins the force and begins learning PC-ALAS. But it's a frustrating process. PC-ALAS has a text-only interface (very strange in this era of graphic user interfaces) and that means that this officer has to keep several huge maps in her office, find the number for a particular intersection, and type it into the map. When she gets results from PC-ALAS, they're also in numerical code, and she has to get out the map again to plot them and look for patterns. And although the more experienced officers assure her that this system is far better than the previous alternatives, she has a hard time believing them. How did this thing get so complicated? Then, at a DOT seminar, she gets a look at a prototype system called GIS-ALAS. In this system, the map is right there on the screen—you run a search and the accidents appear, you click on an accident, and the data pops up in a window. She immediately and enthusiastically signs up as a beta tester.*

In chapters 1 and 2, I discussed the trope of worker-as-victim/designer-as-hero and examined how it led to examinations of work that are primarily done at one level of scope. I will describe a study in chapter 4 in which I use these insights to trace genres across levels of scope. But for now I want to take a detour and trace genres *developmentally*. In this chapter, I examine four periods of accident location and analysis in Iowa (illustrated by the fictional scenarios in the epigraph). In doing so, I provide a macroscopic view of how innovated genres proliferated in an activity and how they were periodically reorganized into new systems. This history helps us to developmentally examine the dynamic nature of an activity system as contradictions form and are mitigated, sometimes by unofficial innovations, sometimes by official action. In the account, I discuss what is entailed in balancing centrifugal and centripetal forces in this activity system and how genre tracing helps us sort all of this out.

But first, a few words on what this study is not. It is not, strictly speaking, a historical study, nor is it situated in the field called "cultural studies." It examines the activity of accident location and analysis by examining retrospective interviews and artifacts (such as documents, interfaces, forms, and maps). In the tradition of other activity theory–based studies (e.g., Bødker 1991; Engeström 1990, 1992; Nardi 1996; Wertsch 1998), it involves examining broad work activity and how that activity changes over time. And it involves tracing genres as they are introduced into these activities, develop, merge, and sometimes disappear.

The study gives us insight into this particular activity and the artifacts and practices that support it, but it also gives us insight into what a macroscopic study involves and how that study might be integrated with other studies to produce integrated-scope understandings of the activity. Thus, in this study I devote equal time to describing the insights of the study and discussing how those insights were reached methodologically. So let's start with a few methodological notes.

As I argue in chapter 2, genre tracing should yield an integrated-scope understanding through a particular unit of analysis, genre. Genre, I argued, cuts across the levels of scope. To understand genres, though, we must do two things. First, we must have a solid understanding or model of activity and how those genres function within that activity. Second, we must be prepared to examine genres not in isolation, but as members of an *ecology of genres*—an interrelated, changing group of genres that comediate work in a shifting variety of ways. This chapter begins that work through a developmental macroscopic study of the ALAS activity system and the genres that comediate it.

One insight reaffirmed in this study is that a given activity never stands still. Activities change. And as we will see, *contradictions*—tensions, imbalances, destabilizations—often appear among elements of an activity system. Activity systems are complex and only temporarily stable: parts of the activity system change continually, and not always in the same ways. Contradictions within these changing activities are typically dealt with first by the sorts of local innovations that I discussed in chapter 1, and only later by more official and centralized responses. Official responses (that is, centripetal reorganizations) are necessary for preserving the system—otherwise it would fragment as individual workers did their own thing—but unofficial innovations are necessary because one size does not fit all. This account tells the story of a cycle in which contradictions are exacerbated, innovations spring up to deal with their effects, then a centripetal reorganization consolidates and standardizes those innovations so that the activity can continue. Any given contradiction is not eliminated in most cases, just abated—and changes in the activity can exacerbate contradictions in various ways, starting the cycle of innovation all over again.

Since the activity is continually developing, official responses tend to become dated quickly, requiring even more local innovations. What was useful and usable at one point in the history is no longer so at other points. So in this chapter I explore systemic changes at the macroscopic level of activity, using the heuristic of activity system diagrams. This macroscopic analysis will be incorporated into the mesoscopic and microscopic analyses of the next two chapters.

In the next section, I discuss how genre ecologies develop, change, and form contradictions, and how these contradictions are related to discoordinations and breakdowns. Then, in the remainder of the chapter, I describe how contradictions arise in the ALAS activity system over the course of three decades. I describe how genres have been imported into, and temporarily stabilized within, an ecology of genres used to mediate this activity system.

STUDYING GENRE ECOLOGIES IN CULTURAL-HISTORICAL TERMS

In chapter 2 I discussed the idea of *genre ecologies*, interconnected and dynamic sets of genres that jointly mediate activities. As Mark Zachry and I describe it, "A *genre ecology* includes an interrelated group of genres (artifact types and the interpretive habits that have developed around them) used to jointly mediate the activities that allow people to accomplish complex objectives. In genre ecologies, multiple genres and constituent subtasks co-exist in a lively interplay as people grapple with information technologies" (Spinuzzi and Zachry 2000, 172). Genres mediate a given activity, but not individually: they are densely connected to each other. "To account for variations across instantiations of a given genre," Zachry and I argue, "a more robust, ecological perspective is required, one that accounts for the dynamism and interconnectedness of genres. In particular, ... the genre ecology framework must account for how official and unofficial documentation genres are animated by and connected through contingency; how the documentation's functionality is consequently decentralized, distributed across the ecology; and how ecologies of genres achieve relative stability despite their contingent, decentralized nature" (Spinuzzi and Zachry 2000, 173).

For instance, James Wertsch (1998, 35) illustrates the development of mediated action by describing the changes in airplane design from the 1960s to the present:

> In the 1960s, the design of a new airplane might have involved dozens of draftsmen working for months or years with slide rules, drafting equipment, and other such cultural tools. Today, the same task might be done in a much shorter time by a single computer operator using the complex hardware and software that makes computer imaging possible. The relevant issue to address in such cases is, "What happened?"
>
> It is fairly obvious that an explanation of the increased productivity cannot be grounded solely in an account of increased intelligence or skill on the part of the individuals involved. Indeed, some might be tempted to argue that the single computer operator today needs less intelligence or

skill than what was required of the engineers using slide rules, complex mathematical formulas, and other instruments several decades ago. What the illustration does suggest is that the intelligence involved is an attribute of the *system* created by the irreducible tension between agent and mediational means.

Many authors have argued, as Wertsch does, that cognition can be distributed among people and artifacts (e.g., Ackerman and Halverson 1998; Hutchins 1995; Salomon 1993; Winsor 2001). But what is intriguing about Wertsch's illustration is that it depicts an entire ecology of tools, including slide rules, drafting equipment, mathematical formulas, and so forth, being replaced by a computer. The ecology's functionality remains, but it is transferred somehow into the computer. How? Are slide rules, drafting tables, and mathematical formulas simply abandoned, replaced by an entirely different computer system? Are they swallowed whole by the computer, where they and their intricate ecology somehow reside—albeit in altered forms—within the interface? Wertsch does not elaborate. It seems to me that this is a highly interesting question for information system designers and evaluators: if genres are indeed imported into the computer interface (as I argue that they often are), we may benefit greatly by tracing them across history and across organizational boundaries, understanding the genres' ecological relationships and how they have been altered. One way to explore the issue is to conduct a study—not merely a snapshot of a genre ecology at one point in time, but a macroscopic cultural-historical study of a genre ecology as it develops over a period of months or years.[1] Such an examination can provide insight into how local innovations are officialized, how they resist officialization, and why they exist in the first place.

Such a study can provide a developmental view, one that can help us to fully understand the operations that the current system requires of workers. As Susanne Bødker (1997, 150) argues, "Artifacts crystallize knowledge so that operations which are developed in the use of one generation of technology may later be incorporated into the artifact itself in the next." To put it in terms of Wertsch's illustration: the mathematical formulas that the airplane designers used in the 1960s have become embedded in the computer systems used by airplane designers in the 1990s.

But these computer systems have incorporated more than just mathematical formulas. As Bødker argues, "One computer application may contain several instruments," instruments that "are juxtaposed in their mediation of a particular activity" (p. 150). That is, the genres that jointly mediated airplane design in the 1960s (mathematical formulas, slide rules, drafting equipment) are not simply *replaced* by a computer system; they are to some extent reproduced, operationalized, and "juxtaposed" in it. The 1960s-era genre ecology has migrated into the 1990s-era computer system, albeit in drastically altered form. When we examine a computer system, sometimes we can still discern the traces of these genres.

The Development of Genre Ecologies

Such migrations do not happen en masse and for only one time; genre ecologies are not entirely stable or static. An activity continually changes and thus the ecology of genres mediating the activity must also change if the activity is to continue.

One way to change a genre ecology is to introduce new genres to mediate activities differently. Yet in entering an ecology, those new genres are themselves changed. Bakhtin (1986, 62) describes such a metamorphosis of genres:

> Secondary (complex) speech genres—novels, dramas, all kinds of scientific research, major genres of commentary, and so forth—arise in more complex and comparatively highly developed and organized cultural communication (primarily written) that is artistic, scientific, sociopolitical, and so on. During the process of their formation, they absorb and digest various primary (simple) genres that have taken form in unmediated speech communion. These primary genres are altered and assume a special character when they enter into complex ones.

Similarly, Charles Bazerman (1994, 20) describes genres being "drawn into" documents:

> In constructing the text, the writer makes visible for the readers some components that went into it, represented in generically appropriate ways and put in relation to other visible elements. Tables, charts, descriptions, and references to other documents are more obvious modes of drawing outside artifacts into documents, but more subtle are the passing mention

of a government office or piece of legislation, the name of a form, or a list of addressees.

Bakhtin and Bazerman see genres as entering a larger genre, yet retaining something of their own history, addressivity (that is, orientation to an activity), and distinctiveness, as well as their interrelations with other genres. When we encounter the genre of the personal letter in Dostoyevsky, or the genre of the table in an annual report, we expect them to be quite similar to the same genres *outside* the genre ecology—although perhaps metamorphosed to fit a niche in the ecology (e.g., tables in reports have table numbers). This genre perspective also allows us to examine in genre terms how local innovations can become centralized and officialized over time—how, for instance, locally produced maps can become an integral part of an information system (as we will see in the study later in this chapter).

Yet neither Bakhtin nor Bazerman deals with how genres enter and are changed by the genre ecology of the computer interface. If a table genre were to enter a computer interface, it would have to be displayed using some sort of interface genre—as a graphic in a window or as a collection of spreadsheet cells, for instance. The genre that migrates into the ecology of an interface must *be combined with* (i.e., become represented or recast in) an existing interface genre. Their union produces what I term a *hybrid genre*: a genre that involves the history, addressivity, and distinctiveness of its parents; that retains the interrelationships with other genres that its parents enjoyed; and that workers perceive as being more-or-less the "same" genre as its parents, so that they can apply habits to it that they have developed for dealing with its parents.

I discuss such hybrid genres throughout this chapter, and in more detail in chapter 5.

Contradictions, Discoordinations, and Breakdowns

All is not always harmonious in a genre ecology. Genre ecologies mediate activity systems, which are constantly destabilized as they are interpenetrated by other activities (Engeström 1992) and as parts of the activity system change. As Marcie Tyre and Wanda Orlikowski (1994, 12–13) describe it,

The introduction of a new technology into an operating environment triggers an initial burst of adaptive activity, as users explore the new technology and resolve unexpected problems. However, this activity is often short-lived, with effort and attention declining dramatically after the first few months of use. In effect, the technology, as well as the habits and assumptions surrounding it, tends to become taken for granted and built into standard operating procedures. This initiates a period of stability in which users focus attention more on regular production tasks than on further adaptation. Later on, users often refocus their attention on unresolved problems or new challenges, creating additional spurts of adaptive activity. In many cases, this episodic pattern continues over time, with brief periods of adaptation followed by longer periods of relatively stable use.

Although Tyre and Orlikowski focus on how technological change leads to this "lumpy" or episodic pattern of adaptation, other changes—changes in organizations or goals, for instance—can lead to destabilizations as well. (See also Wertsch 1998, 43, 59.) Such macroscopic destabilizations, or *contradictions*, are the impetus behind changes in the genre ecology: changes in which workers invent, adapt, migrate, and combine or hybridize genres.

These destabilizations, as I argued in chapter 2, are best understood as coconstitutive. Macroscopic contradictions manifest themselves as mesoscopic *discoordinations*, difficulties in perceiving and managing genres in the ecology. Discoordinations in turn manifest themselves as microscopic *breakdowns*, points at which workers find that they must reinterpret the genres they are using. In fact, the destabilizations that occur in a given activity tend to lead workers not only to reinterpret existing genres, but also to adapt new genres, which lead to a swelling of the genres in a given ecology. To understand changes in the genre ecology, then, we need to understand contradictions, discoordinations, and breakdowns (see table 3.1).

Contradictions   "Between the components of the [activity] system," Yrjö Engeström (1992, 12) tells us, "there are continuous transformations. The activity system incessantly reconstructs itself." This continual reconstruction is fueled by *contradictions*, which are tensions or imbalances in the activity system. Since contradictions occur at the level of activity, they call for a macroscopic analysis of the activity. We will

Table 3.1
Three levels of scope, their activity theory terms, and destabilizations

Level	Activity theory term	Destabilization
Macroscopic	Activity (cultural-historical, unconscious)	Contradiction
Mesoscopic	Action (goal-directed, conscious)	Discoordination (genre perception, genre management)
Microscopic	Operation (habitual, unconscious)	Breakdown

examine these contradictions through the heuristic of the activity system diagram discussed in chapter 2.

Engeström discusses four types of contradictions. The most relevant for this study is that of *secondary contradictions*—that is, tensions *between* components of the activity system. Engeström (1990, 85) explains that "when a strong novel factor [is] 'injected' into one of the components [of the activity system] and it thus acquires a novel quality, pressing secondary contradictions appear between that component and some other components of the system." For instance, when a new information system is introduced into an existing activity system, it is likely that a secondary contradiction will appear between it and the established domain knowledge that has until now governed the activity. In Engeström and Escalante's (1996) study of an automated kiosk, for example, the kiosk's users were able to utilize it to mediate a variety of activities, but to do so they had to learn new domain knowledge for operating the kiosk.

Of secondary contradictions, Engeström (1990, 84) says:

> These secondary contradictions of the activity are the moving force behind disturbances and innovations, and eventually behind the change and development of the system. They cannot be eliminated or fixed with simple remedies. They get aggravated over time and eventually tend to lead to an overall crisis of the activity system.

Contradictions give rise to unofficial, localized innovations (such as changes in the division of labor, the invention of new genres, and the adaptation of old genres for new purposes), and eventually to more standardized (official, centripetal) responses that tend to incorporate and officialize the local innovations.

In the study later in this chapter, I discuss the history of the ALAS activity system, giving special attention to the secondary contradictions that arise and the official and unofficial genres imported into the genre ecology in attempts to ease those contradictions. I examine the unit of analysis, genre, to detect such contradictions, and I use activity system diagrams as heuristics to map out these contradictions. I also point to how these contradictions lead to discoordinations and breakdowns (discussed in more detail in chapters 4 and 5).

Discoordinations *Discoordinations* are difficulties in interpreting artifacts and managing the actions that those artifacts mediate. Since discoordinations occur at the level of action, they call for a mesoscopic analysis that connects macroscopic contradictions with microscopic breakdowns.

Engeström contrasts discoordinations with *coordinations*, in which the normal, expected flow of interaction continues without a hitch. He describes coordination in two ways, which I attempt to unpack below in terms of genre perception and genre management.

Genre Perception Genre perception can be conceived in Engeström's terms as the matching of symbols—that is, the understanding of an artifact in terms of a genre, and the application of genre rules (domain knowledge) to it. Engeström's (1990, 87) comments on discoordinations in discourse, although having to do with spoken communication, are applicable to this sort of discoordination: "When both symbols are identical [e.g., when worker and designer perceive the artifact as being of the same genre], we may say that discourse ... is coordinated." The designer and worker agree on the artifact's genre, and they understand the genre in a similar way. On the other hand, if the worker perceives the artifact as being of a different genre, the result is a discoordination: the worker may attempt to use the artifact with the domain knowledge of the perceived genre, only to find that the artifact reacts unexpectedly. At that point the worker may encounter a microscopic breakdown, a point at which she or he must consciously reinterpret the artifact in terms of another genre.

Genre Management   Genre management involves coordinating the interrelated genres in an ecology in such a way as to comediate the activity at hand. Workers manage genres through genre rules applied within the ecology. For instance, when a worker wants to look up traffic accidents, she uses genres such as a node map and a dialog box. When she applies the genre rules of node maps to this particular node map, the action makes sense only because she uses the result to operate the dialog box. Thus the genres of the node map and the dialog box are interconnected in a mediatory relationship. (Notice also that an entire ecology of interconnected genres needs to be coordinated.)

When workers successfully manage genres, they experience "the normal, scripted flow of interaction. ... The script, coded in written rules and plans or tacitly assumed traditions [here, genre knowledge], coordinates [workers'] actions as if from behind their backs, without being questioned or discussed" (Engeström 1992, 66). Workers go about their work, generating reports that they then interpret to make decisions about the roadway system. But sometimes they do *not* experience "the normal, scripted flow of interaction." As we will see in chapter 4, sometimes they have trouble managing genres: they attempt to apply genre rules, but the genres interact in unexpected ways. The genres are discoordinated. And the discoordination involves an interpretive breakdown: rather than using the entire ecology to comediate the activity, workers find themselves attempting to reinterpret the individual genres of the ecology.

Breakdowns   Points at which a worker finds the present interpretation of an artifact to be inadequate for the task at hand are called *breakdowns*. Breakdowns cause the worker to become aware of an action he or she has operationalized. Since breakdowns occur at the level of the operation, they require a microscopic analysis of the worker's moment-by-moment interactions with the system.

As I discuss above, breakdowns accompany discoordinations (Engeström 1990, 1992). Breakdowns can lead the worker to reperceive and remanage genres. For instance, in the chapter 4 study, a worker named Mike searched for a specific type of accident, only to find that the resulting report listed no accidents whatsoever. Although he did not realize it, the problem was not with the report, it was with the way he conducted the search. Mike's perception of the search function was inadequate for supporting his work. He had to reinterpret it if he was to continue to use it in his activities.

Breakdowns are relatively easy to locate because workers are aware of them and typically call them *mistakes*. One temptation that designers face is to attempt to treat the breakdowns by themselves, rather than taking the time to understand the reciprocal relationship that break-downs have with discoordinations and contradictions. Since the desta-bilizations at these three levels coconstitute each other, treating the breakdown alone might actually exacerbate destabilizations at other levels, destabilizations that will be manifested as still more breakdowns.

To illustrate, in the remainder of this chapter I discuss the history of the ALAS activity system, based on retrospective interviews, examina-tions of historical documents, and analyses of computer interfaces, and supplemented by the studies of chapters 4 and 5. This study lends special attention to the contradictions that arise and the genres that are im-ported into the genre ecology in attempts to ease those contradictions. Chapters 4 and 5 continue the work by studying discoordinations and breakdowns at two points in the activity system's history. Together, these chapters furnish an integrated-scope analysis that uses genre as a unit of analysis, a dialogic approach, and a way to examine system flexibility.

OVERVIEW OF THE ALAS ACTIVITY SYSTEM

Like many states, Iowa keeps rather detailed statistics on the traffic acci-dents that occur on its roads. In fact, Iowa has one of the most extensive systems in the nation. The Accident Location and Analysis System (ALAS) contains data[2] on accidents occurring on every interstate high-way, every state road, every street, and even every gravel road in the state. These data are the object of what I will term the ALAS activity

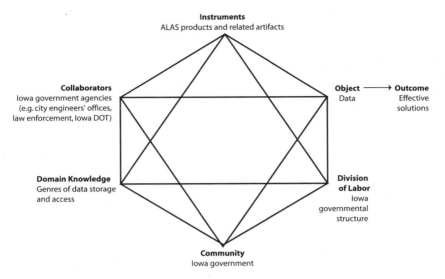

Figure 3.1
The activity of accident location and analysis in Iowa.

system: the statewide activity system devoted to locating and analyzing accidents (figure 3.1).

At this level of granularity, the collaborators are governmental agencies that use various instruments to transform data—for instance, to transform a sheaf of officers' accident reports into a set of statistics suitable for making decisions.

But, of course, this is not the whole story. If we examine the genre-mediated activities of specific agencies, we begin to see that this activity system is the interpenetration of several activity systems distributed in time, space, and culture (Engeström 1992; Russell 1997a; Bødker 1997; cf. Bakhtin 1981; see also chapter 4). For instance, individual agencies transform data in vastly different ways and for different purposes as they labor in their discrete activities. County and city engineers use the transformed data to help them decide whether to regrade roads, raise bridges, and erect stoplights and signs, as well as to respond to citizens who want to see those changes made. Police officers use the data to affect the rate of traffic offenses by deciding where to place officers or what sorts of violations to enforce most vigorously. Emergency response teams use the data to plan routes to and from high-risk areas. The Governor's Traffic Safety Board uses the data to monitor behavioral factors (such as alcohol use) in traffic accidents statewide. Legislators at the city, county, and state levels use the data to decide where they stand on issues such as road improvement and driving laws. And most of these entities use the data when applying for yearly grants from the state and federal governments. These entities all need a tool that enables them to browse through the copious data and select only the data they need to examine.

To make things even more complicated (and we must, if we are going to understand localized innovations in this activity well enough to provide design suggestions), we can examine different eras in the development of the ALAS activity system. Changes in the gathering, processing, and distributing of data have periodically rippled across the system, transforming the overall system itself as well as the activity systems of the individual agencies. These transformations include the data that the agencies seek, the ways they work, the instruments they use (including genres), and even their fundamental divisions of labor.

Below, I discuss four eras of the ALAS activity system. I have defined these eras in terms of major redesign projects—that is, points at which new ALAS products are introduced. These new products each entail the adaptation of large numbers of genres at once in a substantially new operative framework. At the end of each era, internal contradictions in the activity system made a new ALAS product possible, even necessary; at the inception of each new ALAS product, these contradictions were eased, the system was fundamentally changed, and new contradictions began to form. As they developed new ALAS products, software developers of each era mingled the official and unofficial genres of the previous era with interface genres to produce official hybrid genres suitable for mediating the reorganized activity system. Here, tracing the genres involved in the activity allows us to detect points at which large numbers of genres change en masse, and thus to detect and analyze the contradictions addressed by those changes.

A methodological note: innovations by their nature are often transitory and are not formally documented. In places, particularly in the first two eras, it is difficult to determine where and when some innovations arose and what particular events prompted them. When possible, I have identified innovations and discussed them in some detail; in other cases, I clearly mark my speculations about innovations and their origins.

BEFORE 1974: PREAUTOMATION ACCIDENT LOCATION AND ANALYSIS

Before 1974, accident location and analysis in Iowa was rudimentary and done differently at the local level (sheriff's offices and police stations) and the state level (the Iowa Department of Transportation). Accidents were recorded—as they still are today—on two types of reports. If an accident involved fatalities, injuries, or damages over $100,[3] drivers involved in the accident each had to file a driver's report, which was sent to the driver's insurance companies and then to law enforcement. The driver's report included a narrative of the accident and a diagram describing it. In addition, for accidents involving fatalities or injuries, police had to fill out officer's reports, which were more detailed versions of the driver's reports. Both types of reports included information such as location, conditions, number of vehicles involved, type of accident, and a diagram and narrative explaining the accident. Locational parameters were expressed in terms of address (3417 Coy Street), intersection (the corner of Coy and Franklin), or landmarks near which the accident took place (ramp 167 on I-35 southbound) (Wilbur Smith and Associates, 1972, 18–19). If the location was uninterpretable, the Iowa Department of Transportation (DOT) sent a map to the reporting party, who marked the proper location with an X and sent it back to the DOT.

The reports were stored at the local level: in the county sheriff's office or the city's police department. Copies of the reports were forwarded to the Iowa DOT in Ames. This is essentially the same system of collecting data as existed in 1998–1999, when this study was conducted, though at the time I write this chapter, the system is beginning to change radically once again (as I explain later in the chapter).

For various reasons, agencies needed statistics on various types of accidents. For instance, summaries of statistics on deadly accidents were used by law enforcement agents, city and county engineers, and legislators, among others. These statistics were compiled and distributed by hand. They were obtained in two ways: at the local level and at the state level.

At the local level, officials would individually leaf through the reports, counting accidents on the rural secondary and municipal street systems that met certain criteria—for example, how many accidents in the county involved alcohol in 1961, or how many deadly accidents occurred at a given intersection. This technique, which is still used by some local agencies, provided officials with rather crude statistics that were unsuitable for complex analyses. Yet many local jurisdictions did not even perform this level of analysis, and others performed it poorly because of inexperience, lack of training, or lack of detailed accident information (Wilbur Smith and Associates, 1972). Local accident analysis was idiosyncratic, but a systematized response was necessary if the DOT was to produce reliable statistics.

Some local agencies visualized accident distribution by adapting a familiar genre, the map. According to a study conducted in 1971, 62 percent of cities and 49 percent of counties surveyed reported that they maintained spot maps or point maps to summarize accidents by location (Wilbur Smith and Associates, 1972). Workers would mark accidents on these maps with pins or pens—a local innovation that allowed a spatial representation of accidents, making it possible for workers to detect clustering.

At the state level, officials at the Driver's License Division of the Department of Public Safety (DPS) would match all reports covering the same accident and assign a number to the accident. In the early 1970s, workers began clipping official forms to the reports in order to facilitate information storage for automated data processing (Wilbur Smith and Associates, 1972, 19–20). These rural accident slips, which were likely an officialization of earlier handwritten notes, included the county, location, milepost, and other information. When analyzing accidents, personnel at the DOT would leaf through their copies of the reports, counting accidents across the entire state according to a wide range of criteria: fatal accidents involving pedestrians, trains, farming or construction equipment, and so forth. They would summarize and analyze these data by hand and present them in annual reports from the DOT and other related agencies. The DOT would then send the reports to various state agencies. By 1971, the Data Processing Division of the DPS regularly compiled nine statistical summaries (Wilbur Smith and Associates, 1972, 21–22). The reports included prose analyses, tables, bar graphs, pie charts, and a number of humorous cartoons depicting various types of fatal accidents (figure 3.2).

Within each county, workers at the DPS would identify segments of rural roads by two-character codes and indicate the segments ("control sections") on special county maps. The control sections were a centripetal (official) system that standardized ways of talking about roads. Previously, workers would have to identify the sections they wanted to address ("I-30 from SH 69 to the east edge of Story County"), and different workers might use different units. Once the control sections were in place, three clerks organized the reports by segment and attached special forms to them to indicate segment information.

By the early 1970s, as part of the TRACIS initiative toward automation, DPS data entry workers were entering accident data into a mainframe system. That change brought in genres from business computing associated with media such as punch cards and magnetic tape, as well as various automated report genres. DPS workers entered data on punch cards, which were run through a card reader and transformed into data on magnetic tape. Clerks could then copy tapes to send to the Iowa State Highway Commission (ISHC). ISHC personnel generated printouts for the primary road system by category, then manually noted accidents on spot maps (adapted from normal road maps) and Spot Location Accident Summary Sheets (another form that probably developed from handwritten records). The spot maps allowed workers to identify clusters of accidents, which could indicate trouble spots that could be mitigated through engineering changes (e.g., regrading a road, placing signage) or policy changes (e.g., changing the speed limit, focusing law enforcement efforts on particular areas). The genre ecology became much more complicated, and a growing number of workers had to coordinate a growing number of genres originating in different activities.

The hand-calculated (and, later, computer-calculated) statistics provided by the DOT were more standardized and complex than those produced at the local level. But they were quite crude by later standards.

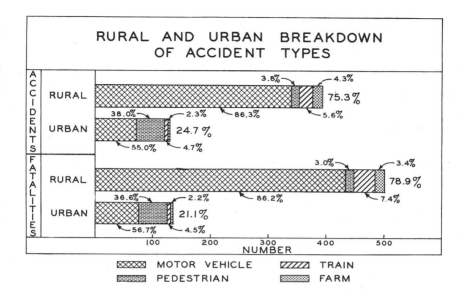

RURAL AND URBAN BREAKDOWN OF ACCIDENT TYPES

	MOTOR VEHICLE	TRAIN
	PEDESTRIAN	FARM

AGE OF DRIVERS INVOLVED IN FATAL ACCIDENTS

ROAD SYSTEM	AGE OF DRIVER	24 AND UNDER	25–39	40–54	55–64	65–74	OVER 75	TOTALS
R U R A L	INTERSTATE	6	8	5	1	—	—	20
	PRIMARY	122	125	101	54	19	9	430
	SECONDARY	95	55	49	29	10	10	248
	TOTALS	223	188	155	84	29	19	698
U R B A N	PRIMARY	43	20	20	6	7	4	100
	CITY STREET	36	22	14	5	7	3	87
	TOTALS	79	42	34	11	14	7	187
STATE TOTALS		302	230	189	95	43	26	885

CONTRIBUTING

CAUSES....

Figure 3.2
Visual displays derived from hand-calculated statistics; a cartoon making light of alcohol-related deaths (Traffic and Highway Planning Department, 1961, 9; 1963, 27, 36). Displays also included column graphs and pie charts. (Reprinted by permission of the Iowa Department of Transportation.)

Analysis

As we have seen, before the early 1970s, the activity of accident location and analysis in Iowa was rudimentary—although even in this rudimentary state, the activity system involved a complex ecology of genres, including printed forms, various types of maps, summary sheets, a variety of reports and data displays, and eventually punch cards, magnetic tapes, and printouts. The ecology of genres was as widely dispersed as the division of labor in the activity system, as I describe below (figure 3.3).

Note that in figure 3.3, the outcome of the activity was not simply "output." Output genres such as reports were important as an aspect of the transformed data, but the data were transformed for a larger purpose: to provide effective solutions to vexing problems.

At both the local and state levels, the activity of accident location and analysis involved a transformation[4] of data: from the actual event to the officers' or drivers' reports, and again to a set of simple counts and categorizations. As has been discussed by others (Lave 1988; Hutchins 1995), such transformations are sometimes necessary for data to be used with existing tools. Statistical tools are not typically useful for parsing a narrative, but if the narrative can be transformed into a set of numbers and categories, statistical tools can be very useful indeed. In this case, by quantifying reports, workers turned thousands of narrative and diagrammatic descriptions into visual data display genres such as pie charts, bar graphs, and tables, each of which could have more impact on public policy than individual narratives could.

As figure 3.3 illustrates, workers at both levels used domain knowledge (e.g., report genres, localized rules for categorizing and counting elements within the narratives) and conceptual tools (e.g., mathematical and statistical formulas) to transform narratives into data reports. But these quantification tools and genres took quite a bit of work. Quantification involved distilling copious narratives into minimal numbers, and thus analysts had to examine file cabinets full of reports to get handfuls of numbers. Narratives had to be individually parsed and transformed into quantitative representations; those representations had to be transformed by hand through statistical or mathematical calculations; and the

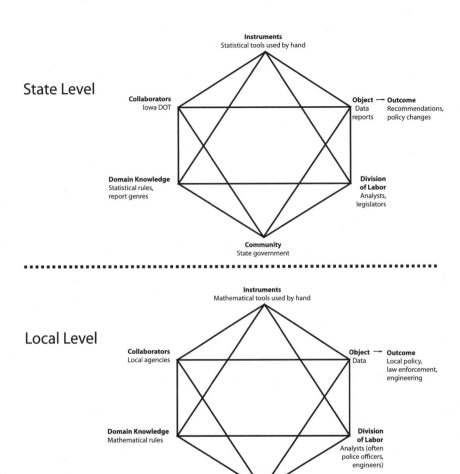

State Level

Instruments
Statistical tools used by hand

Collaborators
Iowa DOT

Object → Outcome
Data   Recommendations,
reports   policy changes

Domain Knowledge
Statistical rules,
report genres

Division
of Labor
Analysts,
legislators

Community
State government

Local Level

Instruments
Mathematical tools used by hand

Collaborators
Local agencies

Object → Outcome
Data   Local policy,
              law enforcement,
              engineering

Domain Knowledge
Mathematical rules

Division
of Labor
Analysts (often
police officers,
engineers)

Community
Local government

Figure 3.3
The activity of accident location and analysis in Iowa before 1972.

results had to be transformed, again by hand, into reports couched in a particular genre. At every step of the process, workers had to decide what to include in the transformation (e.g., the sum of accidents occurring on rural roads) and what not to include (e.g., the sum of accidents at a particular intersection at a particular time of day, individual narratives, diagrams of accidents, and so on).

Once these transformations were completed, however, workers found the data far more versatile and began to see accidents in different ways. By viewing accident data in a new, systematized way, workers found that they could use the transformed data to label dangerous stretches of road, dangerous behaviors, and dangerous classes of drivers. These labels became tremendously important for obtaining grant money, planning roads, establishing law enforcement strategies, and the like—and therefore transformed data became increasingly valued within the ALAS activity system.

As systematized accident data became more widely used, in fact, workers came to want and expect more from them. It is all very well to know general statistics about accidents at rural intersections throughout the state, but is a particular intersection more likely to have accidents than other intersections? What kinds of accidents? Under what conditions? Such questions could not be routinely answered under the labor-intensive preautomation system. The need grew for more data—that is, the object of the activity system became more complex and the outcome more expansive—and two contradictions also grew (figure 3.4).

(A) The instrument for transforming data (counting by hand) was too labor intensive for workers to make use of it often.

(B) Therefore, workers could not transform the data to the desired level of complexity quickly enough, either at the local or the state level.

Engeström (1990, 84) reminds us that such contradictions "are the moving force behind disturbances and innovations." These contradictions began to cause problems that workers initially addressed through local adaptations of genres (spot maps, handwritten labels for grouping) and later through official versions of the same genres. Eventually the problems were addressed through a radical reorganization of the activity system and its ecology of genres, a reorganization centering on automation.

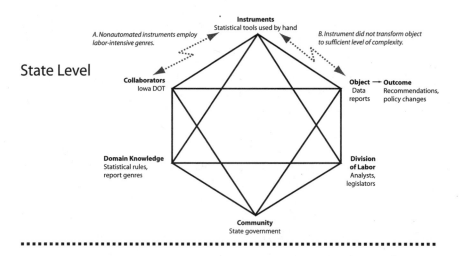

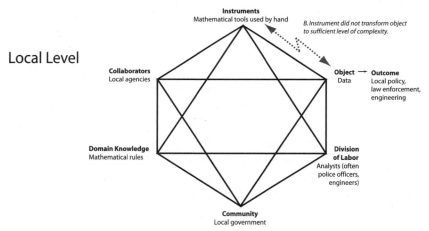

Figure 3.4
Pre-ALAS activity at the state and local levels. The lightning arrows represent contradictions among elements of the activity systems.

The changes that rippled across the ALAS activity system at this point represent attempts to ease the contradictions. We have seen how workers adapted maps, statistical and mathematical genres, report genres, and handwritten routing forms with location codes as they tried to ease the contradictions. But the expanding genre ecology provided more possibilities for discoordinations among genres, discoordinations that were manifestations of contradictions and that in turn manifested themselves as breakdowns. Finally, the Iowa State Highway Commission hired a contractor to automate accident location and analysis, and a massive centripetal reconfiguring of the genre ecology began.

1974: MAINFRAME-ALAS (IBM 3090 MAINFRAME)

In 1974, the DOT adopted an automated system called mainframe-ALAS, which transformed how workers in the state located and analyzed accidents. This transformation was helped considerably by two developments: the node-link system and the data system that became known as mainframe-ALAS. Both were inventions of Wilbur Smith and Associates (WSA), a firm commissioned by the ISHC in 1971 to develop a system for accurately identifying accident locations on all primary, secondary, and municipal roadways in Iowa. WSA's recommendation report, submitted in June 1972, recommended the node-link system for representing accident locations and a data system for manipulating the data.

To automate accident locations, WSA had to quantify[5] the roadway system—turn it into a form that a computer system could easily store and manipulate. In addition, the system had to work with the existing data collection tools: the drivers' and officers' reports, which located accidents by street address, intersection, or distance from landmarks. Quantification, unfortunately, was a two-way street:

> Ideally, accident locations would be reported in a format directly suited to automated data processing. However, a system which is readily usable to a computer may tend to be too abstract for the average motorist to comprehend easily. This is particularly true when a series of special maps is the only source of the necessary identification numbers or coordinates.
>
> However, even if field markers [such as mile point markers] were utilized, it must be admitted that it would seem more natural to identify an accident location by methods with which the motorist is already familiar,

such as street name or route number. The most workable procedure, then, may entail conversion, by state coding personnel, from identifiers used on the accident report to a uniform numerical system suitable for computer processing. (Wilbur Smith and Associates, 1972, 35–36)

Indeed, this is the approach WSA adopted for quantifying the roadway system. And the consequent effect on the nature of the information was the most striking change in the activity. Whereas the multiple genres and narratives of the officers' and drivers' reports had undergone limited quantification before—mainly involving the narrowing or collapsing of multiple narratives and the categorization and quantification of accident factors so that they could be easily compared—now the entire *roadway system* had to be quantified in order for mainframe-ALAS to process the data. WSA assigned each county and city a two-digit designation number, then mapped all counties with a system of *nodes*: coordinates marking all intersections, ramp terminals, railroad crossings, grade-separation structures, bridges, road ends, 90° turns, county lines, major signalized commercial entrances, and interchanges and other multiple-node intersections.

Now workers had to locate accidents in relation to the nearest nodes. Accidents that occurred at a node (e.g., within an intersection) were referenced by the node itself. Accidents that occurred away from a node (e.g., twenty feet away from the intersection) were referenced in a *link* between nodes (e.g., recorded as twenty feet away from the intersection's node, in the direction of a second node). The node-link system, then, was a radical simplification of the accident's location performed to quantify it for further data analysis. And as the roadway system expanded, more nodes had to be identified, numbered, and charted. In 1972, there were about 180,000 nodes in Iowa; in 1998, the year this study was conducted, the number was approximately 240,000.

The node-link system was initially conceived as a centralized system, tightly controlled at the state level: "This system should be used directly only at the state level, by accident-coding personnel. For this purpose, master maps would be printed in limited quantities, containing all node numbers" (Wilbur Smith and Associates, 1972, 41). These "master maps" were the result of overlaying an old, familiar genre—the spot map, an innovation that had up to this point been used idiosyncratically

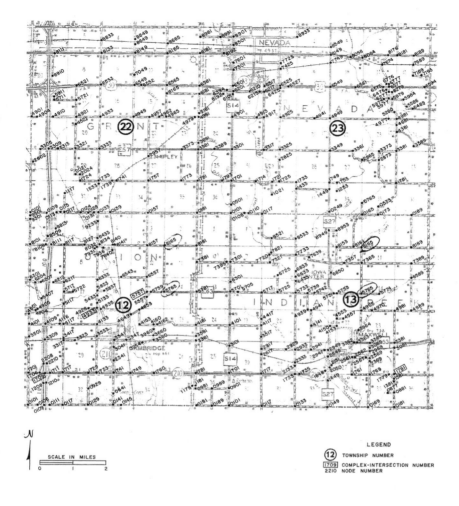

SAMPLE COUNTY MAP
ACCIDENT LOCATION AND ACCIDENT ANALYSIS SYSTEMS

STATE OF IOWA

Smith and Associates

FIGURE

Figure 3.5
A portion of an early node map of four townships in Story County. The diagonally angled numbers indicate nodes. These numbers are hard to read when densely clustered, and that problem was only exacerbated when more roads were built. (Reprinted by permission of the Iowa Department of Transportation.)

by half of the counties and about six-tenths of the cities—with the new node system. The result was a standardized hybrid genre: the *node map* (figure 3.5).

Another new genre was the *node table*, a text-only list of nodes in each county along with a short literal description of each. Node tables were printed from the DOT's node database and bound in books. The books were then used by operators to identify nodes and (more often) strings of nodes. For instance, a worker wanting to gather data on a stretch of Interstate 35 would look up the nodes in a county whose descriptions included the identifier "I-35."

The ALAS activity system required an automated accident location system that could more or less reproduce pre-ALAS work (locating, counting, and reporting accidents) using the alphanumeric data of the node-link system. WSA recommended, and partially implemented, a cutting-edge system that became known as mainframe-ALAS, consisting of thirty-two programs and three permanent tape files (Wilbur Smith and Associates, 1974b). The programs were written in the programming language COBOL, but designers envisioned add-ons written in PL/I or FORTRAN. Mainframe-ALAS was seen as only the basis for a more so-phisticated system. However, WSA was not retained for the second and third phases of development, so the system was not further developed.

Mainframe-ALAS could not take requests or updates in the same way that human operatives could (e.g., through handwritten reports, letters, and telephone calls), so data entry clerks had to enter requests and updates into mainframe-ALAS via punch cards. The system's designers adapted and officialized a variety of genres to translate workers' oral and written requests to machine-readable format: a worksheet for generalized requests (figure 3.6) as well as a variety of forms that guided workers as they filled out punch cards for generalized requests, node-string updates and requests, accident summaries, and so forth. These forms, along with the node maps, were the interface for the workers:[6] genres that addressed their frequent queries in terms of the node-link system, and in doing so standardized those queries. (Sless (1994) argues that paper is still the most prevalent interface for computer applications.) In fact, although node maps were officially restricted to the state level, they soon made their way to city and county agencies, along with node tables and the

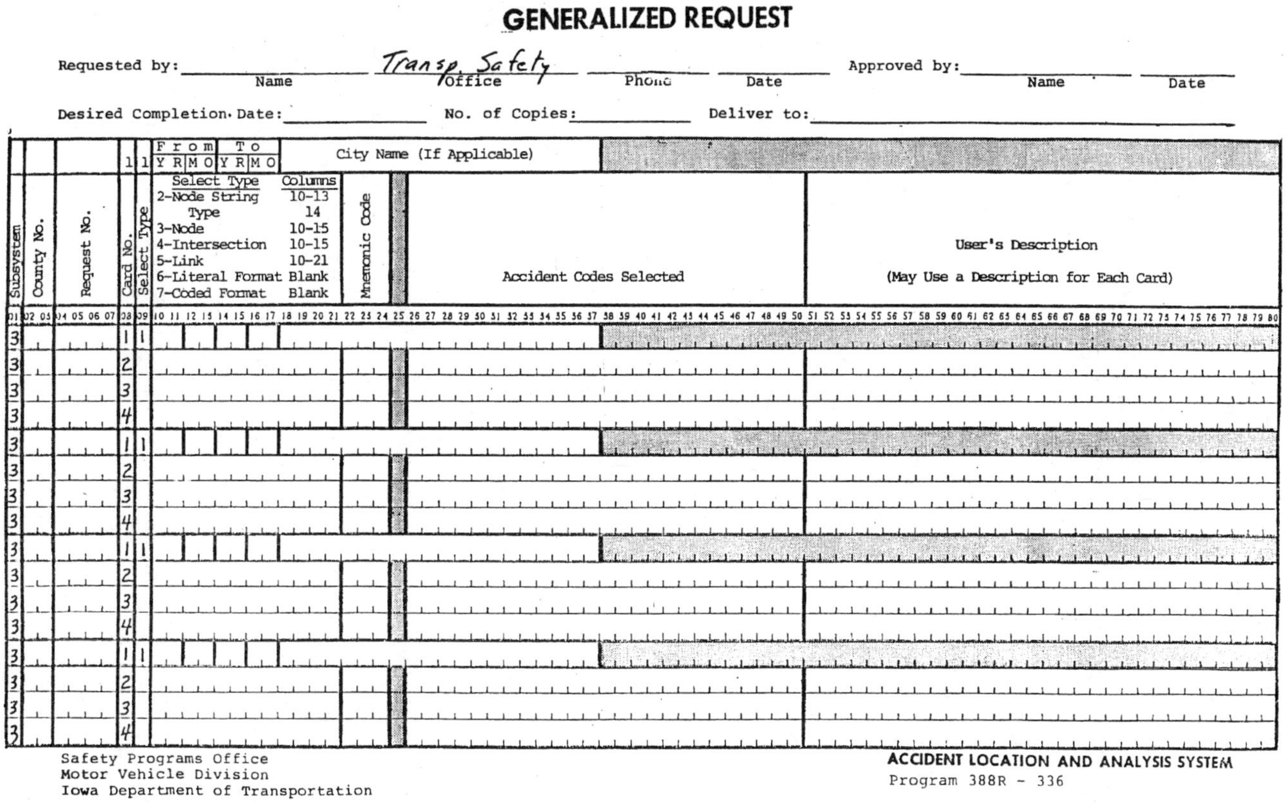

GENERALIZED REQUEST

Requested by: ______ Name   Transp. Safety Office   ______ Phone   ______ Date   Approved by: ______ Name   ______ Date

Desired Completion. Date: ______   No. of Copies: ______   Deliver to: ______

Subsystem | County No. | Request No. | Card No. | Select Type | From YR MO | To YR MO | City Name (If Applicable)

Select Type	Columns
2-Node String	10-13
Type	14
3-Node	10-15
4-Intersection	10-15
5-Link	10-21
6-Literal Format	Blank
7-Coded Format	Blank

Mnemonic Code

Accident Codes Selected

User's Description

(May Use a Description for Each Card)

01 02 03 04 05 06 07 08 09 10 11 12 13 14 15 16 17 18 19 20 21 22 23 24 25 26 27 28 29 30 31 32 33 34 35 36 37 38 39 40 41 42 43 44 45 46 47 48 49 50 51 52 53 54 55 56 57 58 59 60 61 62 63 64 65 66 67 68 69 70 71 72 73 74 75 76 77 78 79 80

Safety Programs Office
Motor Vehicle Division
Iowa Department of Transportation

ACCIDENT LOCATION AND ANALYSIS SYSTEM
Program 388R - 336

Figure 3.6
A worksheet for generalized requests. The Generalized Request Form helped workers recast queries in terms of the node-link system. (Reprinted by permission of the Iowa Department of Transportation.)

forms needed to specify data analyses. That is, mainframe-ALAS genres were unofficially adopted by workers outside the DOT.

We can speculate that these workers also innovated other genres to augment these official genres, such as notes written on scratch paper (as some workers do today). But such innovations were transitory if they did exist, and the only one for which I have evidence is the genre of the help call: workers reported calling each other and the DOT for help in using the mainframe-ALAS genres.

Mainframe-ALAS' output drew on older, pre-ALAS report genres. Output was via printouts in one of two report formats. The High Accident Ranking Report, a "packaged" summary report (Wilbur Smith and Associates, 1974a) with a rigid format, ranked a group of locations by the number of accidents at each location. The Generalized Request Report, a one-time request based on certain parameters, gave detailed information for each accident that matched the parameters. Although both reports were useful, the Generalized Request Report, with its ability to pinpoint specific locations and accident types, was to become the cornerstone of further ALAS development. Both reports were difficult to read, requiring the DOT to train special analysts to interpret them and thus widening the division of labor (as I discuss below).

These report genres were hybrids, combinations of older hand-compiled report genres, officers' and drivers' report forms, and standard computer printouts. The Generalized Request Report in particular resembled the officers' and drivers' reports: the location descriptions and the very narratives written on the reports appeared in the Generalized Request Report, albeit transformed to fit neatly into the ALAS database. The older input and output genres (driver's and officer's reports, DPS reports) migrated into the interface of the new system, mingled with the system's interface genres, and produced a hybrid genre that could be used to mediate new activities, just as the map genre and the node-link system had produced the hybrid node map.

Both the node-link system and mainframe-ALAS changed the activity. Of particular interest is the increasingly complex division of labor. First, *locators* transformed the categorical and narrative data of the officers' and drivers' reports into node data. Locators were DOT personnel whose sole job was to read the reports, pinpoint the accident location on a map, and determine which node number(s) best expressed the location, using genres such as drivers' and officers' reports, node map, and perhaps their own notes. The results (perhaps on scratch paper or on forms—it is not clear from the archived materials) were passed on to *data entry personnel*, who would transform the reports' narrative accounts into database records on punch cards (and occasionally reconcile conflicting narratives based on their own experience or evaluations of the different claims, what Susan Leigh Star (1995, 98) calls "deleting the work").[7] Finally, *analysts* would take local agencies' requests for data via forms or phone calls (probably noting phoned requests on scratch paper), fill out the requests on preprinted forms, key them onto punch cards, and run them in batches to produce reports. These reports were difficult to read, so specially trained analysts were assigned the job of interpreting them. Thus the task of accident analysis, once a relatively solitary affair, became piecework: different specialists had to work together to produce the analyses. And whereas accident analysis once involved fairly traditional tasks of writing and reading in a relatively small number of genres, in the mainframe-ALAS era these traditional tasks were disassembled and divided among workers using a wide variety of genres: one translated the original reports into machine-readable code, one did the same for written or spoken requests, and a third transformed the machine-compiled results into more traditional written and spoken genres.

But if the division of labor was more complex, so were the analyses that were possible from this new system. Access to complex accident data was quicker, easier, and cheaper than ever before. Workers could more easily access statewide accident records. Complex analyses were more feasible and results were more consistent. The centralized database reduced errors in accident reports and counts. Eventually, the DOT produced node maps for all cities and counties to help local officials better understand reported data (thereby officializing the local workers' unofficial adoption of these genres). Report formats became more standardized, and the number of reports and applications of accident data analysis increased (Pawlovich 1996). By 1990 the DOT was regularly sending customized ALAS reports to all ninety-nine counties, including data such as accident statistics on each intersection in the county, as well as filling specific requests from county engineering offices.

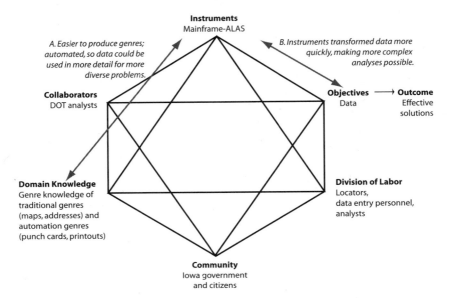

Figure 3.7
The mainframe-ALAS activity system. Straight arrows indicate the easing of contradictions from the previous era.

Analysis

In the early 1970s, then, automation moved into the ALAS activity system and fundamentally changed it. Iowa's accident location and analysis system became more centralized, its data more complex, and its ecology of genres more diversified (figure 3.7). Automation eased contradictions, not by clearing out the existing genre ecology, but rather by importing some genres into the computer's interface and functionality while retaining their history, addressivity, and relationships to other genres in the ecology. Genres like spot maps and reports were hybridized with automation-era genres such as quantified representations of roadways and computer printouts to form a new genre ecology that existed partly within the computer. In the process, they were officialized. Officialization was used to standardize practices at both state and local levels.[8]

Although mainframe-ALAS achieved a greater level of productivity and complexity than ever before, it formed contradictions as well, as illustrated in figure 3.8.

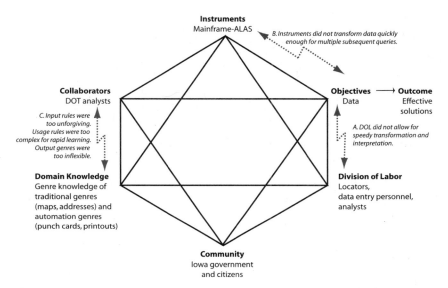

Figure 3.8
The mainframe-ALAS activity system. All queries went through the DOT. Lightning arrows represent contradictions among the system's elements.

(A) Data and analysis tools were deliberately centralized at the DOT, meaning that other agencies had to telephone or mail their query requests to the DOT, then wait days or weeks to have the resulting reports mailed back to them.

(B) The slow response time meant that it was impractical to make multiple subsequent queries: workers could not easily test increasingly specific hypotheses or "snoop around" the data.

(C) Operating mainframe-ALAS was no picnic. There were problems with formulating and processing requests, due partly to the rigid nature of the query language. One character in the wrong column on a punch card could get the query rejected. And since queries were processed in batches, the unlucky operator would have to wait hours to discover errors. Output was in the form of two types of reports: one had an inflexible format and the other had to be interpreted with reference sheets and tabulated by hand (using unofficial genres such as handwritten notes). Finally, mainframe-ALAS took weeks to learn how to operate (Moreland 1992).

Consequently, mainframe-ALAS was never used as widely as one might expect. It was used almost exclusively by the DOT and by some county engineers' offices. Its reports, in fact, were designed primarily for engineers (Iowa Department of Transportation, 1990). And other workers, such as law enforcement officials and legislators, typically needed the data more quickly than the DOT could run the requests.

We have seen how WSA adapted a wide variety of genres, mingling some of them with interface genres to produce hybrids, in a quest to ease the preautomation contradictions. Yet new contradictions formed (figure 3.8). The system became overofficialized. Centralization limited the sorts of requests; since workers did not have direct access to the analysis tools, they were quite limited in the genres they could adapt, data they could request, and reports they could generate. Since request and report formats were centrally controlled and adapted to the work activities of system analysts,[9] they left very little room for workers to produce unofficial alternatives. The centralization also meant that workers were limited sharply in what genres they could adapt.

Despite the contradictions and limitations, mainframe-ALAS endured from 1974 until the late 1980s, when we see another centripetal mass adaptation of genres.

1989: PC-ALAS (DOS)

In 1989 Joyce Emery, who was running the DOT's Traffic Safety Office, hired Scott Moreland as an intern. Moreland, then an eighteen-year-old computer engineering student at Iowa State University, was to serve as a data analyst, running queries and interpreting reports. At this point, mainframe-ALAS' shortcomings were becoming increasingly obvious to Emery and she was interested in a PC-based solution. Moreland's solution, which eventually won him the Iowa Governor's State Top Achievement Recognition (STAR) Award, was PC-ALAS.

Moreland's idea was to create a PC-based ALAS that had the same capabilities as mainframe-ALAS: the ability to read the existing state crash data, run various queries, and generate reports. Whereas mainframe-ALAS had cost millions of dollars to develop and run, PC-ALAS was developed in Moreland's spare time and could be distributed freely to any and all who were interested.

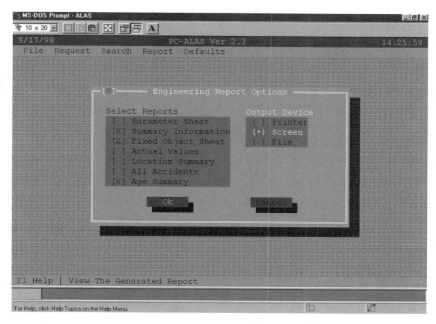

Figure 3.9
A PC-ALAS screen, showing the Windows-like DOS interface. Windows-like features include the horizontal menu; the dialog box with its checkboxes, radio buttons, and OK and Cancel buttons; and the status line at the bottom of the screen.

Moreland developed PC-ALAS using Borland's version of the Pascal programming language, Turbo Pascal 5.0. The original PC-ALAS ran on MS-DOS 3.3 and was pilot-tested in late 1989 and 1990; other versions followed. In 1990 Moreland implemented a more user-friendly interface using Borland's TurboVision package. The new interface, although DOS-based, included Windows-like features such as pull-down menus, dialog boxes, and mouse support (figure 3.9).

Moreland and others who later maintained PC-ALAS also implemented a variety of other options, including canned queries and a report specifically for law enforcement agencies. These genres, then, became diversified based on the input of workers.

PC-ALAS was a revolution of sorts, a low-budget, high-tech assault on the mainframe-centered mentality that dominated the DOT at the time. In an article reporting Moreland's winning of the STAR award, one

DOT publication enthusiastically hailed PC-ALAS as good news for democratic data processing: "Dyed-in-the-wool data processing people still say it's a mainframe world. For the rest of us, namely the computer-illiterate population, personal computers (PC) may be our pathway into the electronic era" (Iowa Department of Transportation, 1990).

The mainframe-ALAS legacy was a centralized information processing system. Although local agencies could make requests and receive reports, most of the work in accident analysis—data entry, requests, execution, and to some extent interpretation—was done at the DOT, by DOT workers. But PC-ALAS meant a certain degree of decentralization for many workers: although data were still coded and consolidated at the DOT, the datafiles were then released—along with a copy of PC-ALAS—to all interested agencies. They were distributed through mail, the DOT electronic bulletin board system, and the DOT circuit rider (an individual commissioned to visit local agencies and disperse DOT materials). A single floppy disk could hold both the program and a county's data file. As local agencies began processing their own requests, the burden on the DOT was initially lightened. Yet the ability of local agencies to process their own requests led to more complex analyses; it raised the bar on what could be considered a good analysis. Soon the DOT was awash in requests, this time from smaller organizations that had not felt the need for complex analyses before and that were not confident in their own abilities to conduct analyses.

Although the interface was new, PC-ALAS borrowed heavily from the genres of mainframe-ALAS. For instance, the mainframe-ALAS Generalized Request Worksheet and Form both had selection types; these types are incorporated into PC-ALAS' Run Location dialog box. Similarly, the mainframe-ALAS Node String Request Form closely resembles PC-ALAS' String Request Parameters dialog box (figure 3.10). Genres that were once the *paper* interface for local workers became the *on-screen* interface, and became more customized. In being recast in the dialog-box genre, forms took on characteristics familiar to Macintosh and Windows users.

Workers found that they could begin using PC-ALAS with minimal training: the standard training class lasted one day, not the several weeks required for mainframe-ALAS training. Workers in local agencies could now conduct their own searches rather than relying on the DOT's analysts. Local agencies tended to assign the job of searching to one person or a small group of people, "PC-ALAS experts" who would field search requests from others in the agency. PC-ALAS had delivered control of accident location and analysis to local agencies, but the task had grown complex enough that local experts were now needed to carry it out.

Using a node map or a node table, workers at local agencies could formulate their own queries or sets of queries and receive the results immediately. Instant feedback made it practical to make multiple subsequent queries, allowing workers to form and test increasingly specific hypotheses "on the fly." They could sift quite specific types of accidents out of the data: accidents involving people over twenty-five, accidents involving dry conditions, accidents involving fixed objects. The accident location and analysis system had suddenly become far more useful for most workers.

The various types of reports also made PC-ALAS useful. In mainframe-ALAS, paper reports were the only form of output and came in two genres: the High Accident Ranking Report and the Generalized Request Report. These were produced at the end of the process and regarded as end products. But with the advent of PC-ALAS, reports were fundamentally transformed in three ways.

First, reports mingled with an interface genre—the scrollable text window—to produce a hybrid genre, the on-screen report. Such reports could be generated, reviewed, and dismissed without ever being printed. And since generating these reports was swift and relatively easy, workers began to generate reports for preliminary results that could be used for further refining queries. The reports were no longer simply end products.

Second, report genres began to multiply thanks to a dialogue between developers and workers. In contrast to mainframe-ALAS, which was developed by outside consultants and code-frozen in 1974, PC-ALAS was developed internally and over a period of years. Consequently, the developers responded to workers' requests by creating several flexible, configurable report formats that were easier to interpret and presented information useful to a wider range of agencies. For instance, the Generalized Request Report split into two genres, the Engineering Report (which focused on the physical roadway system) and the Enforcement

NODE STRING REQUEST

Requested by: _____ Office _____ Phone _____ Approved by: _____

Name   Name   Date

Desired Completion Date: _____   No. of Copies: _____   Deliver to: _____

ALLbbb   — Prints out all Node Strings in State or Selected County.(Columns 11-78 Blank)
UPDATE   — Used in Conjunction with Node String Update Form, Prints out all Node Strings
           that were Added or Updated.(Columns 11-78 Blank)
SELECT   — Prints out Node Strings as Selected Within a County.

Node String Numbers Selected, County Only, Maximum of 17 Node Strings per County

Subsystem	County	Command	01 02 03 04 05 06 07 08 09	11 12 13 14 15 16 17 18 19 20 21 22 23 24 25 26 27 28 29 30 31 32 33 34 35 36 37 38 39 40 41 42 43 44 45 46 47 48 49 50 51 52 53 54 55 56 57 58 59 60 61 62 63 64 65 66 67 68 69 70 71 72 73 74 75 76 77 78

ACCIDENT LOCATION AND ANALYSIS SYSTEM
Program 388R - 206

Safety Programs Office
Motor Vehicle Division
Iowa Department of Transportation

Figure 3.10

The mainframe-ALAS Node String Request form (top) mingles with the screen genre of the dialog box to produce a hybrid, the PC-ALAS String Request Parameters dialog box (bottom). Some features, such as the county specification and the columnar format for node entry, persist. Other features are distributed among other interface genres or are not handled by PC-ALAS (e.g., updating). (Form reprinted by permission of the Iowa Department of Transportation.)

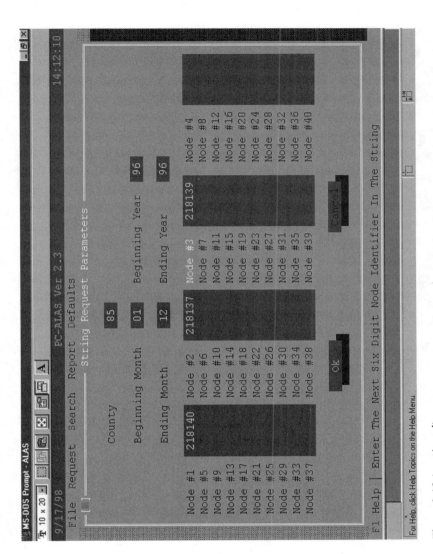

Figure 3.10 (continued)

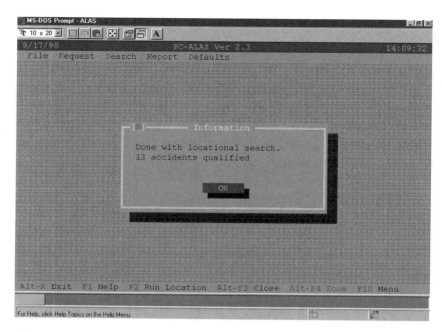

Figure 3.11
A message dialog box showing the number of accidents retrieved by a request.

Report (which emphasized behavioral factors). The Ranking Report, while remaining a single genre, was given new options to make it more flexible. And other genres were developed: the Driver Matrix Report, the Injured Matrix Report, and a report that simply listed city and county numbers. Each served specific needs of various agencies and external clients.

Third, part of the reports' duties were redistributed to another interface genre, the message dialog box (figure 3.11). In PC-ALAS, message dialog boxes informed the worker how many accidents are found in a given location, and how many are found when searching the location by specific characteristics. Both functions had once been the domain of the reports, which were the primary output method for mainframe-ALAS. But by adding the message dialog boxes, Moreland made it possible for workers to monitor their data on the fly. For instance, a PC-ALAS worker who wanted to view all accidents at an intersection no longer had to run the request *and* print a report to discover whether such accidents exist; she could find out simply by running the request. As chapter 4 argues, message dialog boxes became important resources for workers trying to develop hypotheses about their data.

PC-ALAS became a success. Police departments, local legislators, and engineers began to use accident data with increasing frequency. And they could do so knowing that their work was consistent with the work of others, as one DOT manager pointed out in an interview:

> PC-ALAS is a tool for communication among all units of government. A problem location can be studied simultaneously by the city traffic engineer and traffic law officer, by the Iowa DOT district local systems engineer and Safety Bureau, and soon by the FHWA [Federal Highway Authority] and Governor's Traffic Safety [Board] offices, each office knowing they are operating upon the same database with the same software. Each one may be using those tools differently, based upon the agency's expertise and purpose, while retaining the ability to reproduce each other's work.

Analysis

In 1989, the contradictions that bedeviled mainframe-ALAS led a DOT worker to develop PC-ALAS, which again transformed the ALAS activity system in significant and far-reaching ways. Perhaps the most significant change was that the genre ecology expanded radically as mainframe-ALAS genres mingled with PC-based interface genres—menus, dialog boxes, message windows, and text windows—to form new hybrids. Automated report genres multiplied. At the same time, workers invented and adapted other genres such as handwritten notes and manuals. (Chapter 4 discusses the PC-ALAS interface in more detail and evaluates it based on participants' use.)

As figure 3.12 indicates, PC-ALAS genres were still genetically connected to mainframe-ALAS. Workers still used mainframe-ALAS' node-link system, and in fact it became far more widely known and used than ever before. Local agencies began to see the road system in its terms. And workers began to use (and adapt) the genres linking preautomation and automation-era representations of the road system—node maps and node tables—even more frequently at their local agencies.

Furthermore, the genre of data entry forms used for querying mainframe-ALAS survived after a fashion: the forms migrated into the

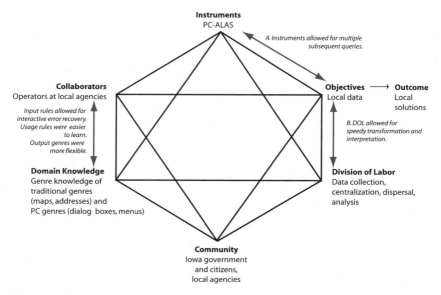

Figure 3.12
PC-ALAS activity system. Queries now go through local agencies.

PC-ALAS interface, mingling with the genre of the dialog box to produce hybrids. We can trace these genres from older to newer versions. Recall that the mainframe-ALAS forms themselves were genres that addressed frequent queries in terms of the node-link system. These queries had migrated into the interface—first as paper mainframe-ALAS forms, then as PC-ALAS dialog boxes. The PC-ALAS dialog boxes are not simply metaphors for the "real" forms. Rather, they are qualitative trans-formations of the older genres, perceived and used in much the same way, designed with similar genre rules, and mediating the same activities. The older genres have mingled with interface genres to produce hybrid genres suitable for the new ecology: forms become dialog boxes, reports become scrollable text windows, and routine procedures are fixed within menus, just as routine queries were fixed within ALAS forms in 1974.

The last part bears closer examination. The PC-ALAS menu structure separates ALAS actions into requesting, searching, and reporting infor-mation, and in doing so, provides a way for workers to conceive differ-ent groupings of ALAS data. This tripartite division was *implicit* in the

Table 3.2
Groupings of data and how they are acquired through PC-ALAS

Grouping	Description	Acquired through
Universe of data	All data stored in the PC-ALAS database.	
1. Requested data	Subset of the universe of data pertaining to a particular county, city, intersection, or other area.	Request menu
2. Searched data (optional)	Subset of the requested data meeting criteria such as accident conditions, vehicle characteristics, or driver characteristics.	Search menu
3. Reported data	All found data, represented in a chosen report genre. (If the worker did not search for data, *all* requested data are represented.)	Report menu

separate boxes on mainframe-ALAS forms, but the division was *conceptually separated* in the PC-ALAS menu system (table 3.2).

This tripartite separation serves to structure workers' actions. Workers begin at the left menu and work their way to the right (see figure 3.11). (Yet, as chapter 4 discusses, workers often find it difficult to remember which grouping of data they are using, a discoordination that contributes to numerous breakdowns.)

Although PC-ALAS made for a far more widespread and decentralized use of accident data than mainframe-ALAS ever had, it still had some contradictions, contradictions that became obvious by the mid-1990s (figure 3.13).

(A) Off-screen genres were physically and conceptually difficult to use with PC-ALAS. These genres included cumbersome node maps (created in CAD format by the DOT and distributed to local agencies) and node tables (printed in book form from the DOT's database). Workers first had to acquire these off—screen genres (sometimes a feat in itself—one

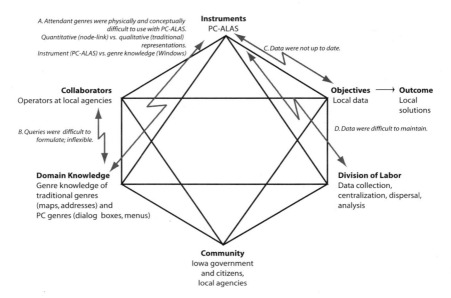

Figure 3.13
PC-ALAS activity system. Lightning arrows represent contradictions among elements of the network.

worker I observed in 1998 still used a node map from 1983). Then workers had to learn how to interpret and use them in conjunction with PC-ALAS. Not only were these genres difficult to coordinate with PC-ALAS, they were physically difficult to deal with, especially the maps. The node maps were three by three feet square, about the size of the top of an office desk when unrolled, and required about that much space. In addition, they tended to roll back up, necessitating the use of other artifacts to keep them flat (e.g., paperweights, coffee cups, small office equipment) or other innovations for representing the data (e.g., photocopying a frequently used part of the map onto a flat piece of paper). One worker showed me the coffee stains on his map that resulted from his habit of using his coffee cup as a paperweight (figure 3.14).

In addition, node maps and node tables had to be used with each other and with PC-ALAS' text-based interface, meaning that workers had to convert between these off- and on-screen representations. (As we saw at the beginning of chapter 1, this work was frequently done through

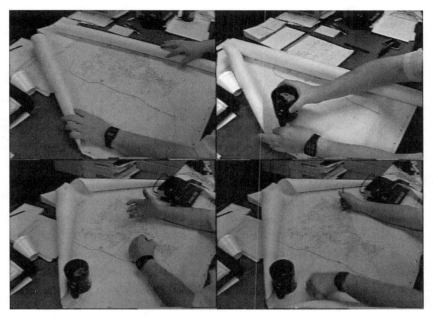

Figure 3.14
Various artifacts are enlisted to hold down the 3 × 3′ node map and to point out
and mark nodes.

unofficial genres such as handwritten notes.[10]) Reports were also text-
based and thus required further coordination with the node-map and
node-table genres. Report genres, although far more flexible than their
predecessors, did not address the activities of all workers. And the mingling of off-screen and on-screen genres was not seamless. For instance,
input entry dialog boxes looked and functioned differently from the
standard dialog boxes that workers had encountered in Microsoft Windows, as we will see in chapter 4.

(B) Queries were inflexible and difficult to formulate. Despite the
changes in the user interface, PC-ALAS came to be seen as cumbersome
and inflexible by many. The queries were characterized as "tedious"
(Pawlovich 1996, 25). Part of this perception, undoubtedly, came from
workers' experience with other, newer programs.

(C) Data were not up to date and were sometimes inaccurate. Errors
in the data entry process were propagated in local databases. And since

the same data were used to plot new nodes, node maps were not always accurate, and even in low-growth areas, tended to quickly become out of date. Databases were not usually up to date either: the PC-ALAS workers I observed in the spring of 1998 were working with data up to 1995—a limitation that had important implications for how workers perceived and employed PC-ALAS, as I discuss in chapter 4.

(D) Data were difficult to maintain, just as they had been in the mainframe-ALAS era. Officers, drivers, locators, and data entry personnel all had a hand in transforming accident reports into database records. This attenuated division of labor, and the intensive and complex nature of the labor, bred errors that were then propagated to the database and node maps.

Finally, PC-ALAS itself had become difficult to maintain. Although Turbo Pascal had been a popular computer language in 1989, by the mid-1990s it was for all practical purposes a dead language, so updates to the original code became extremely difficult to make. Moreland and the other programmers had all gone on to other jobs. And DOS-based programs themselves had gone the way of the 5.25-inch floppy disk.

In the late 1990s, the waning days of the PC-ALAS era, the ALAS activity system had begun to collapse under the weight of its own contradictions. Workers were beginning to develop unofficial genres to deal with PC-ALAS' limitations, from handwritten notes to customized databases and geographic information systems, as they attempted to cope with PC-ALAS' contradictions and take over some PC-ALAS duties. One of these unoffical projects, a thesis project begun in 1995, obtained funding in 1997 and became the official successor-in-development: GIS-ALAS.

1996: GIS-ALAS (WINDOWS)

Like PC-ALAS, GIS-ALAS was developed by an innovative Iowa State student. In 1995, Michael Pawlovich, a master's student in civil and construction engineering, was working at the Center for Transportation Research and Education (CTRE). He became involved with distributing PC-ALAS disks, training workers in PC-ALAS, and extracting PC-ALAS data for a CTRE project. This project brought to Pawlovich's attention some of the problems with PC-ALAS:

> So we were getting accident information out of [PC-]ALAS, which involves a long, arduous process, as most people know. And then I had to put all that information on a map, which made the process all that much more arduous, and it occurred to me that perhaps these [the program and the map] could be put together, and it would be a lot quicker.

Pawlovich did so by adapting an off-the-shelf geographic information system (GIS), a database that allows queries and displays results through an on-screen map. He developed a version of the product, dubbed GIS-ALAS, as his 1996 thesis project and as a project for CTRE. Using the programming language FORTRAN, Pawlovich extended the GIS' capabilities to read PC-ALAS crash data and perform standard PC-ALAS functions. The result was an on-screen map that could be configured to show accidents of various types. (I discuss GIS-ALAS' dual heritage in more detail in chapter 5.)

CTRE obtained funding for the GIS-ALAS project in the fall of 1997. With the help of an undergraduate assistant, Pawlovich moved GIS-ALAS to another GIS, ArcView (figure 3.15), and rewrote its routines in ArcView's macrolanguage, Avenue. The ArcView version was undergoing testing and development during this and the following studies, and was subsequently completed in fall 1999.

The map is a natural candidate for migration into the interface. Edward Tufte (1983, 16) enthuses:

> Only a picture [such as a map] could carry such a volume of data in such a small space. Furthermore, all that data, thanks to the [map], can be thought about in many different ways at many different levels of analysis— ranging from the contemplation of general overall patterns to the detection of very fine county-by-county detail.

This flexibility of analysis was quite desirable for ALAS workers: the advantage of automation is that workers can quickly form and test hypotheses, but the map had been a weak link because, until the GIS-ALAS era, the map could not be automated. Workers could manually mark spot maps if they wanted to contemplate overall patterns or examine spatial relations in detail, but without automation the process was labor intensive and involved converting from the node-link system to the map genre, a process that introduced conversion errors. With GIS-ALAS, Pawlovich successfully automated the map.

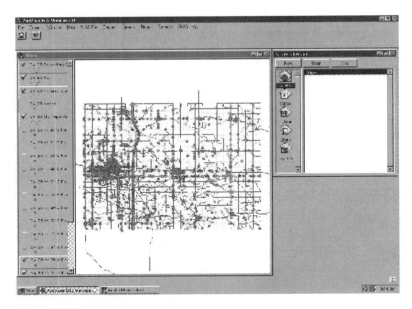

Figure 3.15
The ArcView-based GIS-ALAS interface, including horizontal menu (top), map
window (left), and control window (right). These genres are versions of older
genres found in the PC-ALAS interface, which in turn are versions of still older
genres. (See chapter 5 for a more detailed analysis.) (Reprinted from *Computers
and Composition, 18*, Spinuzzi, " 'Light green doesn't mean hydrology!' ", pp.
39–53, copyright (2001) with permission from Elsevier Science.)

Pawlovich (1996, 5) said that "the chief advantage of GIS [is] the
ability to view and select nodes and links through a spatial graphical user
interface." But perhaps GIS-ALAS' chief advantage was that workers
could begin to forget about nodes and links altogether. Although
workers could still run queries based on node numbers, GIS-ALAS made
it easy for them to simply click on a node (represented as a glowing dot
on a screen map) instead. Workers could also select a group of nodes
simply by clicking and dragging the mouse appropriately. Better yet,
workers could elect not to use nodes at all: they could select areas of
interest on the map instead, such as actual accident locations. Finally,
queries resulted in highlighted spots on the map (the genetic descendants
of marks made on spot maps since the earliest days of the ALAS activity

Summary Sheet - Time of Day/Day of Week

Day	Period1	Period2	Period3	Period4	Period5	Period6	Period7	Period8	Period9	Period10	Period11	Period12	All
	0000 0159	0200 0359	0400 0559	0600 0759	0800 0959	1000 1159	1200 1359	1400 1559	1600 1759	1800 1959	2000 2159	2200 2359	All Times
Sunday	0	0	0	0	0	0	0	0	0	0	0	1	1
Monday	0	0	0	0	0	0	0	0	0	0	0	1	1
Tuesday	0	0	0	0	0	0	0	2	0	0	0	0	2
Wednesday													
Thursday	0	0	0	1	0	0	0	0	1	0	1	3	
Friday	0	0	0	0	0	0	0	0					
Saturday	0	0	0	0	0	0	0	0	0				
All Days	0	0	0	1	1	0	0	2					

Summary Sheet - Accident Numbers

Field1	Field2	Field3	Field4	Field5	Field6
0	Fatal Accidents	0	Fatalities	0	Injuries
3	Personal Injury Accidents			4	Injuries
9	Property Damage Only Accidents				
12	Total Accidents	0	Fatalities	4	Injuries

Summary Sheet - Driver/Vehicle Related Contri...

Value1	Item1	Value2	Item...
	*** Driver/Vehicle Related		Contributing Circl
0	Animal in Roadway	1	Improper Lane C
0	Ran Traffic Signal	2	Following Too Cl
0	Ran Stop Sign	0	No Signal or Imp
0	Passing Where Prohibited	0	Disregarded Wa
1	Passing Interfered w/ Other Ve	0	Reckless Driving
1	Left of Center - Not Passing	0	Improper Backin
0	FTYROW - Uncontrolled Inters	0	Illegal or Improp
0	FTYROW - From Stop Sign	1	Not Under Conti
	FTYROW - From Yield Sign		Hand Lights

Figure 3.16
GIS-ALAS summary sheets. Whereas in PC-ALAS the report genres were made more flexible with optional sections, in GIS-ALAS the sections are displayed in separate windows altogether. Each window is printed separately.

system) as well as tabular descriptions descended from the reports of mainframe-ALAS and PC-ALAS.

With GIS-ALAS, genres continued to be imported into the genre ecology. The map is the most obvious example, but the old PC-ALAS dialog boxes, queries, reports, and menu system were also hybridized. For instance, the node map combined with the online map genre common to GISes to form the GIS-ALAS map (figure 3.15). Points of interest showed up as dots; map features such as roads, railroads, and bodies of water were conceived of as different "themes" that could be displayed or hidden; the map could be enlarged or shrunk. Reports (figure 3.16) were now produced as series of discrete tables (displayed in their own windows) rather than as complete documents. PC-ALAS menus were adopted in partial form, but coexisted with ArcView menus.

GIS-ALAS promised to transform the ALAS activity system once again, and in significant ways. It reduced the need for workers to know node numbers, masking the competing representations that had caused trouble for PC-ALAS workers. It visually displayed map features. And the rank-and-file workers had to transform data less: rather than looking up and entering node numbers to inspect certain intersections, for example, they could simply select the appropriate intersections on the online map.

GIS-ALAS made use of the familiar map genre that workers had often and skillfully employed to transform their objectives. In doing so, it minimized the work of translating report results back to the map genre. Furthermore, these maps could be updated more quickly: rather than printing maps on request and sending them to each of the ninety-nine counties, the DOT could simply post the updated maps to its website.

Analysis

Even in its prototype state, GIS-ALAS began to form contradictions within the ALAS activity system (figure 3.17). These contradictions are explored in chapter 5.

(A) Contradictions began to develop in the ways that GIS-ALAS presented information in its hybridized genres, as we will see in detail in chapter 5. For instance, even though the node-link system was theoretically rendered obsolete by the map window, workers still needed to understand it if they were to understand the hybridized genres of the

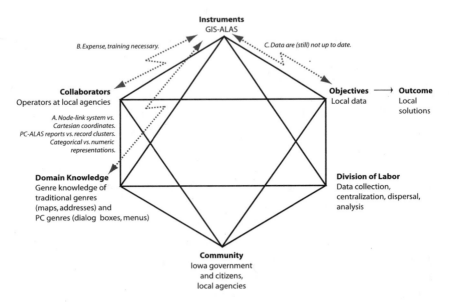

Figure 3.17
GIS-ALAS activity system. Notice the changes in genres available.

map window and the information window, whose data displays were still based on nodes. In addition, these data displays were often cryptically named, leading workers to immediately suggest adopting documentation genres to mediate them. Essentially, when the traditional ALAS genres were imported into the GIS interface, they were hyperconstrained by the GIS, which was built to meet very different needs (see chapter 5). The genres became radically deformed—some were consolidated, some were atomized, others were changed almost beyond recognition.

(B) GIS-ALAS was more difficult to distribute because it represented substantial investments in money and training. Since it was based on ArcView, workers had to purchase ArcView to run GIS-ALAS. ArcView retailed for over $1,000 in 1998, putting it out of the price range of many smaller agencies. In addition, many small agencies did not own computers that were fast enough or had enough memory to run GIS-ALAS, necessitating a substantial investment in hardware. Finally, ArcView was a complex program, so local agencies would need to train workers thoroughly. The study in chapter 5 suggests that workers may begin to adapt new genres to deal with the complexities posed by the new system.

(C) Finally, the data were still not up to date. Although the MARS initiative was anticipated to narrow the division of labor needed to enter data, shortening data turnaround and improving accuracy, it was only in the testing phase in 1998. The slow updating and inaccuracies that plagued previous activity systems would continue in the GIS-ALAS activity system, at least in the short term.

At the time of my studies, GIS-ALAS was the latest ALAS software. Since then, Access-ALAS has been developed, based on Microsoft Access and including a basic map interface. VB-ALAS, written in Visual Basic, is tentatively slated for development.

CONCLUSION

The study above indicates that interrelationships among genres develop over time. As people use computers, they collectively develop ecologies of genres: they adapt existing genres to help mediate between other genres in the ecology. In doing so, they find new ways to perceive the adapted genre and develop new ways to manage the relationship between that genre and the others in the genre ecology. That is, they learn a new way to interpret the genre, and that way involves using it to mediate between other genres.

People find that they must frequently import genres into their genre ecology. Such adaptations of existing genres are necessary to address deep contradictions among elements of their activity system—contradictions that manifest in discoordinations and breakdowns, as I demonstrate in chapters 4 and 5. Such importations can be official, but they most often start out as unofficial. At some point, the activity changes enough that a system is not flexible enough to support it; the resulting critical mass of workaround genres eventually gives rise to the new, official system.

Sometimes new information systems are developed to help mediate an activity, and when that happens, the traditional off-screen genres often are imported to the computer screen, where they are combined with on-screen genres to produce hybrid genres. Hybridized genres, the result of mingling off-screen and on-screen genres, tend to retain their history, their addressivity, and their relationship to other genres in the ecology. But as off-screen genres are imported into the interface, workers continue to adapt new off-screen genres.

These points are demonstrated in this chapter's study. Over the span of four decades, an ecology of genres has grown around the activity of accident location and analysis in the state of Iowa. This genre ecology serves to mediate the transformation of accident data into analyses, analyses that are then used in mediating other activities. Within the ecology, genres serve to mediate the use of other genres: mainframe-ALAS request forms and, later, PC-ALAS dialog boxes mediated between the node maps that workers used and the printed reports they wanted to produce. The genre ecology constantly develops as workers adapt still other genres to mediate those that already occupy it.

At three points in the history of the activity system, secondary contradictions became so severe that agencies developed information systems to remediate the activity by transforming the system. In all three cases, the developers transformed genres of the existing genre ecology by importing them into the computer interface, where they were combined with other genres to form hybrids. Just as accident report forms were combined with mainframe query forms to produce the hybridized mainframe-ALAS request forms, those request forms were later combined with the screen genre of the dialog box to produce the hybridized PC-ALAS dialog box. Yet despite these radical transformations, the genres retain their history, addressivity, and relationships with other genres. They are perceived and managed in substantially the same ways as their predecessors.

When these new information systems are developed, the developers tend to attempt to import many or most of the genres from the ecology into the interface. This attempt is most pronounced in the GIS-ALAS interface. Yet workers continue to innovate, adapting centrifugal genres to supplement the official (centripetal) genres; the ecology continues to develop.

In this chapter, the macroscopic analysis has helped us to see and understand tensions in activities and how those tensions relate to the many genres that mediate those activities. When workers adopt a great number of centrifugal genres, they do so because their activity has built up considerable tension. Radical design efforts, such as the major introductions of new information systems, indicate centripetal efforts to ease those tensions.

In the next two chapters, I draw on this macroscopic analysis as I take a closer look at centripetal and centrifugal genres. By tracing these genres across levels of scope, we can gain further insights into the destabilizations that characterize the activity, into how those destabilizations constitute design challenges, and into how designers can help meet those challenges.

4

Tracing Genres across Levels of Scope: A Study of PC-ALAS Use

Mike, a city engineer for a medium-sized city in northern Iowa, has been asked to investigate patterns of traffic accidents around a high school. The question he must answer is whether these accidents can be mitigated by adding signage and/or signalization. Mike suspects the answer is no: in his experience, traffic accidents around a high school are the result of inexperienced driving behavior rather than the lack of stop signs and traffic signals. But Mike understands that he must first diagnose *the problem—determine whether his hypothesis is correct—and then be prepared to* argue *his diagnosis in a city council meeting.*

Mike begins by starting a specialized database of traffic accidents called PC-ALAS. Then he asks me to hand him a node map: a three-by-three-foot rolled map of the area, showing the intersections he wants to investigate as well as numbers overlaid on the map. The numbers indicate locations. He writes down some of these numbers, then rolls up the map and sets it aside. Next, he types one of the numbers into a PC-ALAS dialog box and runs a search for accidents that have occurred there for a span of five years. (The span does not include data for the last two years, because those data have not yet been compiled.) Since Mike suspects that accidents at this intersection tend to be the result of inexperienced driving, he generates an enforcement report *(which shows the relationship of accidents to traffic violations) rather than an* engineering report *(which shows the relationship of accidents to road conditions such as weather).*

As he reads the report, he interprets it for me. "As far as the traffic control, there's not much you can do. There's fourteen people that run the light. And this one here's another common problem [points to the twenty-one accidents that involve a failure to yield right of way]. And that [pointing to another part of the report] depicts that as, in that hour of the day. That's the highest, at 3:00 when school gets out."

Chapter 3 traced genres developmentally through eras of an activity's history. In this chapter, I trace genres across levels of scope, using genre as a unit of analysis to help make sense of how the levels of scope coconstitute each other. I describe how workers in the ALAS activity system—a loose alliance of government agencies that share the objective of transforming traffic accidents into local solutions—performed their activities through the mediation of genres, how they encountered destabilizations at the three levels, and how those destabilizations and workers' innovations can be studied through an integrated-scope perspective.

In this chapter, I first discuss tracing genres (and the destabilizations associated with them) across levels of scope. I elaborate the concept of compound mediation and discuss how genre furnishes a suitable unit of analysis for investigating this concept. Finally, I describe a study I conducted to trace genres across the three levels of scope, particularly examining the innovations of users and the consequences of those innovations.

First, a word about this study. Although genre tracing can support a rigorous empirical study—by virtue of drawing on genre theory and activity theory—the study here is an informal one in the tradition of contextual studies used in software documentation and development: contextual design, participatory design, and studies involving ethnographic methods (e.g., Beyer and Holtzblatt 1998; Engeström and Escalante 1996; Schuler and Namioka 1993; Wixon and Ramey 1996). The study is meant to illustrate the methodological principle of integrating scope; the principle can also be applied to more formal studies.

GENRES AND DESTABILIZATIONS: ISSUES IN TRACING GENRES ACROSS LEVELS OF SCOPE

As I argued in chapter 2, genre provides an integrated-scope unit of analysis, one that works well for studying the sorts of subversive interactions that have often been glossed over by fieldwork-to-formalization methods. Since rhetoricians are familiar with theories of genre, it provides a useful entry point for examining information design issues. Genre is flexible enough to examine both official and unofficial artifacts. And, of course, genre theorists have provided a wealth of scholarship tying genre to the different levels of scope, as we saw in chapter 2.

Furthermore, genre can be seen as both the *product* (object) and the *mediator* of repeated activity (Geisler 2001; Spinuzzi 1996; cf. Bødker 1996). A genre is the product or material residue of problem solving. For instance, Charles Bazerman (1988) demonstrates that the genre of the experimental article is the result of centuries of cyclical activity in which experimenters gradually agreed on what sorts of proof are needed to argue for a particular proposition. Genre thus reflects the work that has gone into solving problems, as well as the values and assumptions held by the problem solvers. It provides a sort of social memory (see Bakhtin 1984, 87; Bakhtin 1981, 249; Medvedev and Bakhtin 1978, 133–135).

But genres also *mediate* cyclical activities. As the material residue of problem solving, genres provide a ready-to-hand solution for recurrent problems (Berkenkotter and Huckin 1995). They keep their users from having to "reinvent the wheel," from having to negotiate unique solutions for each instance. Of course, by their very use, they reaffirm the values and assumptions reflected in them.

For instance, consider the traffic report form discussed in chapter 3. This form allows drivers, who typically have little experience in describing traffic accidents, to describe their own accident in ways that are useful to the ALAS activity system. In following the form, all drivers are led to use the same incorporated genres (a diagram, a narrative of the accident, and so on) in the same ways. (Imagine how different the results would be if drivers were simply asked to describe the accident on a blank sheet of paper.) By filling out the form, drivers supply information that has historically been important to the ALAS activity system (e.g., the accident location, road conditions, a particular type of pictorial representation of the accident, a narrative description) while eliminating a wide range of information deemed irrelevant[1] (e.g., the brand of tires on each car, the color of each car, what the driver had for breakfast). DOT workers can consequently interpret and code this information into the PC-ALAS accident database. This *historical* solution of consolidating genres into a form also allows drivers and DOT workers alike to *address* each individual accident: the solution that has been worked out in the past can be applied to various types of accidents in the present. The solution is flexible enough to address (accommodate) most accidents.

In this example, we see how in genre, history and addressivity are inseparable. When a worker applies genre knowledge, she is taking a solution that has worked in the past and applying it to a current problem. The solution is sometimes applied in a routine way (as above), but sometimes in an innovative way that stretches the genre's capabilities. Workers (as we saw in chapter 3) might need to supplement the genre with other genres to produce a satisfactory solution. In fact, it is difficult to think of any reasonably complex social transaction that does not involve several genres working together to collectively mediate the activity. Witness the accident report, which is coordinated with drivers' licenses, proof of insurance, street addresses, and a variety of other genres—and which is itself a conglomeration of older genres.

These many disparate genres form an ecology that, ideally, mediates the many sorts of actions that go on in the activity. One might imagine that with the right balance of genres, the activity would function like a Swiss watch. But there are two things that keep this from happening.

First, as we have seen, genres are shaped by their history; they tend to reflect the values and assumptions of those who shaped them. Given that any reasonably complex activity employs a variety of genres, any number of these genres might reflect very different values and assumptions, and thus may tend toward shaping the activity in a particular way. When the Iowa Department of Transportation elected to automate its paper-based accident analysis system in 1974, for example, it did so by adopting a variety of genres (punch cards, automated reports, and so on) from business computing. Those genres shaped the ALAS activity system in ways very different from the more traditional genres (for instance, by making it necessary to quantify the landscape using the node-link system). Similarly, the accident report both reflects the information valued at the time it was designed and shapes the information later workers see as valuable.

And that leads us to the second point. As we saw in chapter 3, the activity itself constantly changes. Contradictions constantly open in the activity system as its parts continually mutate and realign and as it encounters other activities. The Iowa DOT developed mainframe-ALAS, for instance, after years of struggling with a paper-based system that became inadequate. The paper-based system had worked reasonably well at first, but as more detailed information became more important to more agencies and entities (eventually expanding to include federal agencies, lawmakers, and governors' commissions), the system developed the contradictions described in chapter 3.

The genres of an activity, then, are caught between history and addressivity—between offering the solutions of the past and responding to the exigencies of the present. It is this bind that makes genre such an interesting unit of analysis, since genres tend to be points at which such binds become visible. Not only are genres the points at which activities meet (as I demonstrate in chapter 5), but genres innovated by workers tend to embody the ways those workers attempt to remediate (Hasu and Engeström 2000, 65) the destabilizations in their activities.

Destabilizations

I use the term *destabilization* as I did in chapter 3, to emphasize the multilevel gaps and mismatches that develop in an activity or in the meeting of activities. As we have seen, activities are always off balance, always changing, always coming into contact with other activities. Change spawns destabilizations at various levels of scope. In chapter 2, I described three levels of scope and the destabilizations that can occur at each level, and I argued that the three levels coconstitute each other. Chapter 3 told the history of the ALAS activity system in a way that emphasized the macroscopic destabilizations—the *contradictions*—that developed during that history.

Since the levels of scope are coconstitutive, destabilizations at the different levels are similarly coconstitutive. The macroscopic contradictions described in chapter 3, for instance, do not form a causal layer of which mesoscopic discoordinations and microscopic breakdowns are merely symptoms. Rather, destabilizations appear at all levels of scope and can be traced across the levels—in this approach, by tracing genres, the points at which destabilizations often become visible and are often addressed.

Workers often address destabilizations by adding or altering genres, either centripetally or centrifugally. The centripetal impulse is to attempt to stamp out destabilizations by centrally consolidating and regulating genres. For instance, at crucial points in the history of the ALAS activity system, agencies developed new systems, categories, forms, and computer systems that both consolidated the solutions of the past and regulated how those solutions were applied. This centripetal impulse tends to result in commonly used, official genres (such as the drivers' report) and routines. But it can also lead to inflexible tools, stasis, and ossification. The set of official genres is by definition difficult to change, since official genres are meant to weather change. On the other hand, the centrifugal impulse is to multiply conflicts, to locally resist the official channels, to try out *any* solution. This impulse results in local innovation, local empowerment, and customized solutions (such as Barbara's sticky note), but can also lead to a loss of standardization and a loss of solutions, since local solutions might not be promulgated. Unofficial genres are meant to change and mutate; they are highly reactive stopgaps. They typically do not transfer well. And when they do, they are on their way to becoming official genres.

In chapter 3, I describe a repeated cycle in which an agency centripetally consolidated genres into a new information system that workers then supplemented with centrifugal innovations that eventually had to be consolidated again. In this chapter, I take a closer look at the end of this process—at the end of the PC-ALAS era, just before the DOT centripetally consolidated genres into GIS-ALAS—to examine the locally innovated genres and trace how they respond to the destabilizations in activities.

To perform this action of tracing, I examine systemic destabilizations at the different levels, then juxtapose them through the heuristic of the CDB table (see table 4.1).

In table 4.1, the three understandings of genre that I discussed in chapter 2 are juxtaposed, offering a methodological outline for examining genres at each level of scope, then integrating the levels. For example, at the macroscopic level of activity, we can understand genre as social action by examining how it affects the entire activity in which it plays

Table 4.1
A contradiction-discoordination-breakdown table, including the understandings
of genre that it helps to integrate

Destabilization	Understanding of genre
Contradiction in macroscopic activity	*Genre as social action.* Look for changes in the activity system: the object of activity, instruments, division of labor, community, and so on.
Discoordination in mesoscopic actions	*Genre as tool-in-use.* Look for new genre adaptations and new ways of interpreting and using existing genres.
Breakdown in microscopic operations	*Genre as collection of habits.* Look for new formation of operations.

a part and the contradictions in which it is involved (see chapter 3 for a first attempt at such an analysis). And by examining a genre in terms of the three levels simultaneously, we can examine how destabilizations are manifested in genres at each level and how additional genres have been adapted to address the destabilizations.

Table 4.1 provides a blueprint for the analysis I conduct in the latter part of this chapter, and in fact tables similar to table 4.1 appear at the end of the chapter. But before we get to that analysis, we need to better understand compound mediation.

Compound Mediation

Examining one genre in isolation can lead us to understand the genre as a tool-in-use (at the mesoscopic level) to the exclusion of the other levels of scope. That is, when we focus on a single genre (say, a computer interface) to the exclusion of the other genres that workers coordinate with it, we may come to believe that the genre is the linchpin of the system: if only we could redesign that one genre properly, it seems, the entire system would function more smoothly at all levels of scope.

But we never really deal with linchpins. No genre can function as a linchpin because genres are densely coordinated in what I have metaphorically termed an *ecology*. In a genre ecology, intercoordinated genres intermediate each other and any change in the ecology (such as altering, introducing, or removing a genre) can change the entire dynamic. In the headnote at the beginning of chapter 1, for instance, Barbara added a sticky note to the genre ecology. She used that innovated genre to mediate between the node map and the dialog box, and in doing so, dramatically changed how the genre ecology mediated the activity—pushing the node map to the margins of the activity and disassociating the nodes from the spatial representation of the map. (We will further explore the implications of this innovation later in the chapter.)

To maintain an integrated-scope perspective, then, I suggest using the notion of genre ecology to help us conceptualize this dynamic system of genres that has grown up around any given activity. Doing so allows us to explore how each genre mediates other genres. Furthermore, it allows us to examine *ecological niches* that are opened by changes in the activity and the genres that workers innovate to fill those niches.

When workers coordinate interrelated genres in an ecology, they manage these genres through domain knowledge applied within the genre ecology. For instance, PC-ALAS users employed dialog boxes in conjunction with node maps: they used a node map to look up the intersection for which they wanted data, then typed the node number into the dialog box. Perceiving an artifact as being the member of a certain genre entails managing those existing genre connections. The connection between the node map and the PC-ALAS dialog box echoed the much older connection between the node map and the mainframe-ALAS form (figure 3.10).

Figure 4.1 depicts the PC-ALAS genre ecology. The lines indicate mediatory relationships among genres, the ways workers coordinated them as they accomplished their activities. These relationships made the genres cohere as an ecology and allowed them to comediate workers' activities. Workers *perceived* genres (interpreted the genres themselves, represented by the genres' names in the figure) and *managed* genres (maintained and coordinated the mediatory relationships among genres, represented by the lines in the figure). For instance, Mike used handwritten notes to mediate between the node map and the dialog box.

Now that we have reviewed these two heuristics, let's apply them to the study.

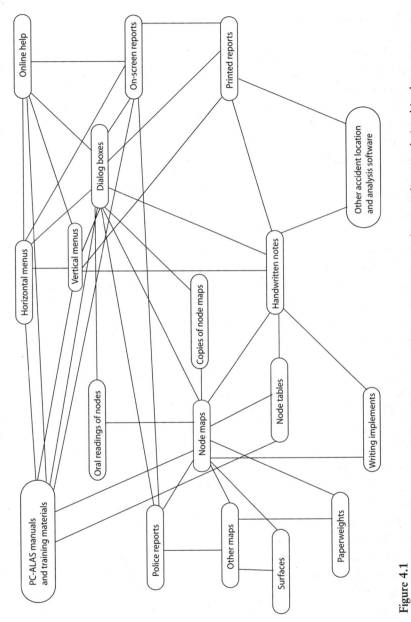

Figure 4.1
The genre ecology used for locating and analyzing traffic accidents. Lines indicate mediatory relationships between genres. (Spinuzzi, *Journal of Business and Technical Communication* 16.1, p. 25, copyright © 2002 by SAGE Publications. Reprinted by Permission of SAGE Publications, Inc.)

TRACING GENRES IN THE ALAS ACTIVITY SYSTEM

In this field study of PC-ALAS use, I asked the following questions: How do participants come to encounter destabilizations in perceiving and managing genres? How can we trace those genres and their related destabilizations across levels of scope? To answer these questions, I observed encounters that PC-ALAS users had with genres during work and walkthroughs. In addition, I observed and interviewed participants to determine what destabilizations they experienced when using PC-ALAS.

Methods

I collected all data from twenty-six participants[2] at various state and local agencies such as the Iowa Department of Transportation, the Federal Highway Authority, the Governor's Traffic Safety Board, city and county engineers' departments, sheriffs' offices, and police departments.

Ten participants completed questionnaires describing their experience with their activities, the ALAS family of software, and other types of online products with which they were familiar. Answers to the questionnaires became the basis for interviews exploring their experiences with the ALAS family of software, including PC-ALAS.

In addition, five participants demonstrated activities ancillary to PC-ALAS use, including the entry of crash reports into the PC-ALAS database, the entry of crash information into the MARS database, the use of node maps, and the use of PC-ALAS data to write an environmental impact report for a government agency. They also filled out questionnaires and completed interviews afterward.

Twelve participants completed the same questionnaires and were observed as they either completed actual work with PC-ALAS or walked through data similar to those they would normally process with PC-ALAS. (One of these participants also took part in a previous telephone interview.) I videotaped the computer screen during these observations and also took field notes. After each observation, I interviewed participants about their general experiences with PC-ALAS and their specific experiences during each observation.

Once I had collected the data, I analyzed them in three ways. Through a macroscopic analysis, *participant profiling*, I drew on all three types of data as well as the analysis in chapter 3 to construct detailed profiles of the participants and the local activity systems in which they worked. Through a microscopic analysis, *videocoding*, I categorized the artifacts, actions, operations, and breakdowns of the twelve observed PC-ALAS participants. And I constructed mesoscopic analyses, *chronological accounts*, through a qualitative and simple quantitative examination of the twelve participants' sessions in terms of their local activity systems and the genres they used. I describe each of the three analyses in more detail below.

Participant Profiles   Although the historical analysis in chapter 3 gave a general description of the ALAS activity system, local agencies such as sheriff's offices, county engineers' offices, and traffic safety organizations have their own local activity systems as well. They participate in the activity of locating and analyzing accidents, but in terms of their own desired outcomes (law enforcement, engineeering, traffic safety). I attempted to learn more about some of these local organizations at the macroscopic level through participant profiling.

Participant profiling, in this study, involved the following steps:

   • **Categorize local objects and outcomes.**   First, I examined questionnaire and interview data in terms of the participants' activities. In particular, I studied their organizations' desired outcomes and how the participants transformed the object of their labor (PC-ALAS output) to produce those outcomes, which indicate interpenetrating activity systems.

   • **Summarize demographics.**   Next, I examined questionnaire and interview data in terms of participants' demographics, including age, gender, years using PC-ALAS, frequency of PC-ALAS use, and years using various operating systems. I categorized these by outcomes.

   • **Transcribe usage comments.**   I reviewed interview data and field notes, transcribing portions relating directly to the following issues: what tasks the participants were trying to accomplish, how participants coordinated PC-ALAS with other artifacts, how participants used PC-ALAS reports in their work, and what complaints the participants had about PC-ALAS. These transcribed portions served to more fully profile participants.

I stored these data in a database, which I could easily arrange, sort, and explore.

Videocoding   To provide a microscopic analysis, I coded the twelve videotaped PC-ALAS observations in terms of interface artifacts used by the participant and their genres (including menus, dialog boxes, and the like), actions performed on the artifacts, operations used to perform the actions, and breakdowns encountered by the participant.

This videocoding scheme is based on that of Susanne Bødker (1996).[3] But whereas Bødker coded events by *breakdowns*, I coded events by *actions*. Consequently, I could compare successful as well as unsuccessful actions, and associate them with the genres and artifacts within which they occur.

Table 4.2 describes the coding scheme and shows a sample episode that has been coded. In this sample episode, the *action* is the entering of a county number into a field of an *artifact*, the City/County Request dialog box (an instance of the genre of the data entry dialog box). The action of entering the number could have been performed with a variety of differ-

Table 4.2
Videocoding categories

Coding category	Artifact	Action	Operation(s)	Breakdown
Description	The segment of the interface involved in the current action	A conscious goal-directed activity	Habitualized strategies that are used to fulfill actions	An unexpected focus shift
Example: detailed	City/County Request dialog box	Enter county number	Click on field, type	Input not entered
Example: simplified	Data entry dialog box	Enter number	Click on field, type	Input not entered

Note: Detailed coding was used for precise accounting of artifacts and actions. Simplified coding was used for measuring interrater reliability.

ent *operations*; here, the participant clicks on the field and types. But the participant encounters a *breakdown*: the number is not entered into the field. This particular breakdown occurs frequently in the data: workers have trouble properly selecting fields with the mouse.

I coded both simplified and detailed information. The detailed information included names of specific artifacts and precise descriptions of actions performed on those artifacts; coding this detailed information required an intimate knowledge of PC-ALAS. The simplified information included artifact genres (types of artifacts) and generic actions; coding this simplified information required only a general knowledge of PC-ALAS, so it was suitable for checking interrater reliability.

I tested interrater reliability to determine whether the coding scheme was systematized enough to be teachable to other raters. One rater was trained during an hour-long session by viewing and coding two five-minute segments of an observation, viewing and coding another five-minute segment, and then comparing the result with my coding. The subsequent training sessions helped me to refine my coding scheme.

After the training, the rater coded the first eight minutes of each work session, or if the session was shorter than eight minutes, the entire session. The rater coded 21.1 percent of the total video data. Table 4.3 indicates that the rater reliably applied the coding scheme.

Once I had coded the video data, I entered it into a database. I then generated reports and graphs to visualize relationships among the coded elements and with the participant profiles.

Chronological Accounts   After constructing profiles and videocoding, I used them to construct chronological accounts of all workers' sessions.

Action Sequence Graphs   Using the videocoding data, I generated graphs showing participants' action sequences (requesting data, search-

Table 4.3
Cohen's kappa for the four categories

Artifact	Action	Operation	Breakdown
0.935	0.927	0.919	0.807
(93.5%)	(92.7%)	(91.9%)	(80.7%)

ing data, generating reports) in the order that they occurred within the sessions, along with breakdowns that occurred within those action sequences. These data allowed me to visualize participants' typical action sequences and clusters of breakdowns, meaning that I could associate breakdowns with parts of the sequences as well as with individual artifacts or genres. For instance, one worker encountered multiple breakdowns with vertical menus while reporting, but not during other action sequences. This unusual clustering led me to examine the video data and the stimulated-recall interview; both suggested that these breakdowns occurred because the worker could not remember how to print, not because the menus were difficult to use per se.

Examination of Participants' Breakdowns   Once I had spotted clusters of breakdowns in the graphs, I triangulated the videocoding database with (1) the videotape where the breakdowns occurred, (2) the field notes taken at that point in the observation, and (3) portions of the stimulated-recall interviews dealing with that breakdown or type of breakdown. These data provided evidence that I used to determine which breakdowns could be attributed to genre expectations. For instance, at various points in separate observations, two workers examined PC-ALAS' File menu before moving on to other menus. Both indicated in stimulated-recall interviews that the desired act—printing—was usually handled in the File menu of Windows-based programs; they expected the File menu to handle such functions likewise, even though they had used PC-ALAS in the past and knew that the functions were handled elsewhere.

Comparison of Action Sequences and Artifact Use across Participants   Finally, I categorized participants by data in their profiles: object (how they wanted to transform the data), outcome (the desired result of engaging in the activity), and demographic data (such as frequency of PC-ALAS use and number of years of Microsoft Windows experience). Then I compared participants' action sequences and genre-related breakdowns across categories. Doing so allowed me to examine users' recurrent actions in terms of the genres, objects, and outcomes involved; this mesoanalysis gave me added insight into the discoordinations that users faced as they perceived and managed genres.

After relating the levels of scope in these ways, I constructed the genre ecology diagram in figure 4.1, a consolidated picture of the many genres used by workers and how they mediate each other. I also developed CDB tables to provide individual and consolidated views of how destabilizations appear at different levels of scope.

Genres-in-Activity: Examining Macroscopic Contradictions

At the macroscopic level, genres are understood as social action (Bakhtin 1984, 1986; Bazerman 1988; Miller 1984; Yates 1989). Genres are the material residue of a community's problem solving as it engages in an activity; they shape the activity. Genres embed community values and beliefs as well as problem solving. Thus, at the macroscopic level, genres can be understood as they help to mediate the many parts of the activity. For instance, in figure 3.13, we can see that PC-ALAS (with its many genres) mediates each worker's efforts to transform the object of the activity system.

As chapter 3 suggests, the ALAS activity system was experiencing macroscopic destabilizations, or contradictions, at the point that this study was conducted. These contradictions had become so severe, in fact, that the activity was nearing the point at which it had to change or disintegrate. (As chapter 3 discusses, the Iowa Department of Transportation later changed the activity by adopting GIS-ALAS.) At this point of extreme tension, I expected and found many signs of the contradictions that had developed.

I detected three contradictions by looking at changes in the activity system. These changes included how workers understood the object of their activity, the way they divided their labor, the new domain knowledge they developed as they performed the activity, and the new instruments they adapted. From the genre tracing perspective, the last two—domain knowledge and instruments—are the most important, since they involve repurposing or reconstruing old genres and adapting new ones. When new and repurposed genres begin to proliferate in detectable patterns, as they did in this study, they indicate that a contradiction is reaching a critical stage and must be addressed if the activity is to continue. In the ALAS activity system, the Iowa Department of Transportation had typically addressed such contradictions by centripetally reorganizing and consolidating genres (see chapter 3).

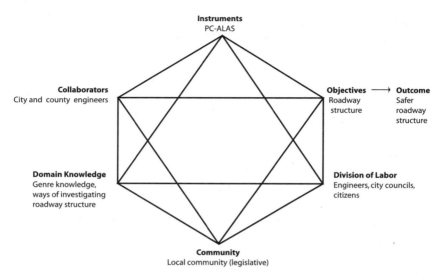

Figure 4.2
City and county engineers' activity.

In this section, I examine genres-in-activity. I draw on the analysis in chapter 3, but also on the participant profiles, which offer a close look at this activity at the end of the PC-ALAS era. I found that three contradictions were particularly influential: among interpenetrating activities, among representational systems, and among interface paradigms.

Contradiction 1: Among Interpenetrating Activities First, participants encountered a contradiction among the multiple activity systems that interpenetrate the ALAS activity system in question (city/county engineering, law enforcement, and traffic safety). Each interpenetrating activity involves transforming the same object—the ALAS data—but in different ways, to achieve different outcomes using different genres developed for the given activity (figures 4.2 through 4.4). (For instance, engineers used the engineering report, interacted frequently with city councils, and consulted references and regulations involving things such as road grades; law enforcement officers used the enforcement report, sometimes examined the actual drivers' reports, and wrote grants.) As Bowker and Star (1999, 135) point out, "In many ways software is frozen organizational

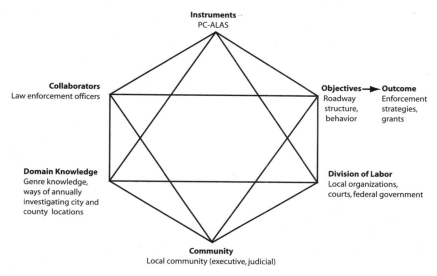

Figure 4.3
Law enforcement officers' activity.

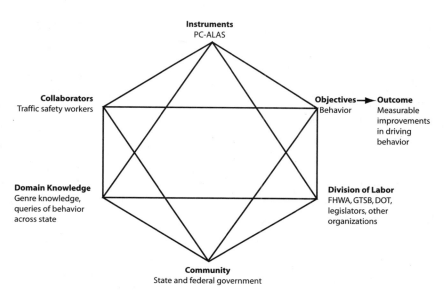

Figure 4.4
Traffic safety workers' activity.

and policy discourse," and software that is used to mediate multiple activities thus intrudes on the discourse of those different activities. In this study, different participants sometimes encountered different discoordinations and breakdowns, depending on the different activities in which they were engaged. In other words, variations in activities—and the interactions among those activities—can have tremendous consequences for the disruptions that workers encounter as they use designed information. Rather than focusing on a single overarching set of conditions (such as the work structure sought by Contextual Design), genre tracing examines the disparities among activities and how those disparities are addressed by workers' localized innovations.

The disparities in the ALAS activity system are broad, as table 4.4 suggests. One key indicator of interpenetrating activities is that the same data—traffic accident statistics—are transformed quite differently to achieve different outcomes, such as changes in the roadway structure (erecting traffic signals, regrading roads, raising bridges) or changes in drivers' behavior (new legislation, targeted enforcement of traffic laws, initiatives against drunk driving).

Although these activities all used PC-ALAS to transform accident data, they differed in important ways, including the genre knowledge they used

Table 4.4
Interpenetrating activity systems, objects, and resulting characteristics

Interpene-trating AS	City/county engineering	Law enforcement	Traffic safety
Object	Roadway structure	Behavior of local motorists; roadway structure	Behavior of statewide motorists
Queries	Complex, one time only, generally focusing on location	Complex, repeated for different years or locations, focusing on location	Vary in complexity, focusing on areas or ranges of locations
Problems	Easements, signalization	Enforcement strategies, grants	Ecological impact, legislative impact, grants
Scope	One city or county	One city or county	Many (or all) cities or counties

to transform the data and the outcomes toward which they worked. These differences can be illustrated more concretely by the differences in questions that the twelve participants investigated (table 4.5).

As table 4.5 shows, participants approached their sessions with certain questions to investigate. These questions indicated differences that can be attributed to the interpenetrating activities in which they were engaged (see table 4.4). For example, city and county engineers were concerned with structural (engineering) matters. Five of the six engineers were observed investigating specific locations that may need to be reengineered; only two were observed investigating a range of locations, and in both instances, they were investigating stretches of roadway. Traffic safety workers, on the other hand, were concerned with behavioral (policy) matters and investigated those matters statewide[4] (Rod, Sherry), county-wide (Ellen), or along specific routes (Ellen, Tina); none of the traffic safety workers were observed investigating by specific locations. The law enforcement officers looked at both structural and behavioral factors in specific locations; neither was observed investigating an area or range of locations.

Other indicators similarly pointed to the differences among activities. For example, traffic safety workers were interested in safety patterns across the state. In the study, two traffic safety workers were observed running a request-and-search combination across the state, and a third reported doing so; no engineers or law enforcement officers were observed or reported running such combinations. Similarly, engineers were interested primarily in structural causes, while traffic safety workers were interested primarily in behavior. In the study, five of the six engineers used an engineering report, which emphasized structural factors; only two used an enforcement report, which emphasized behavioral factors.

These differences in activities led to tensions because, as figures 4.2 through 4.4 show, the different groups involved in these activities needed very different things from PC-ALAS. Indeed, at almost every point in the activity system, tensions existed. PC-ALAS simply had not been—and arguably could not be—centripetally fine-tuned to support these different activities equally well.

At the mesoscopic level, these contradictions manifested as disco-ordinations such as choosing the wrong dialog box from the menu.

Table 4.5
Participants, their interpenetrating activities, the ways they transformed the data, and the questions they investigated

Participant	Activity	Question to investigate
Danny	City/county engineering	When starting a new project, are there accident patterns of which we should be aware? (structural)
Ed	City/county engineering	When reengineering a particular roadway, are there accident patterns of which we should be aware? (structural)
Jason	City/county engineering	Should this low bridge be raised? (structural)
Mike	City/county engineering	Does this intersection need signalization? (structural)
Roger	City/county engineering	Is this intersection really dangerous? (structural)
Todd	City/county engineering	Is this intersection dangerous? If so, what are possible causes? (structural)
Barbara	Law enforcement	What contributing circumstances are associated with accidents? What patterns of accidents occur at specific locations? (behavioral, structural)
Roland	Law enforcement	What areas most need grant money for improvements or enforcement? (structural, behavioral)
Ellen	Traffic safety	How does the total number of accidents compare with accidents involving a specific contributing circumstance (e.g., teenage drivers)? (behavioral)
Rod	Traffic safety	Have safety programs been effective? (behavioral)
Sherry	Traffic safety	Are driver inspections for commercial vehicles taking place? (behavioral)
Terri	Traffic safety	Do discernible accident patterns exist in this area? If so, what are likely causes? (behavioral)

For instance, six of the twelve workers brought up a dialog box only to cancel it because it was not the one they expected (a total of thirty-five instances). Another example is the difference in innovated representations of the roadway. Workers sometimes had different discoordinations —and developed different innovations—based on their activities. For instance, Barbara, Danny, and Mike had to locate specific locations (spatial), so they used innovations that helped them convert specific locations into nodes. Ellen, Sherry, and Tina had to locate ranges of locations; they used reports (nonspatial). Rod also had to locate ranges; he used a conventional map to identify the route, then a node table to look up the route's designation. At the microscopic level, the contradictions and discoordinations were manifested as breakdowns involving incorrectly chosen dialog boxes and repeated searches.

Contradiction 2: Between Representational Systems The contradiction between representational systems (and hence among genres used in the two systems) came about because automation had required a way of representing accidents and roadways that was very different from the traditional ways used before 1974. The two representational systems— the traditional and the quantitative—had to be brought together for the activity to work.

The *traditional, qualitative system* was the one with which drivers and police are familiar. Its components included genres such as street addresses, accident reports, and maps, which had been developed to describe street layout. As chapter 3 points out, this representational system had been around far longer than ALAS had, and was so widespread that most citizens could use it—including the drivers and police officers who reported accidents and the citizens, legislators, traffic safety workers, engineers, and law enforcement officials who requested accident statistics. The qualitative representational system represents accidents *spatially*: it is meant to help people envision locations in geographic relation to each other.

The *node-link system* was used exclusively by those in the ALAS activity system. Its components were six-digit node numbers as well as two-digit city and county numbers. As we saw in chapter 3, this representational system was invented in the early 1970s by a consulting firm so that accident statistics could be entered into a computer system. The node-link system, which had its roots in business computing, followed the conventions of that discipline by abstracting data quantitatively, through genres such as punch cards, forms, and (later) dialog boxes. It did *not* represent accidents spatially—in fact, without a reference that converts nodes to the qualitative representational system (a genre such as a node map or a node table), there was no way to associate any given node with a spatial location.

The two representational systems had been brought into contact with PC-ALAS, which required workers to use both as they located and analyzed accidents. As figure 4.5 shows, tensions had built between the representations: they required different literacies, different tools, and different sorts of expertise.

Despite the tensions, workers had to labor to reconcile the systems every day, since they could not be combined otherwise. That labor was sometimes quite difficult. To investigate a roadway, for example, a worker would look up the roadway on the node map (working with

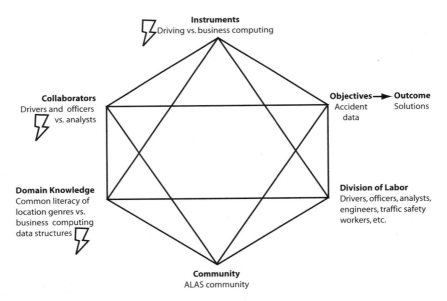

Figure 4.5
The PC-ALAS activity system. Lightning bolts indicate nodes at which the contradiction between representational systems is manifested.

a traditional, spatial representation). Once she found the roadway, she would then open a dialog box and type the county and city numbers from the top of the map, then the node numbers from along that stretch of roadway (working with the quantitative, nonspatial representation). The process was tedious and sometimes error-prone, because the worker had to make sure not to transpose digits, skip a number, or enter numbers in the wrong order. Once these numbers had been typed in, the worker would then generate a report detailing the accidents that had been found along the stretch of road. Supposing the string of numbers had been entered correctly (a dicey assumption, since PC-ALAS would not necessarily catch such errors), the report would list all of these accidents. If the worker wanted to pinpoint the accidents on the roadway, she would then have to reverse the process by finding the node nearest to which the listed accident had taken place.

This conversion process between the two representations was fraught with opportunities for errors. Ten of the twelve workers experienced a total of forty-six breakdowns related to entering wrong input (including incorrect node, county, and city numbers). In addition, nine of the twelve observed workers reported difficulties coordinating the node map with PC-ALAS. These ranged from complaints about having to juggle resources to descriptions of strategies for avoiding node maps. Most had heard of the GIS-ALAS prototype (then under development) and seven expressed interest in a map "linked to" the data. Two even described the problems they had encountered when trying to obtain node maps.

Not only did workers frequently complain about the node-link system, but nine of the twelve developed innovations that allowed them to spread the conversion process across unofficial genres. (I discuss these innovations later in this chapter.)

The contradiction between representations manifested at the mesoscopic level as difficulty managing the genres of the node map and the dialog box. At the microscopic level, the contradiction manifested as breakdowns in typing in node, city, and county numbers as well as breakdowns in using innovations.

Contradiction 3: Interface Literacies   Finally, the third contradiction has to do with interface literacies. In figure 4.6, this contradiction is portrayed as being between instruments (the PC-ALAS interface) and genre knowledge (learned from Windows). As chapter 3 explains, PC-ALAS was a DOS-based interface rather than a graphical user interface (GUI), though it imitated GUI conventions such as menus, dialog boxes, and a mouse pointer. It did not imitate those conventions consistently or exactly, however. Consequently, workers found themselves drawing on two literacies: a GUI literacy and a PC-ALAS literacy. Genres that were widely used in GUI interfaces, such as menus, dialog boxes, and message windows, were reproduced in the PC-ALAS interface, but with important differences. These differences frequently confused new users and required them to learn a new literacy (i.e., a set of genre knowledge) very similar to the old one.

Those literacy differences showed up in different ways at different levels. At the mesoscopic level, they took the form of discoordinations in genre perception: in how Barbara and Jason expected the Print command to be under the File menu, in how Sherry interpreted search parameters, and in how Barbara interpreted radio buttons, for instance. At the microscopic level, they took the form of the breakdowns that nearly every worker encountered when entering input. Given the nature of conventions, this contradiction was coconstituted most strongly at the microscopic level.

Summary: Contradictions   The three contradictions were tensions that had developed in this activity over time. At this particular point, the contradictions had become so severe that they had led to several ad hoc innovations, yet they continued to threaten the integrity of the activity. In the next section, we will see examples of how these contradictions were coconstituted at the mesoscopic level.

Genres-in-Action: Examining Mesoscopic Discoordinations

At the mesoscopic level, genres are understood as tools, strategies, or tactics (Russell 1995, 1997a; Schryer 1993, 2000; Hovde 2000). Genres are not only the result of a community's problem solving, they are the implements used to perform the many goal-directed actions in which community members are engaged. Any given genre—the accident report, the node map, the dialog box—is a tool that can mediate the goal-directed actions of a worker.

Just as macroscopic destabilizations crop up among parts of the activity system, mesoscopic destabilizations crop up among tools and the expectations that workers have for those tools. Mesoscopic destabilizations are known as *discoordinations*, or difficulties in interpreting artifacts and managing the actions that those artifacts mediate. Engeström (1990, 1992) compares them with *coordinations*, in which the normal, scripted flow of interaction continues without a hitch. Discoordinations can happen for a variety of reasons, but when workers consistently encounter discoordinations with a given artifact or set of artifacts, as they did in this study, they often attempt to minimize those discoordinations by adapting new genres.

As they transformed the data in different ways to meet different objectives, the participants encountered several discoordinations involving how they perceived and managed genres. They responded to them with various innovations. Being centrifugal, these innovations sometimes diverged wildly. Yet by examining them we can find some common themes. Below, I focus on two discoordinations: between the genres of the node map and the dialog box, and between expected and actual outcomes of searches.

The Node Map and the Dialog Box   The first discoordination has to do with managing genres: participants had difficulties getting the genres of the node map and the dialog box to work together. The resulting innovations were meant to bridge these genres.

By *genre management*, I mean that workers—and sometimes designers—coordinate interrelated genres in an ecology in such a way as to comediate the activity at hand. They manage genres through domain knowledge applied within the genre ecology. For instance, workers employed dialog boxes in conjunction with node maps: they used a node map to look up the intersection for which they wanted data, then typed the node number into the dialog box. Such connections between genres spring up throughout the ecology. And perceiving an artifact as being the member of a certain genre entails managing those existing genre connections: the connection between the node map and the PC-ALAS dialog box echoes the much older connection between the node map and the mainframe-ALAS form. Problems (discoordinations) in genre management come about when these connections are disrupted and the genres do not work together as desired.

Workers consistently indicated that they had trouble coordinating the genres of the node map and the dialog box, and in fact, of the twelve participants, only three used the standard-issue $3 \times 3'$ node maps directly with PC-ALAS. The $3 \times 3'$ maps were not only unwieldy; they required workers to convert from the spatial representation of the node-map system to the quantitative representation of the node-link system. (That is, this discoordination is the mesoscopic manifestation of the macroscopic contradiction between representations.) Consequently, workers tended to minimize contact with the node map and distribute the labor of conversion among other people and artifacts.

This distribution of work happened via several innovations. For example, when investigating whether a certain bridge was associated with particular types of accidents, Danny had a coworker look up the relevant nodes and read them to him. The coworker used a spatial representation, the node map, allowing Danny to use just the quantitative representation, the node-link system. Barbara and Mike distributed the conversion work among artifacts rather than people, reading the maps and writing down the node numbers so that they no longer had to think about the problem spatially. Sherry and Terri referred to reports rather than maps, cutting out the spatial representation altogether. And although Ellen used maps for the first pass in each county search, for the second pass she would use the printed report generated during the first pass.

Others used maps but still found ways to mediate between the unwieldy $3 \times 3'$ node map and PC-ALAS. Ellen would look up the appropriate county and location on the node map, then photocopy the relevant sections—producing a flat letter-sized map that she could easily use and, later, archive in an office folder. Jason and Ed both used smaller $1 \times 1'$ folded node maps; Ed's had been issued by the Iowa DOT in 1983. In contrast, Rod used a poster-sized conventional map of the state, which had been pinned to one wall, in conjunction with node tables. This turned out to be a sensible alternative since, as a traffic safety worker, he simply had to identify state highways and the counties through which they traveled.

Notice that these innovations did two things. First, they pushed the node map, which had officially been conceived as a central genre of the PC-ALAS system, to the periphery. In most cases, workers routed around the 3 × 3′ node map. Second, in the process, many of the innovations *disassociate* the spatial and quantitative representations of the roadway system that had been unified by the node map. This disassociation happened more frequently when a large area was under investigation as opposed to a specific location (Ellen, Rod, Sherry, and Terri, all of whom were in traffic safety) or when a location was to be monitored over time (Barbara).

Workers did not describe how they developed these innovations, but there is no doubt they found the innovations helpful in managing genres. For instance, Mike described his innovation as "the easy way out."

Expected and Actual Outcomes of Searches   The second discoordination had to do with genre perception. As participants attempted to conduct searches, they often interpreted the genres associated with searches in ways at variance with the results of using the genres.

By *genre perception*, I mean that workers understand a given artifact in terms of genre and apply their knowledge of the genre to it. For instance, when PC-ALAS was developed in 1989, those who had used the mainframe-ALAS request forms were able to understand some aspects of PC-ALAS because PC-ALAS dialog boxes closely resembled the earlier forms. Workers perceived the forms and the dialog boxes as members of the same genre. Consequently, they could draw on their established genre knowledge for using the new interface. Problems (discoordinations) with genre perception come about when workers unsuccessfully draw on genre knowledge—that is, when their perception of the genre does not match how it actually reacts.

One such example is that of searches. When a worker used PC-ALAS, she first *requested* a data set on a county, city, or set of nodes. Then, if she chose, she could *search* that data set for accidents related to circumstances (such as alcohol, driver age, time of day, and so on); searches narrowed the data set incrementally, so if the worker conducted two searches in a row, the second search was conducted on the narrowed data set from the first search. Finally, she generated a *report* that summarized the data set.

Searches were optional: if a worker was interested in *all* accidents involving a given location (Barbara, Danny, Ed, Jason, Terri, and Todd), she did not need to run a search at all. But if the worker was interested in examining a particular factor or in making comparisons—for instance, to answer Ellen's question of what percentage of accidents in a given county involve teenage drivers—she needed to run a search (Ellen, Mike, Rod, Roger, Roland, and Sherry). Three of the four traffic safety workers ran a search, while only two of the six engineers did, likely because traffic safety workers are interested in behavioral factors, while engineers typically are not.

Figures 4.6 and 4.7 show the differences in PC-ALAS sessions that did not involve searches versus those that did. These figures were generated from the videocoding database. Each unit represents an action performed on an artifact as time progresses from left to right. (Although some sessions were longer than others—Ellen's session lasted about twenty-six minutes, for example, while Barbara's lasted about two—I made the graphs all the same width so that general patterns could be compared. Thus units in one graph may seem larger and farther apart than units in other graphs.) Comparing figure 4.6 to figure 4.7, we see two kinds of PC-ALAS use. The sessions that did not involve searches (figure 4.6) tended to involve shorter sequences of actions and followed a simple request-report pattern: workers requested data, then ran a report, always in that order and sometimes in a repeated cycle (e.g., Danny, Jason). The sessions that involved searches (figure 4.7), on the other hand, tended to involve more complicated and varied patterns such as request-search-report (Sherry), request-report-search-report (Ellen), and request-search-report-search (Mike). The videotapes and field notes suggest that sessions involving searches tended to involve comparative studies.

The graphs not only demonstrate that sessions involving searches tended to be more complicated, but they indicate points that can be further investigated by triangulating the graphs with field notes, videotapes, and interviews. For instance, in figure 4.7 we see that Sherry's coded actions involved proportionately more searching (61.3%) than Mike's

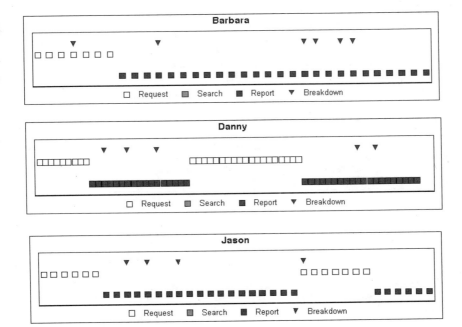

Figure 4.6
Three of the six observations that did not involve searches. Inverted triangles indicate breakdowns, which will be discussed in the next section. These graphs show a straight request-and-report pattern.

(50.0%) or Ellen's (30.4%). By triangulating the graphs with the field notes, videotapes, and interviews, I found that the differing patterns were related to differing perceptions of the genres involved in PC-ALAS searches (a discoordination related to the macroscopic contradiction between interface paradigms). In fact, the six workers who conducted searches encountered either breakdowns (detected mistakes) or undetected mistakes in a relatively high 17.4 percent of their actions involving searches.

For instance, during his investigation of an intersection, Mike decided to explore a subset of the intersection data: accidents involving pedestrians. He found only two pedestrian accidents and generated a report to examine them. At this point he made the mistake of forgetting to clear the previous search. Consequently the second search was performed only on the two accidents found from the previous search. Mike conducted

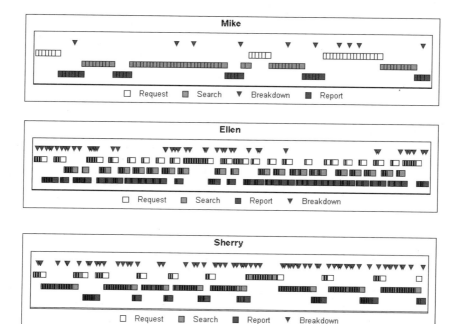

Figure 4.7
Three observations that involved searches. These sessions involve more complicated patterns that were triangulated with field notes, videotapes, and interviews to reveal different objectives—and different misconceptions about the system.

three more searches and each time was surprised by the results: the first search turned up only one match, and the next two turned up no matches at all. Since Mike had not cleared the previous search, each subsequent search was conducted using the narrower data of the last. Finally, he double-checked by generating a report, which confirmed that no accidents have been found. "Well," he said, "something happened. Let's go back."

Rather than discovering how to clear the search, Mike simply re-requested the intersection data (in effect, clearing the search by replacing the current narrowed data with the original pool of requested data). This time he conducted a search—on drivers between the ages of fourteen and nineteen—without incident, then generated and interpreted another report.

Mike's mistake in not clearing the search went undetected for so long because PC-ALAS provided no genre to monitor the current scope of a search. That is, an *ecological niche* existed that had not yet been filled by an innovation. Workers were expected to mentally keep track of what searches they had executed and what parameters they had used. And that brings us to Sherry's session. Like Mike, Sherry had trouble executing searches, but unlike Mike, Sherry believed that PC-ALAS *did* furnish a genre to monitor search scope: the dialog boxes that she used to specify search criteria.

Since Sherry requested new data each time, she did not encounter the narrowing multiple searches that Mike encountered. However, she did encounter difficulties with searches. In PC-ALAS, sometimes dialog boxes showed *all settings as deselected*; they showed a "blank slate" that the worker had to fill out. Sherry assumed that since the options were deselected in the dialog box, they were by default never selected until she selected them. In fact, the opposite was true: in these dialog boxes, by default, PC-ALAS selected *all* options (figure 4.8).

Furthermore, Sherry perceived search options not as *restrictive* (that is, narrowing a wide pool of data) but *additive* (that is, adding types of data to an initially empty pool). Therefore, each time she requested new data, she was compelled to fill out series of dialog boxes: she specified a search on days of the week and selected *all* days; she specified a search on contributing circumstances and selected *all* circumstances. The laborious nature of this job led her to suggest, "You really need to invent something to do 'em all at once." (Roger made a similar statement.)

Summary Workers encountered various discoordinations in genre management and perception during their observations. Here, I have discussed two that proved particularly troublesome. Workers dealt with these by innovating when possible and muddling through when not. Their innovations—even the most successful, such as Barbara's sticky note—were stopgaps. They made the system more usable, more customized for the activity, but they did not lead to a utopian system. Indeed, the proliferation of innovations indicates that the official genres no longer sufficed, and that workers were growing more idiosyncratic in how they used the system. We can imagine how Mike's conception of the

Figure 4.8
The Contributing Circumstances dialog box, which comes up with all items unchecked. By default, it includes all items unless the worker specifically selects items. Sherry assumed that it would include *none* of the items, so she spent a lot of time clicking on every item in every dialog box involved in the search.

search process, for instance, could potentially lead to wrong assessments and improper changes to the intersection! Remember, the study took place at the end of the PC-ALAS era, when such destabilizations had reached critical mass and a centripetal reorganization of the activity's genres was pending.

Genres-in-Operation: Examining Microscopic Breakdowns

At the microscopic level, genres are understood as unconscious collections of operations (Bazerman 1997; Engeström 1995; Freedman and Smart 1997; Spinuzzi 2001a; Schryer 1993). At this level, genres are learned habits or responses on which a worker unconsciously draws as she routinely interpret texts.

For instance, suppose the worker is entering information into a dialog box, using habits she has developed in her previous encounters with dialog boxes: she starts at the field in the upper-left corner and clicks on each field with her mouse to select it, then types in the appropriate text for each field. If her habits produce results consistent with the worker's interpretation of the genre—for instance, if clicking on a field really does activate it, if typing in the text really does result in that text appearing in the field—then the worker is not conscious of these interpretive habits. She continues to look "through the interface," in Susanne Bødker's (1991) memorable phrase, concentrating on the goal at hand (in this case, specifying nodes to be investigated). But if her habits *do not* produce the expected results—for instance, if she attempts to click on a field or type text and nothing happens—she encounters an interpretive breakdown: a point at which the worker finds her present interpretation of an artifact inadequate for the task at hand.

I use the term *breakdown* as it is used by Bødker (1991), who draws it from Winograd and Flores (1986) and Engeström (1990). According to Bødker, a breakdown happens when an artifact that has become operationalized ("ready-to-hand") suddenly does not behave as expected. At this point, the worker becomes conscious of the artifact and her unconscious operations on the artifact consequently become conscious actions. The artifact, which was used to mediate the worker's actions on an object, now itself becomes "unready-to-hand"—it is now the object of the worker's actions. The worker must reinterpret the artifact if she is to continue to use it to mediate her activities.

Since breakdowns interrupt work by making operationalized (unconscious) actions *conscious*, workers in this study tended to innovate at the microscopic level to avoid breakdowns. That is, they learned new operations (i.e., operationalized actions, as I discussed in chapter 2) that would not result in breakdowns. For example, in the headnote in chapter 2, Rod dealt with the problem of clicking in fields—a problem that causes breakdowns for nine of the twelve workers—by learning the new operation of clicking on labels.

In this study, I found that breakdowns were widespread. I coded 15 types and found a total of 180 breakdowns in the videotaped observations, or about 10.3 percent of all interactions (table 4.6). Furthermore, workers tended to develop innovative new operations to avoid such breakdowns.

Table 4.6
Breakdowns encountered by observed workers

Breakdown	Danny (C/CE)	Ed (C/CE)	Jason (C/CE)	Mike (C/CE)	Roger (C/CE)	Todd (C/CE)
Confused about report results	1			1		
Dialog box doesn't dismiss				2		
Dialog box not relevant/desired				1	1	
Entered incorrect data	1			3	2	
Error when scrolling report	1					
Input not entered	2		2	1	4	
PC-ALAS crashes		4		1		
Relevant help topic not found						
Selected wrong text or number field						
System reports input error		1	1		2	
Unexpected search results		3				
Vertical menu does not appear						
Vertical menu does not close						
Vertical menu does not stay open						
Vertical menu not relevant/desired		3	1	1	3	1
Total breakdowns	5	11	4	10	12	1
Total actions	67	91	38	116	51	17
% of breakdowns to actions	7.47	12.09	10.53	8.63	23.53	5.89

Barbara (LE)	Roland (LE)	Ellen (TS)	Rod (TS)	Sherry (TS)	Terri (TS)	Total break-downs	en-coun-tering	% encounters/P
				1		3	3	25
		4		1		7	3	25
	1	23	2	7		35	6	50
		8		7		21	5	41.67
				6		7	2	16.67
1	1	5		36	2	54	9	75
	1	4				10	4	33.33
				1		1	1	8.33
				2		2	1	8.33
1	5			2	1	13	7	58.33
	1					4	2	16.67
	1		1			2	2	16.67
	2					2	1	8.33
			1	1		2	2	16.67
4	2		2			17	8	66.67
6	14	44	6	64	3	180		
33	67	624	148	457	36	1745		
18.19	20.9	7.06	4.06	14.01	8.34	10.32		

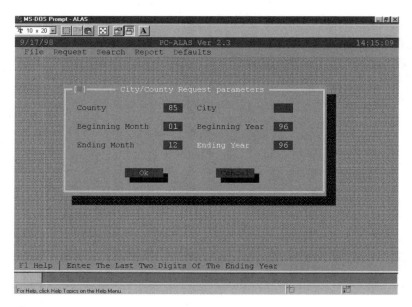

Figure 4.9
The City/County Request Parameters dialog box has text/number input fields as
well as OK and Cancel buttons.

These microscopic breakdowns were often related to the macroscopic
contradiction between the PC-ALAS interface and the graphical user
interface with which most users were familiar: Microsoft Windows. In
the rest of this section, I examine breakdowns related to two on-screen
genres: dialog boxes and menus.

Dialog Boxes   PC-ALAS dialog boxes are rather similar to Windows
dialog boxes. Both variants of the genre provide more-or-less the same
sorts of input devices: text/number fields for entering alphanumeric
characters; radio buttons that allow one of a series to be selected;
checkboxes allowing one or more of a series to be selected; and OK and
Cancel buttons allowing users to accept or reject the dialog box. (See
figures 4.9 and 4.10 for examples.)

Yet for all their similarities, the PC-ALAS and Windows variants of
this genre differ in important ways. Dialog boxes are the locus of 119
breakdowns—the most of all the genres. This abundance of breakdowns

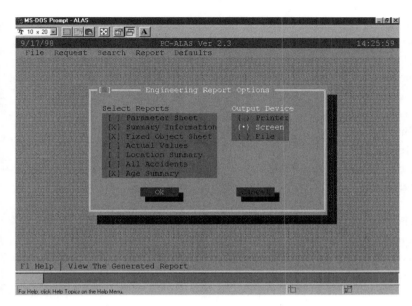

Figure 4.10
The Engineering Report Options dialog box includes checkboxes (left) for multiple selections and radio buttons (right) for mutually exclusive selections.

has much to do with the role dialog boxes play in the PC-ALAS genre ecology. Whereas menus provide a gross management of artifacts necessary to transform raw data into processed reports, dialog boxes provide a fine control over particular points in the transformation. To provide this fine control, dialog boxes sport a number of different input devices (text/number fields, radio buttons, checkboxes). These input devices allow participants to coordinate each dialog box with other artifacts: node maps, node books, notes, other dialog boxes, and reports that are eventually generated from input. Of the sixty-eight on-screen artifacts (i.e., dialog boxes, menus, reports) that participants encountered, forty-six (67.6%) were dialog boxes.

Given the dialog-box genre's central place in the PC-ALAS ecology, breakdowns associated with dialog boxes are especially troubling.

Nine of the twelve participants encountered breakdowns when they unsuccessfully attempted to enter input into dialog boxes. Their attempts failed primarily because PC-ALAS does not give the user precise control over mouse input: the mouse pointer is as large as a character, as are most of the input fields, so a successful attempt at input requires the user to click in exactly the right spot, with no leeway. In contrast, although Windows input fields tend to be smaller than PC-ALAS', the Windows mouse pointer is even smaller. Consequently, Windows users are able to be more precise in their input and at the same time do not have to make a "bull's-eye" to activate an input field.

However, two participants avoided unsuccessful input attempts because they had operationalized their actions differently from the others. Whereas most participants clicked the mouse cursor on input fields, two did not. Rod clicked on field *labels*—a strategy that has the same effect as clicking the fields themselves, but affords a bigger target (fields tend to be one or two characters wide, while labels are several characters wide). Ed, on the other hand, did not click at all: he had no mouse, so instead he controlled his input entirely through the spacebar and the Tab, Enter, and Shift keys. Some of the other participants had learned these alternative operations, but often clicked directly on fields as well. Sherry, for instance, believed erroneously that some fields could be directly clicked on while others could not, so when she failed in an attempt to click directly on a field, she would click on the next field and shift-tab back into the desired one. (Sherry selected and deselected search parameters in sixty-eight different dialog boxes, and encountered input breakdowns on thirty-six of those screens, or 52% of the time.)

One might be tempted to suspect that a larger repertoire of operations helps users: the larger the repertoire, the more flexible the data entry. Yet Rod and Ed did not appear to have broad repertoires at all. Rather, the opposite was the case: they each used only *one* way to enter input. Those ways worked presumably because they took less fine-motor control. And that brings us back to genre perception: all participants were steeped in the genre of Windows dialog boxes, in which fine-motor control is facilitated by the interface so they could rely on entirely mouse-driven input. Most of the participants perceived PC-ALAS dialog boxes as variants of the Windows-based genre, and therefore best controlled (or *solely* controlled) by clicking the mouse on the input field. For some participants, alternative forms of control simply did not exist.

Participants encountered other breakdowns with dialog boxes as well, and these had to do largely with how dialog boxes were coordinated with other genres. Seven of the twelve encountered a system error resulting from incorrect entry in a dialog box—for example, they entered a wrong city or county code (resulting from discoordination with a node map or other mediating genre representing the road system), or a wrong month or year (resulting from discoordination with a report or note they used to guide their search). Additionally, a bug in PC-ALAS ensured another sort of breakdown: if a nonexistent city or county number was entered into the City/County Location dialog box (resulting from a discoordination with the node map), PC-ALAS crashed.

Horizontal and Vertical Menus   Participants encountered several breakdowns when using horizontal and vertical menus, primarily breakdowns in which users selected the wrong item. Nine of the twelve participants encountered a total of twenty-one breakdowns (that is, 1.2% of all actions, or 11.7% of all breakdowns) when operating the menus. And when improper dialog-box and report choices are factored in, the menu system arguably had a hand in sixty-five breakdowns (3.7% of all actions, or 36% of all breakdowns). Taken by themselves, these breakdowns were not very serious, since they typically involved hesitations and incorrectly chosen options—consequences that could be easily caught. However, they added up to major delays, confusion, and frustration. Each breakdown reminded workers that the PC-ALAS interface was considerably different from, and arguably inferior to, a modern graphical user interface such as Windows.

PC-ALAS was chiefly controlled through its horizontal menu and the vertical menus that dropped down from it. Both horizontal and vertical menus are genres with variations in DOS, Microsoft's Windows, Apple's MacOS, and programs running on various other operating systems.

The genres of the horizontal and vertical menu were important to PC-ALAS users because their chief purpose was to help workers coordinate their work with all of PC-ALAS' many genres. They established the structure of the activity, just as do menus in GUIs. In doing so, they guided workers' activities. Yet since PC-ALAS' menus diverged in key ways from GUI menus, they introduced possibilities for breakdowns.

For instance, workers tend to start and end their interactions with GUI applications at the left, with the File menu; they perform the next most frequent actions in the next menu over, the Edit menu; and so forth.

Participants in this study, who tended to have considerable Microsoft Windows experience and used Windows far more frequently than they did PC-ALAS, expected PC-ALAS' menus to work similarly. For example, in Windows, workers tend to open the File menu at the beginning of their work sessions because it allows them to load data (hence the menu item's name and placement). But in PC-ALAS, the File menu had nothing to do with that function—the Request menu did. Similarly, in Windows the File menu contains the Print command. In PC-ALAS, printing was done through the Report menu. This particular difference resulted in breakdowns for two of the participants. Jason described his experience this way:

> A lot of times I hit the File menu almost automatically, cause that's where—you print out of there most of the time, and that's just where I normally—first place I go. It's just habit, I guess, on that. It's not—I gotta do that in about all Windows-based application type things.

Similarly, Barbara described her attempt to print through the File menu as "just going back to my Windows thought again."

Both participants were aware of how the PC-ALAS menu system worked. Yet they went "back to [their] Windows thought again." Although they were aware of the difference, they had not used PC-ALAS with enough frequency to construct operations that would help them interpret this menu in such a way as to avoid breakdowns. And since the horizontal menu was a means for calling up other genres, these breakdowns led to discoordinations in genre management.

Participants relied on the menu system to help them manage (i.e., locate and string together) artifacts of different genres in a sensible way, especially when they did not remember or know what artifacts they must deal with. For instance, a participant who knew that she wanted to request data selected the Request menu and chose an option—perhaps Run Location—that set her on a path in which one dialog box led to another dialog box, and then to a message window. Once the menu choice was made, the artifacts more or less coordinated themselves in a preprogrammed procession.

Yet the menu does not always give users enough assistance in that initial coordination. Of the twelve participants I observed, ten encountered breakdowns related to the menu system. Eight users opened vertical menus only to close them because they were not relevant or desired—that is, the sought-for option was not accessible through them. Participants who selected options sometimes decided that the choices were wrong: half of the participants brought up a dialog box, only to cancel that dialog box because it was not the one they wanted.

Summary   At the mesoscopic level, innovations tended to be new genres that were brought into or repurposed within the genre ecology: notes, reports, maps, and so forth. At the microscopic level, however, innovations tended to be newly learned operations that workers employed to interpret and use existing genres: clicking on labels rather than fields, establishing new routines, and otherwise differentiating PC-ALAS genres from their Windows analogues.

Although breakdowns are fairly easy to detect and analyze through videocoding, workers' innovations are not: such innovations are behavioral rather than physical, and can be detected only through comparative study. For instance, tabulating the videocoded breakdowns allowed me to detect a commonly encountered breakdown, in which input is not entered, and led me to closely examine why certain participants did *not* encounter it. But in cases in which breakdowns are less plentiful and widespread, it is more difficult to determine when workers have innovated new operations. For example, only two workers seemed to treat the PC-ALAS File menu like the Windows File menu. Does that mean that the other workers have successfully innovated different operations, such as habitually opening the Request menu to load data? Perhaps they never learned the Windows genre habits to begin with. More studies may provide more certain answers.

In any case, innovated operations are stopgaps that can make the system more usable, as we see in Rod's and Ed's examples. And again we can see that users' experiences with the system will be quite different depending on how successful they have been at learning different operations.

Integrating the Levels of Scope

As we have examined the different levels of scope and the destabilizations appearing at each level, doubtless readers have begun to link the different levels. In this section, I link them more formally through the heuristic of the contradiction-discoordination-breakdown (CDB) table. The levels of scope are not linked in a simple causal relationship, as they would be in a single-scope analysis, but coconstitutively.

For instance, table 4.7 links destabilizations related to representational systems across the three levels of scope, allowing us to see how destabilizations coconstitute each other. Table 4.7 also shows how a local innovation reconfigured the activity.

With this integrated view, for instance, we can see how microscopic breakdowns such as improperly entered node numbers relate to macroscopic contradictions between different roadway representations and mesoscopic discoordinations between the genres that have been developed to instantiate and support those representations.

Furthermore, table 4.7 shows how Barbara's innovation affected all three levels, changing how she worked and how she conceived of her work. Notice that with minor changes to this table, we could examine other innovations here, such as Mike's handwritten note and Sherry's report. These innovations responded to the same destabilization, the gulf between the spatial and node-link representations. Each worker's innovations added genres to the genre ecology, and in doing so, filled ecological niches that had been opened by the contradiction between their activity and the one PC-ALAS was invented to serve. Each innovation changed the dynamic balance of the genre ecology and the activity it mediated for them—making some tasks easier, others harder.

Table 4.8 provides a second example, which integrates the destabilizations related to interface literacies. This destabilization, I want to emphasize, does not "start" at a given level, but is coconstituted at each level: the microscopic breakdowns and the macroscopic contradiction are different views of the same destabilization.

Here, destabilizations across all three levels became pervasive and disruptive enough that individuals often remarked on the difference between the two interfaces and wished for a Windows-based system. In 1997, the Center for Transportation Research and Education began sharing beta versions of such a system, GIS-ALAS. As I discuss in the next chapter, GIS-ALAS minimized destabilizations involving interface literacies, but did not eliminate them—and introduced a host of new destabilizations.

Table 4.7
Contradiction-discoordination-breakdown table showing destabilizations across levels of scope linked to representational systems and the changes resulting from an innovation

Macro	PC-ALAS designers provided node maps because they envisioned workers investigating spatial locations—the sort of problem solving done by city and county engineers. But Barbara (and others) did not need to relate the data spatially, although their results were reported in ways that others could later relate spatially if they wanted.
Meso	PC-ALAS' official genres were geared for spatial locations of accidents. Thus the genres included the node map, the primary genre for relating the traditional (spatial) and node-link (nonspatial) representations of accidents. Since the map is not only unwieldy but also unnecessary for Barbara's work, it introduced discoordinations having to do with genre management.
Micro	Barbara encountered breakdowns in trying to use the map in conjunction with other genres. Everyone encountered these breakdowns, but she may have especially disliked them because she did not get anything out of coordinating the map genre with other genres: she did not need to spatially relate points. The labor was divided at the macroscopic level in such a way that someone else would do that work.
Innovation	*Permanent Post-It note in file (an adaptation of the file system).*
Micro	Barbara had less trouble because she was using a simple, familiar genre that did not involve coordinating traditional (spatial) and node-link (nonspatial) representational systems.
Meso	And that genre was easier for her to coordinate with other genres (such as the dialog box). It cut out a genre (the map) primarily useful for spatial location. It obviated the conversion work that was normally a part of using the node map.
Macro	Thus the contradiction was eased. By adapting a genre to reroute around a difficult part of the software, Barbara had partially transformed a piece of software that was intended to facilitate *spatial problem solving* into software that primarily facilitated *textual reporting*. It now mediated her personal work more effectively because it mediated that work differently. Yet the contradiction still existed. We can see it, for instance, in the exceedingly complex report options, which were geared to support spatially oriented investigations. We can imagine how, with repeated use, Barbara might adapt still more genres (e.g., cheat sheets) to further transform the software.

Table 4.8
Contradiction-discoordination-breakdown table showing destabilizations across levels of scope linked to interface literacies and the changes resulting from an innovation

Macro	A contradiction between the interface literacies of PC-ALAS and Windows (figure 3.14). For some, this contradiction led to the perception of the PC-ALAS interface as inferior to that of Windows.
Meso	Consistent, pervasive genre discoordinations. Workers encountered discoordinations in entering information into fields, wrong menu items being clicked, wrong dialog boxes being selected.
Micro	Breakdowns related to Windows operations (including cursor precision and menu selections).
Innova-tion	*GIS-ALAS: An ALAS product developed as a Windows application.*
Micro	Reduction or elimination of breakdowns related to Windows operations (including cursor precision).
Meso	More familiar genre relationships, coordination.
Macro	Minimizing of contradiction between interface literacies.

CONCLUSION

In this chapter, I have traced genres and the destabilizations associated with them across the levels of scope to examine how the levels of scope coconstitute each other. In doing so, I believe I have provided insight into innovations that would not be possible through single-scope approaches. By using genre as a unit of analysis that cuts across levels of scope, I have been able to analyze the observational and interview data at the three levels, then connect the levels. Doing so has led me to an integrated-scope explanation of why workers encountered destabilizations, why they innovated genres in response, and how those genres transformed their work. I have been able to examine the very different (centrifugal) innovations and discern patterns that indicate systemic destabilizations. In sum, the genre tracing approach has allowed me to trace genres and the destabilizations associated with them, and in doing so, to understand how the destabilizations are coconstituted across levels of scope.

This study took place in the waning days of PC-ALAS, when a number of destabilizations threatened the ALAS activity system. These destabilizations led workers to develop various centrifugal innovations, stopgap measures that alleviated but did not solve the destabilizations. One of the more ambitious innovations, GIS-ALAS, was soon sponsored by the Center for Transportation Research and Education, then designated PC-ALAS' heir apparent by the Iowa Department of Transportation. GIS-ALAS was an official, centripetal response to the destabilizations in the activity. In the next chapter, I investigate how workers and students used two prototypes of GIS-ALAS.

5

Embedded Contradictions: Two Studies of GIS-ALAS Genre Hybrids

Terry, a worker at the Iowa Department of Transportation, is using a prototype of GIS-ALAS to look up and print data on the highest accident locations in a small town. He examines the previous records he has of this town (which are kept in a folder), then brings up a map of the town in the prototype. He causes the map to show the nodes, then prints the map. Next, he enters node numbers into PC-ALAS to generate a report of accidents at various nodes. Later, he plans to provide the data to a consultant. Terry is not impressed by the prototype. It's harder to use in conjunction with PC-ALAS than a standard paper map is.

Of course, the developers intended GIS-ALAS to replace PC-ALAS. Whereas Terry sees the prototype as an electronic map, the developers want him to treat it as an updated PC-ALAS with new display capabilities. According to the developers, Terry shouldn't use PC-ALAS at all anymore.

In the incident above, there is a fundamental confusion about exactly what role GIS-ALAS is to play in Terry's activity. Should it be seen as an electronic catalog of maps? Or an entire accident location and analysis system? How should it be integrated into the existing genre ecology? Or should it actually *replace* the ecology as a stand-alone program that encapsulates the totality of genres within itself? In sum, what are the implications of pulling existing genres into the computer interface?

In this chapter, I describe two studies that I conducted specifically to answer the last question. We have seen in previous chapters how activities can intersect and how genres belonging to one activity can be adapted for another. Here, I describe how an entire ecology of genres, including the node map, was imported into an interface originally developed for a very different activity. And I discuss how importing genres entails more than simple reproduction: it entails developing hybrid genres that resemble parents from the different activities. Tensions between those activities are in a sense embedded in each hybrid genre. I discuss how the centripetal act of hybridization can result in fragmentation as these tensions engender multileveled destabilizations in the activity, destabilizations clustered around the hybrid genres that serve as meeting points for the different activities. Understanding this process should help us in two ways.

First, in understanding hybrid genres as embedding tensions between activities, we can anticipate destabilizations associated with those genres. We can trace how hybrid genres can pull in the activities in which they were developed and the associated genres from those activities.

Second, we can anticipate innovations. Although it is not easy to predict what innovations workers will adopt, we can nevertheless examine how hybrid genres bring activities into conflict and anticipate ecological niches. In some cases, we can see the beginnings of new innovations as workers start to search for genres to fill those niches.

The two studies in this chapter capture a snapshot of GIS-ALAS as it was in 1999. Since then, GIS-ALAS has been developed in ways that obviate many of the problems discussed here. Before we get to these two studies, let's explore the notion of hybrid genres further.

IMPORTING GENRES, MAKING HYBRIDS, FORMING CONTRADICTIONS

Hybrid genres are genres that emerge from the unification of two or more disparate activities. They resemble parent genres from the different activities. For instance, the node map was a hybrid genre that resulted from the union of accident location and business computing in 1974. It provided a bridge between the two activities, allowing traffic workers to convert their representations into something the DOT mainframe could process, as well as to interpret the reports that resulted from requests to the mainframe. Similarly, PC-ALAS dialog boxes represented the meeting of two different computer literacies, combining the genres of mainframe punch cards and GUI-style dialog boxes. Indeed, whenever a new computer system is developed, "separate historical layers and perspectives meet and interact" in the transfer from developers to users (Hasu and Engeström 2000, 65), and that bridgework is frequently done through hybrid genres.

A hybrid genre is often the result of a genre that has been imported into the computer interface. For instance, PC-ALAS dialog boxes resulted from the importing of paper forms into the interface, where they mingled with the existing genre of the dialog box. This mingling is not simply the pouring of content into a form. (In fact, Bakhtin (1986, 165) argues that what we call *form* is really content that has become "congealed" or standardized over time.) In importing a genre, designers often have to make it fit the logic and connotations of the genre with which it mingles. Sometimes that is very difficult. For example, in chapter 4, Sherry had trouble understanding how search dialog boxes worked because they did not follow the logic of the Windows dialog boxes with which she was familiar.

It is important to bring up Sherry's experience here because GIS-ALAS, the Windows-based version of PC-ALAS, was developed in large part to address the destabilizations related to interface literacies that I discussed in chapter 4. GIS-ALAS was to provide the *functionality* of PC-ALAS (the content) with a friendlier, more useful, and more intuitive *interface* (the form). It would accomplish this goal in large part by importing official genres—most conspicuously the node map, dialog box, report windows, and menus—and mingling them with Windows-based interface features to produce hybrids. Along with the genres, certain practices governing them were automated in the interface: GIS-ALAS allowed workers to point and click on traffic accidents to obtain corresponding accident data. In this way, the developers hoped to resolve the many differences between interface literacies that I discussed in chapter 4.

Although these developers were not trained in formal user-centered design approaches, in some ways they hewed quite closely to the assumptions of some user-centered design approaches described in chapter 1. They saw the messiness of PC-ALAS use and developed a centripetal solution, one in which workers could use familiar official genres in prescribed and often narrowly bounded ways. They thought of imported genres as *metaphors,* thus following the lead of many user-centered designers who see metaphoric design as a way to effectively bridge the familiar and unfamiliar (Erickson 1990; Beyer and Holtzblatt 1998; Hackos and Redish 1998; cf. Spinuzzi 2001b). Similarly, they took advantage of the workers' familiarity with Windows (see chapter 4) to embed the genres in an intuitive "point-and-click" Windows interface. At first glance, GIS-ALAS appears to be a user-centered upgrade: a cleaned-up, optimized version of the messy PC-ALAS genre ecology. The developers appeared to have rescued the workers from the tyranny of a chaotic, standardless system.

But on closer examination, the centripetal reorganization of the genre ecology seems more problematic. Genres carry with them the histories and interconnections in which they were developed. In the case of GIS-ALAS, its hybrid genres were the meeting points of at least two sets of activities: the activities of accident location vs. geographic location, and the activities of using standard databases (such as PC-ALAS) versus visualization tools (such as GIS-ALAS). (See table 5.1.) These activities are contradictory, and the hybrid genres consequently embed the contradictions, destabilizing whatever activity they mediate. Below, I trace the development and outlines of these hybrid genres, showing how contradictions have become embedded in them. Later, in the two studies of this chapter, we will see how these contradictions constitute mesoscopic

Table 5.1
Two contradictions embodied by GIS-ALAS hybrid genres

Contradiction	Points at which the contradiction manifests
Between accident location and geography	Between genre rules and division of labor
Between standard databases and visualization tools	Between genres: static reports vs. dynamic displays
	Between objects: finished analyses vs. on-the-fly analyses
	Between mediational means and rules: serial vs. interactive data exploration, manual vs. automated genre management

differences in genre perception and genre management. And we will see points where workers are likely to develop innovations.

The First Contradiction: Accident Location and Analysis vs. Geographic Location

The first of these two embedded contradictions is between the activities of *accident location* and *geographic location*. This contradiction becomes embedded in GIS-ALAS' hybrid genres in part because of the division of labor struck by the developers of GIS-ALAS, a division of labor that limited developers' abilities to design genres. As we will see in the two studies in this chapter, this contradiction between accident location and geographic location is associated with numerous discoordinations and breakdowns.

In 1996, when Center for Transportation Research and Education (CTRE) workers decided to develop a new information system for accident location and analysis, they used on-screen genres that had been developed for a quite different activity: that of geographic location (studying the relationship between geography and other factors such as environment, pollution, road and city planning, census data, and emergency response times). Rather than building GIS-ALAS from scratch, CTRE based it on an existing geographic information system (GIS) developed by a software company, ESRI. Consequently, CTRE was quite restricted in how much it could adapt those on-screen genres for the needs of the ALAS activity system. Thus, GIS-ALAS' hybrid genres embedded a contradiction between *genre rules*, which had to be adapted to the activity of accident location and analysis, and *division of labor*, which included developers of GISes designed for the very different activity of geographic location.

Since CTRE's developers based GIS-ALAS on this existing GIS, they had to combine PC-ALAS genres (oriented toward accident location) with the GIS' existing on-screen genres (oriented toward geographic location). Figure 5.1 gives some idea of the radical restructuring of the genre ecology as PC-ALAS' genres were hybridized with the GIS' genres to produce GIS-ALAS hybrid genres.

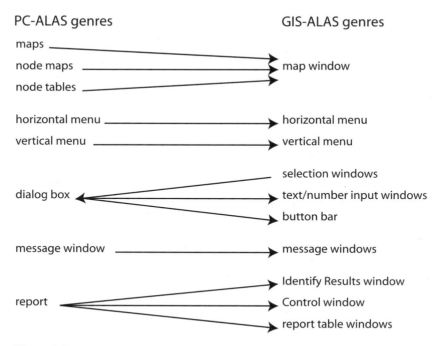

Figure 5.1
PC-ALAS genres and their GIS-ALAS descendants.

   Although the GIS genres are oriented toward a *general* exploration of *geographic* data, they were combined with PC-ALAS genres, genres oriented toward a *more specific* exploration of *accident* data. The resulting genres are doubly oriented, a change that is more than skin deep; it involves more than shuffling functionality from one genre to another. The previous ALAS information systems used complex points of data, too complex for the GIS to handle well. The GIS was built for analyses using simpler data points—an indicator of how different accident location and analysis is from geographic location. To get the GIS to work with the old ALAS data, CTRE had to reconfigure ALAS' *underlying data structure*. This reconfiguration has consequences for both spatial and textual displays.

Consequences for Spatial Displays   To understand the nature of these changes for spatial displays, let's revisit how data are stored in the node-

Table 5.2
Data on three accidents stored in the node-link system

Reference node	Direction node	Distance	Accident data
1560	1660	3	(All data related to this accident)
1560	1660	1	(All data related to this accident)
1661	1561	4	(All data related to this accident)

link system used by mainframe-ALAS and PC-ALAS. In the node-link system, workers at the Iowa DOT have designated *nodes*—six-digit numbers that represent points in the roadway system such as intersections, bridges, and entrance ramps. These node numbers are overlaid over a paper map to form that hybrid genre, the node map.

It is important to note, though, that the nodes' *spatial relationships* are not stored in the node-link data. That is, PC-ALAS "knows" that an accident is associated with a particular node, but it does not "know" *where* that node is. The data are fundamentally oriented toward explicating accidents, not toward explicating their spatial relationships. (This is a legacy of the preautomation system, in which statewide reports focused on types of accidents rather than accident locations.) Table 5.2 shows an abstraction of the stored data.

In table 5.2, the accident data for each accident are stored in a *record*, a data structure that holds two node numbers, a distance between the two, and data associated with the accident that the record describes. For instance, the first row of table 5.2 describes an accident that occurred near a point designated 1560, three units (three hundredths of a mile) toward a second point, 1660. These data are alphanumeric, not spatial, so there is no way to reconstruct the spatial location of the accident simply from this information—a human being has to plot it on a node map (figure 5.2).

In figure 5.2, a worker has traced the road running between nodes 1560 and 1660. He has located the accident (the X) three units from node 1560 in the direction of node 1660, and in doing so has related the nodes *spatially*—something that could not have been accomplished with the node-link data alone. (See Pawlovich and Souleyrette 1996 for more on the node-link system.) Notice that the accident's placement is not

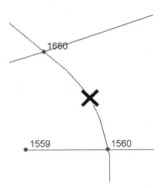

Figure 5.2
A worker has plotted the accident three units from node 1560 toward 1660 along the road.

exact by any means. Not only is the placement based on the worker's estimate (or best guess), but the original accident data are themselves based on the estimate of a driver or police officer (who might "guesstimate" that the accident happened about 150 feet from an intersection). This lack of precision is not a problem because ALAS workers are interested in clusters of accidents; as long as the placement is within a dozen yards or so, the precision is high enough to serve the workers' purpose.

Compare the underlying data structure of the node-link system with that of the GIS. Since the GIS is oriented toward geographic location, GIS data represent an *absolute positioning* of an item on a grid (Herzog 1999). After all, in geographic location the important thing is to know precisely where each represented feature is in relation to the others—within centimeters, if possible, although M. T. Herzog (1999, 12) allows that "positional accuracy to a couple of meters is acceptable." If a river is located exactly twenty feet from the road, the GIS should depict exactly that distance between the two features. Thus the items are *always, fundamentally* related spatially through the grid, and their positioning is represented through coordinates that we can think of as x (horizontal) and y (vertical) coordinates. Table 5.3 shows an abstraction of how accident data are stored in the GIS.

Here, the data are all tied to specific spatial coordinates rather than related to node numbers. Therefore a worker does not need to manually

Table 5.3
Data on a single accident in the GIS

x (horizontal) coordinate	y (vertical) coordinate	Point data
624	840	Accident record (A)
624	840	Accident record (B)
624	840	Accident record (C)

Note: The x and y coordinates tell the GIS where to plot the accident horizontally and vertically on the map. The A, B, and C records refer to different aspects of the same accident (see next section)

plot the accident on a map: the GIS has enough information to plot the accident itself.

How do the data—approximately 700,000 accidents occurring over the previous ten years—become converted from the low-precision node-link system to the high-precision GIS data structure? The CTRE developers created a simple program to combine the old data with the nodes' coordinates, resulting in the GIS data. This system worked quite well when an accident was located *at* a particular node (e.g., in an intersection). But when the accident was at a link between nodes—for example, 158 feet from node 1560 in the direction of node 1660—the conversion program plotted a straight line between the two nodes rather than following the road, as a worker would (figure 5.3). What resulted was a display of accidents that appeared to be located *off the road*.[1]

We see the contradiction between accident location and geographic location, then, in the central genre of the map window (figure 3.15). The map window was a hybrid of the node map and the GIS' online map. As I discussed in chapter 4, the node map itself embodied the contradiction between qualitative and quantitative roadway representations (that is, between workers' traditional ways of talking about accidents—in terms of addresses, intersections, landmarks, and maps—and the node-link system). Both representations contradicted a third representation, the coordinate representation that the GIS used for geographic location (table 5.3). We might anticipate—and the studies below verify—destabilizations across the levels of scope as participants used the online map, a genre oriented toward both accident location and geographic location.

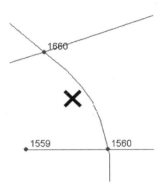

Figure 5.3
In GIS-ALAS, the accident is plotted in a straight line between the two nodes, rather than on the road.

The reconfiguration of the underlying data structure that I have described, then, reassigned some of the labor of accident location from the worker to the machine, and in the process introduced some inconsistencies in how data were *spatially* displayed. This reconfiguration also had consequences for how data were *textually* displayed.

Consequences for Textual Displays   In the PC-ALAS era, all types of data for a given accident had been stored in *records*, data structures that consisted of numbers and characters. These records, cryptic in themselves, were converted by PC-ALAS into information that workers could understand. For instance, the number 2 in a particular slot of the record would be read by PC-ALAS and converted into categorical data: in a PC-ALAS report it would indicate that the driver sustained "moderate injuries."

But when CTRE developed GIS-ALAS, the developers had to split each record into three types of records: one for the accident information itself, one for each vehicle involved in the accident, and one for each injury sustained in the accident. These three new record types were called A, B, and C records. These records, like the PC-ALAS records from which they were derived, were full of data that appeared cryptic until translated by the information system. However, since CTRE's developers were limited in what they could do with GIS-ALAS' genres—genres oriented

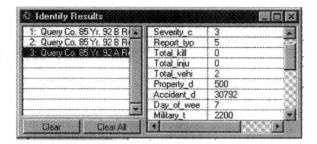

Figure 5.4
The Identify Results window.

toward geographic location, with its simpler tabular data—they could not always make sure the records were translated appropriately. The results were data displays that were often quite difficult to decipher. For instance, in figure 5.4 the Identify Results window shows A, B, and C records for a single accident (left pane) and cryptic information for the accident (right pane). Notice that categorical data (e.g., "Severity_c") are represented by numbers whose categorical meanings are not apparent.

Since CTRE built on ESRI's tool, CTRE's developers had quite limited choice over the look, feel, and function of GIS-ALAS. Thus, CTRE's developers were limited in how much they could adapt genres; they had less chance to mitigate the contradiction between accident location and geographic location.

The Second Contradiction: Standard Databases vs. Visualization Tools

Up to this point, I have discussed how GIS-ALAS hybrid genres embodied the contradiction between accident location and geographic location. But a contradiction also existed between GIS-ALAS, a data visualization tool, and PC-ALAS, a standard database. This contradiction, as we will see in the two studies later in this chapter, was embedded in certain hybrid genres; the resulting double orientation was associated with destabilizations across the levels of scope.

PC-ALAS and GIS-ALAS were quite different tools. PC-ALAS was essentially a database with canned queries and static displays (paper and online reports, message windows). GIS-ALAS, on the other hand, was a *data visualization tool,* which Barbara Mirel (1998b, 491) argues is a fundamentally different type of program because "data visualizations are interactive and linked dynamically." The interactivity and dynamism of data visualizations, she suggests, allow workers to accrue certain benefits not available within standard databases:

> With visualizations, users can see the data that database, spreadsheet, statistical, and graphing programs report only textually or present through static displays. Instead of having to spend hours or even days searching through 50 or more pages of reports to analyze the relationships they need for a decision, users may interact with the data visualizations to quickly retrieve and interpret data from a 10,000-foot view and from a close-up detailed view almost at the same moment. (p. 492)

PC-ALAS workers had to visualize data by reading from static displays and converting the node-link system back to the map genre; they sometimes even marked accident locations on an off-screen genre, a spot map. In contrast, GIS-ALAS was interactive: users really could take a "10,000-foot view" showing all accidents, and they really could obtain a "close-up detailed view" of a particular cluster of accidents in the next moment. And since the map window was dynamic, when workers requested and searched accidents, the accidents appeared immediately on the map. Furthermore, GIS-ALAS workers could show and hide *themes,* layers of mapped data that overlap each other like transparent layers of acetate. For instance, workers could choose whether to view or hide primary, secondary, and municipal roads, and accidents by year, by clicking on their appropriate themes.

In other words, whereas PC-ALAS was geared to producing static genres (reports) that represent *finished products* of a given search, GIS-ALAS was geared to producing dynamic genres (maps, information windows) that represent *on-the-fly analyses.* (Although GISes could provide static reports of a kind, they were far less developed than PC-ALAS' because they were not the point of the system; they did not represent the primary activity of on-the-fly data analysis.)

The GIS' orientation toward instant data analysis had an effect on how genres were managed. Genre management between the map genre and other genres had been largely automated in GIS-ALAS. This automation was a centripetal response to the difficulties of coordinating genres: the designers had taken that work, which used to be accomplished through various ad hoc innovations, and regulated it through the compliant agency of the computer. With PC-ALAS, workers had to personally manage the map genre in conjunction with PC-ALAS on-screen genres (menus, dialog boxes, report windows)—a difficult and laborious process that required converting between two representations of the roadway system, and that engendered unofficial innovations such as the sticky note Barbara used. In contrast, GIS-ALAS automatically managed the map window's relationship with other genres. It plotted the accidents, not with pins or pens, but with pixels. And by further limiting human involvement in genre management, it ensured that genres would be managed in regularized, predictable ways.

This fundamental shift from a static database to a dynamic visualization tool had repercussions for the entire genre ecology. The static genres in the PC-ALAS ecology—node maps, horizontal and vertical windows, dialog boxes, message windows, and reports—originated in a standard database, but were imported to the interface of a visualization tool and mingled with that tool's existing genres to produce hybrid genres. Some of these hybrid genres remained static while others became dynamic, in the process embedding the contradiction between static and dynamic representations. Sometimes the double orientation even fractured genres: one genre, the report, split to produce both static hybrids (the Control window, the report table) and a dynamic hybrid (the Identify Results window). And the map, once at the periphery of the genre ecology (witness the workers' heroic attempts to minimize its use through mediating genres in chapter 4), was now the central genre.

These hybrid genres, then, were sites of contradiction because each genre was doubly oriented, oriented toward contradictory activities. Thus they became sites of multilevel destabilizations, as we will see in the studies below.

GIS-ALAS AT WORK

In this illustrative study of four ALAS workers, we will see specific instances of how the hybrid genres become sites of contradiction due to their double orientation. I will show how these contradictions manifested in discoordinations and breakdowns as I did in chapter 4, but the point is to examine how these discoordinations and breakdowns cluster around the hybrid genres themselves, like tremors around an epicenter.

I conducted naturalistic observations of four participants using an early GIS-ALAS prototype[2] in their workaday tasks. In these observations, I focused particularly on how participants perceived and managed genres. I videotaped these participants, but since there were only four participants, I chose not to videocode these sessions.

Participants used a limited GIS-ALAS prototype (Prototype A). Prototype A allowed participants to view and customize node maps in map windows and to examine accident data in the Identify Results window, but it did not offer ALAS-specific menus or reports or ALAS-style search capabilities.

Participants

I studied how four participants from the ALAS activity system conducted actual work using Prototype A. Although they were part of the initial beta-testing group for the prototype, these participants were unfamiliar with it, having used it quite rarely before these sessions. Consequently, unlike the study in chapter 4, this study was primarily concerned with how workers interpreted the prototype, how they planned to use it to conduct their work, how they imagined it fitting into their genre ecology, and how they began to adapt it to their information ecology through initial, experimental innovations.

Mark and Dan were jointly working on an engineering project that required them to assess the accidents along a stretch of 13th Street. They had used PC-ALAS for some of this work (see chapter 4) but elected to use GIS-ALAS to visualize the accidents. GIS-ALAS was new to their department: They were beta testers. Traditionally, Mark and Dan had used PC-ALAS to generate printouts of accidents at a location, then store the printouts in a file along with a photocopy of the appropriate map section.

Sam was attempting to assess the accidents at a particular intersection. On the morning I observed him, he had been told that the intersection may need structural modifications and that he should examine the accident history to determine which modifications might be most beneficial.

Terry, the only nonengineer of the four, worked in Traffic Safety at the Iowa DOT. He was providing help to a consultant who was performing a study on high-accident locations in a small town. The consultant needed printed data on the highest-accident locations. As it turned out, Terry had kept a file on this city that included older reports and a photocopy of a map section. Terry's role was to look up the accidents and print them for the consultant.

These workers all had experience with PC-ALAS, and during the observations, three of the four used file folders containing data generated from PC-ALAS.

Methods

The four workers completed questionnaires and were observed using Prototype A to conduct their normal work. After the observation, workers were interviewed about their use of the prototype.

1. *Questionnaires* were used to explore the participants' experience with their activities, the ALAS family, and other types of online products with which they were familiar. The questionnaires made it possible to compare the workers in this study with those in the chapter 4 study, allowing me to confirm that both sets of workers had generally similar backgrounds and experiences and engaged in generally similar activities. I distributed and collected the questionnaires before each participant's session.

2. *Observations* were recorded in field notes as well as on videotape. Participants used Prototype A to conduct work that they would normally conduct with PC-ALAS. Unlike other observations, these were not coded. I chose not to code these observations because unlike the observations in chapter 4, these observations were of only three sessions (since two workers shared a session), involved very different tasks, and involved the learning of a new interface. Consequently, I did not believe that videocoding would turn up coherent, meaningful patterns across workers. However, the observations gave me context for understanding the workers' actions and activities as well as their perceptions of how the prototype should fit into those actions and activities.

3. *Stimulated-recall interviews* were conducted immediately after the observations and involved reviewing the participants' work during the observation as well as in general. Special attention was

given to how workers perceived the prototype and how they might fit it into their future work, as well as to the breakdowns they reported encountering during the session. Participants were also asked to compare the interface with those of PC-ALAS and related information systems. Interviews were audiotaped. I transcribed selected portions to profile participant activities and the use of Prototype A during those activities.

I analyzed these data through participant profiling (a macroscopic analysis) and chronological accounts (a mesoscopic analysis). Although I did not conduct a formal microscopic analysis for this study, I recorded breakdown types based on the workers' comments in the stimulated-recall interviews.

Participant Profiling   I profiled participants in much the same way that I did the PC-ALAS participants in the chapter 4 study. Participant profiling, in this study, involved the following steps:

1. *Characterizing local objects and outcomes.*   First, I examined questionnaire and interview data in terms of the participants' activities. In particular, I studied their organizations' desired outcomes and how the participants transformed the object of their labor (Prototype A output) to produce those outcomes.

2. *Summarizing demographics.*   Next, I examined questionnaire and interview data in terms of participants' demographics, including age, gender, years using PC-ALAS, frequency of PC-ALAS use, and years using various operating systems. These data helped me to understand the broad activities in which workers were engaged.

3. *Transcribing usage comments.*   I reviewed interview data and field notes, transcribing portions relating directly to the following issues: what tasks the participants were trying to accomplish, how participants coordinated Prototype A with other artifacts, how participants used Prototype A in their work, and what complaints the participants had about Prototype A. These transcribed portions served to more fully profile participants.

I stored these data in a database, where I could easily arrange, sort, and explore them.

Chronological Accounts   After constructing the participant profiles, I used them to guide my exploration of the data. I completed the following steps:

1. *Categorizing other genres.*   First, I examined the videotape to identify other genres that participants adapted as they used Prototype A. This analysis allowed me to map out the genre ecology and hypothesize how it might develop over time.

2. *Examining breakdowns.*   Next, I examined the videotape to identify breakdowns reported by the participants during the interviews, associating them with the genres involved. For instance, when Sam described a breakdown interpreting the map window, I reexamined the portion of the videotape where the breakdown took place and particularly how he interacted with the map window.

3. *Examining genres that workers had described as problematic in the stimulated-recall interviews.*   Finally, I examined the videotape for points at which participants used particular genres that they had described as problematic in the stimulated-recall interviews. This analysis provided another view of breakdowns and discoordinations, since it allowed me to examine workers' successful as well as unsuccessful encounters with difficult genres.

Once I had conducted these analyses, I was able to assess how experienced PC-ALAS participants might react to Prototype A.

The Map Window: Interpreting the Map

When interpreting the hybrid genre of the map window, these workers encountered breakdowns and discoordinations that cluster around this genre, which embodies the two contradictions I discussed earlier: accident location versus geographic location and standard databases versus visualization tools. As we see below, Sam grappled with the first contradiction as he dealt with a map that combined three contradictory representations of the roadway system. Terry grappled with the second contradiction, understanding Prototype A as a static database rather than a dynamic visualization tool. After examining the hybrid genre of the map in terms of its embedded contradictions, I suggest how designers might address these contradictions to encourage productive use and innovations.

Sam's Session: Grappling with Three Contradictory Representations   In GIS-ALAS, the GIS map replaces the genre of the paper node map with its awkward manual linkage to PC-ALAS dialog boxes (see chapter 4).

These four workers certainly saw the on-screen map window as an advantage in terms of visualization and accuracy, as this comment by Sam illustrates:

> Sam: I kinda like being able to see where I'm at on the GIS-ALAS. With the PC-ALAS, you had to know that node number and have the map right there, and if you typed the wrong number in you were getting information possibly for what you thought was an "intersection A" and it might have been a block away. So I guess I enjoy, or I like being able to physically see and know that that's the intersection I'm wanting.... You're less likely to make mistakes in that regard.

On the other hand, workers did experience breakdowns associated with this hybrid genre, breakdowns that can be traced to the embedded contradictions between activities. GIS map windows display coordinates on a grid, whereas the node-link system requires plotting accidents in reference to two nodes (e.g., twenty feet from node x in the direction of node y). The conversion between the two representations is not precise—for example, figure 5.5 shows how traffic accidents that occurred on Iowa roads appear to have taken place in a cornfield.

Sam reported encountering breakdowns while attempting to interpret the map; these were associated with the first contradiction between accident location and geographic location, with their different ways of representing map data. In one incident, he examined a municipal street appearing in the map window. In the map window, the street's terminus approached but did not appear to touch a perpendicular state road. Sam was familiar with the area; I was not. Later, during the interview, we attempted to interpret the map's themes (layers of mapped data).

> CS: Well, let's start with how you were looking for results at this particular node. Um, this is—it looks like a node at the end of a street?
>
> Sam: Uh, T-intersection.... I've noticed that some of them [themes] don't line up just exact, but when I, I'm familiar enough with the community that I know that it's, they're off a little bit, but I—
>
> CS: That's really odd.... But at least you knew where the node was, you identified it, and you spent a lot of time trying to figure out how to get the information out of it. What did you try first?
>
> Sam: Basically, I was trying to have it show—I've found in some of the different places different nodes I've looked at, they'll list the accidents 1 through however many. And I know that this had, this is only showing me one accident. And I'm pretty sure there were probably more than just one accident [at this intersection in 1994].

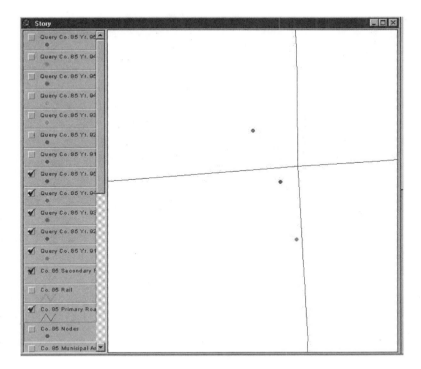

Figure 5.5
Accidents (points) are imprecisely plotted on the roads (lines).

In this dialogue, Sam drew on his knowledge of the county's roads to interpret the map, despite the errors in the map's display (e.g., the T-intersection being displayed as two unconnected roads). Sam's "embodied knowledge" (Haas and Witte 2001) of local accident history told him that other accidents have occurred in that area. What Sam did not know was that when the map depicts multiple accidents at the same spot—as it did here—*the symbols overlap each other* and appear to be one accident.

Sam found that he had to reinterpret the map window innovatively, by connecting it with his knowledge of local accidents, because it appeared to present information he knew was inaccurate. This breakdown was connected with a discoordination between the map window and the node map, genres that represent accidents in very different ways. The

Table 5.4
Contradictions, discoordinations, and their relations to Sam's breakdowns in interpreting the map window

Contradiction	Among three types of roadway/accident representations (originating in different activities):
	Qualitative. Traditional maps coupled with Sam's knowledge of roads, addresses, and accidents (traditional accident location and analysis).
	Node-link system. Fixed locations arbitrarily assigned numbers; accidents plotted between those locations (computer science).
	GIS (coordinate) system. Roads and accidents plotted on a grid with no reference to locations or features (geography).
Discoordinations	Between paper map genre and map window (road representations):
	Paper maps. T-intersections are represented with connected lines on a single sheet.
	Map window. Data for primary, secondary, and municipal roads are represented in layers that do not always precisely overlap.
	Between paper map genre and map window (accident representations):
	Paper maps. Each pin or pen mark represents a single accident.
	Map window. Points overlap each other exactly; one visible point may represent several accidents.
Breakdowns	Sam interprets the map window as presenting highly inaccurate information.

discoordination between these genres was in turn associated with the contradiction among the three representations of the roadway system (qualitative, node-link, and Cartesian coordinate), representations that originate in different activities (table 5.4).

Breakdowns like the one in this instance led Sam to distrust GIS-ALAS. He innovatively drew on, and would likely continue to draw on, other genres (maps, perhaps printed reports, and PC-ALAS, in addition to his own knowledge) that were more "reliable" to supplement the discoordinated genres. Doing so could exacerbate the contradiction by bringing the three systems into even more direct conflict.

Breakdowns can be opportunities for growth and change, so were Sam to continue using GIS-ALAS, he might eventually reinterpret these phenomena in a way that allowed him to make better sense of the data. But the breakdowns were interconnected with destabilizations at other levels of scope. Eliminating them may change the character of the overall destabilization, but it will not necessarily go away. For instance, this incident proved to Sam that he could not trust the online map's representation of the roadway system. When using the online map in the future, Sam may find himself double-checking by consulting other maps and other roadway representations—that is, he may feel the need to constantly reinterpret the map window, and he may bring other genres into the ecology to help him do that.

Terry's Session: Static Database vs. Visualization Tool   Like Sam, Terry also encountered breakdowns and discoordinations involving the hybrid genre of the map window, but these breakdowns and discoordinations for the most part reflected the second contradiction: the contradiction between the static database and the dynamic visualization tool. Terry understood the GIS-ALAS map window to be a static database representation rather than a dynamic visualization tool, so he was more limited in his use of GIS-ALAS.

Unlike Sam, Terry was unfamiliar with the county depicted on his screen. He was providing accident information to a contractor for a small rural county, a county he had not even visited before. To interpret the map window, Terry turned to more familiar genres. He used a folder of county information, which included relevant PC-ALAS reports and a photocopy of the county's node map. During the observation, he sat with the report folder to his left and the map on the desk between him and the screen. At times, he would trace a road on the paper map with his finger, then trace the same road in the map window. When I asked him about the paper map, he said:

> *Terry:* It was just luck that I already had that in the file, [which we started] when the location was first mentioned. And now it's come back that the consultant has met with these people from the city, and they said, okay, we're going to do this study. And they sent us the PC-ALAS request, that's what they're used to getting, so they say, just send us that information.... Normally I'd try to avoid [using the paper map] by using

> [the GIS-ALAS prototype], but then it'd still have to take—print this, print the [prototype's] nodes on a piece of paper, then go to PC-ALAS.

The last sentence is arresting: normally workers would be expected to use the GIS-ALAS prototype as a *substitute* for PC-ALAS, not as a way to produce additional printed node maps. But during the interview it became clear that Terry did not regard the prototype as a PC-ALAS substitute. He had to perform some complex searches, and the prototype he was using did not (yet) have the standard ALAS-type searches programmed into it. Terry regarded the prototype as a flexible online database of maps that he could use to mediate his normal interactions with PC-ALAS. His critique of the product centered on its ability to do that job:

> *Terry:* Sometimes [the prototype] saves me the, looking up the paper copies of the node numbers. But even then these printouts, this one is actually a pretty good one as far as being able to read the node numbers, but as soon as they're crowded like that you can't read them anymore.

So, far from making Terry's task simpler, the GIS-ALAS prototype made it more complicated and more difficult for Terry to use. Rather than *replacing* PC-ALAS, it *mediated* PC-ALAS—and it itself required mediation through the Terry's file folder. He ended up using the map on file to identify and print the online map.

In this session, Terry also reported encountering breakdowns while trying to construct and print appropriate maps—that is, maps that include readable lettering and proper labels for map features such as nodes and streets. These breakdowns were associated with the discoordination between the static paper node map and the dynamic map window: the GIS map window genre is oriented toward dynamic, on-the-fly data visualizations, but the node-map genre is oriented toward simple, static road representations, and Terry—who was most familiar with node maps—understood the second orientation much better. This discoordination in turn was associated with the contradiction between standard databases and visualization tools. The designers saw Prototype A as a *visualization tool*: the only (or at least the primary) tool mediating the activity of accident location and analysis. Terry, on the other hand, saw it as a *standard database*: a tool that provides static maps that he can use as input for PC-ALAS (table 5.5).

Table 5.5
Contradictions, discoordinations, and their relations to Terry's breakdowns in interpreting the map window

Contradiction	Between standard databases and visualization tools: *Terry*. The prototype is a standard database that *supplements* PC-ALAS and its genre ecology. *The designer*. The prototype is a visualization tool that *replaces* PC-ALAS and its genre ecology.
Discoordinations	Between map genre and map window: *Paper map*. Detailed information; high resolution; used in itself. *Map window*. Less detailed information; poor resolution; produces paper maps of lower quality than existing node maps.
Breakdowns	Terry had difficulty constructing and printing a map that has the features he expects from a node map.

In his use of the prototype, Terry grew increasingly frustrated. If his manager had not encouraged him to use this prototype, Terry might have abandoned it. As is, he used the GIS, not to replace the map as the designers envisioned, but to supplement it. The contradiction was handled by creating an ecological niche for what Terry took to be the genre's purpose; the designer's purpose went by the wayside. This misconstrual can itself be seen as an innovation: Terry was able to take the tool and use it in ways the designers had not envisioned. If he continued to use the prototype after this session, perhaps he invented new, unofficial innovations that allowed him to coordinate PC-ALAS, paper maps, and the GIS-ALAS prototype. Those innovations may have caused him to understand the prototype in ways increasingly at variance with the designers' vision.

To sum up, in this section we saw that the map window, a hybrid genre, was the center of a *cluster* of breakdowns and discoordinations because it embodied contradictions. By tracing this cluster back to the hybrid genre, we can discern the contradictions embedded in it, and we can begin to see the overall shape of destabilizations in the emerging activity. We will see something similar with the Identify Results window.

The Identify Results Window: Obtaining Accident Information

All participants clicked accidents on the map to display accident data in the Identify Results window. For Mark and Dan, these data were the heart of the observed activity: they needed detailed information on each of the accidents occurring at or near a particular intersection so that they could understand how factors such as weather, road structure, signage, and behavior influenced accidents. Yet they encountered breakdowns when attempting to perform this activity and obtain this information. These breakdowns can be traced to discoordinations in genre perception and genre management, and from there to the differences in the ways that PC-ALAS and GIS-ALAS represented data.

Their genre-perception difficulties centered on the way the data were presented. Since the Identify Results window showed the underlying structure of the data (the A, B, and C records) rather than the more processed view given by PC-ALAS reports, Mark and Dan had to learn that underlying data structure. This took a while. Near the end of the session, after looking at several accidents and various A, B, and C records, it dawned on Mark what the different records were for:

> *Mark:* So one of 'em has to do with the people involved and others with, with the accidents or vehicles.

Mark was correct: each accident was represented by one A record (information on the accident itself), along with a B record for each vehicle involved and a C record for each injury. Yet this structure only began to make sense after Mark and Dan looked at over a dozen accidents. It was not apparent in the record identifiers.

Neither was it apparent in the field labels displayed within the records. These labels were cryptic, and the data within the fields were often represented by numerical data (e.g., Vehicle_ty = 1; Severity_c = 3; see figure 5.6).

In figure 5.6 the detailed accident information in PC-ALAS reports is hybridized with the GIS' Identify Results window. The two genres are oriented toward very different activities: reports facilitate the interpretation of complex underlying data for accident location, but the Identify Results window displays the underlying data structure "as is," since it

```
Reference Node: 218140       Direction node: 999999    Distance: 9.99    1/18/96
Case #:6004663               Property Damage: $ 1500.00      Thu  Time: 1530
Fatalities: 0                Injuries [Major: 0   Minor: 1   Possible: 0]
Vehicles Involved: 2         Report Filed By - Officer     Story

VEH #  1 Initial Direction of Travel: East      ** FTYROW making Left Turn
         Vehicle Action: Turning Left
         Vehicle Type: Passenger Car
         Vehicle Defects: No Defects
         Drivers Sex: M  Age: 23
         Driver Condition: Apparently Normal
VEH #  2 Initial Direction of Travel: Unknown    ** Ran Traffic Signal
         Vehicle Action: Going Straight
         Vehicle Type: Passenger Car
         Vehicle Defects: No Defects
         Drivers Sex: M  Age: 22
         Driver Condition: Apparently Normal

Accident Type:     Broadside / Left Turn              Hit & Run :N
Light Conditions:  Day                   Weather Conditions: Snow, Strong Wind
```

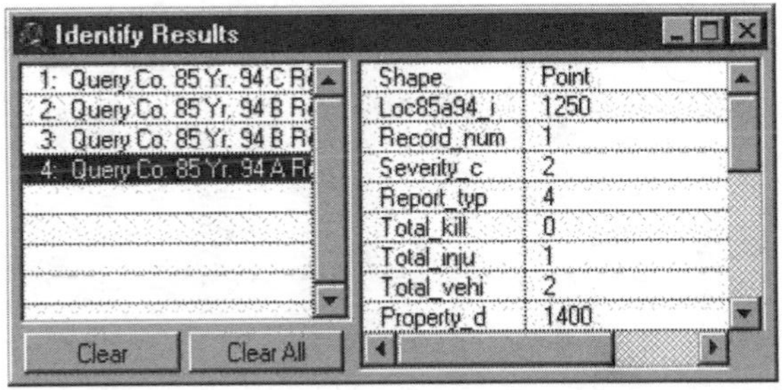

Identify Results		
1: Query Co. 85 Yr. 94 C R	Shape	Point
2: Query Co. 85 Yr. 94 B R	Loc85a94_i	1250
3: Query Co. 85 Yr. 94 B R	Record_num	1
4: Query Co. 85 Yr. 94 A R	Severity_c	2
	Report_typ	4
	Total_kill	0
	Total_inju	1
	Total_vehi	2
Clear Clear All	Property_d	1400

Figure 5.6

(*Top*) Detailed accident information from a PC-ALAS report, which repackages the underlying data structure for easy reading. (*Bottom*) The Identify Results window, which reveals the underlying data structures.

assumes the simple, easy-to-interpret data usually employed in GISes for geographic location.

In the mainframe-ALAS and PC-ALAS eras, the data were stored in abbreviated, primarily numerical formats (records). When the computer was asked to produce a report, it would convert the data, providing appropriate labels and explanatory text to help workers interpret the data. The top of figure 5.6 shows such a report; categorical data such as the day of week the accident occurred, represented here in a readable abbreviation ("Thu"), were stored in the database as numbers. The bottom of figure 5.6 shows similar data in the Identify Results window, which did far less in converting the data ("Day_of_wee = 7"). Other data were even more cryptic ("Severity_c = 3"):

> *Mark:* We don't know what those codes mean. You know, some have the severity or whatever, and it has "3" ... if we had a table that explained what the different codes with each of the things were, you know, you could get a lot more information about an accident.

Mark's remark about "a table that explained ... the different codes" (a proposed innovation) is interesting in that it points to a discoordination in genre management. The field data are meant to fill the same role as the detailed section of a PC-ALAS report. But since Mark found the field data to be cryptic, he saw an unfilled niche and suggested that he might fill it by *adapting another genre* for mediating the field data, such as a table or a legend. This seems to be one way that genre ecologies expand, as we saw in chapter 4.

To sum up, breakdowns and discoordinations clustered around the hybrid genre of the Identify Results window. These were manifestations of the embedded contradiction between accident location and geographic location. The hybrid genre was oriented toward both accident location (workers need complex textual data) and geographic location (workers need simple alphanumeric data). Thus workers found it difficult to interpret data according to the familiar genres and had trouble understanding the GIS' ways of interconnecting the new genres. Consequently, they tended to limit their interpretations of the data they received, either partially completing their interpretive attempts or abandoning those attempts outright (table 5.6).

In the incident described above, breakdowns led to ad hoc coordinations with existing genres (e.g., PC-ALAS reports) and open speculation

Table 5.6
Contradictions, discoordinations, and their relations to breakdowns in obtaining accident information

Contradiction	Between data representations:
	PC-ALAS. Accidents represented in primarily qualitative ways, with text descriptions (for human use and management).
	GIS-ALAS. Accidents represented in primarily quantitative ways, with alphanumeric identifiers (for computer use and management).
Discoordinations	Between familiar and unfamiliar genres, including the identifiers used by those genres.
Breakdowns	Workers had difficulty interpreting data according to familiar genres.
	Workers had difficulty understanding the GIS' ways of interconnecting the new genres.
	Workers' attempts to interpret records and fields were often only partially completed or abandoned outright.

about adapting other genres. Such innovations could lead to reframing (though not resolving) the contradiction between data representations as additional genres are adapted to "translate" between the two representations.

Summary: Destabilizations Encountered by ALAS Workers

In this study, I have argued that certain hybrid genres in GIS-ALAS have embedded two contradictions: between accident location and geographic location, and between standard databases and visualization tools. Because hybrid genres embody contradictions, they are epicenters around which discoordinations and breakdowns are manifested. Such destabilizations are troubling, not just for the workers, but for all who are concerned about the safety of Iowa's roads. If workers have difficulty interpreting the map, the accidents, and the accident data—if they find themselves routinely miscounting accidents or abandoning their interpretations of accident information—the results of their work may mislead them and others in related activities. Engineers may not become aware of the need for signage; law enforcement officers may fail to lend the proper attention to particularly dangerous areas and behaviors; legislators may believe that their initiatives have worked when in fact they have not.

The workers in this study are very new to GIS-ALAS, and we see very different patterns emerging among them. As GIS-ALAS becomes more widely adapted in the ALAS activity system, Sam, Mark, Dan, Terry, and other workers will likely begin to stabilize their interpretations and uses of GIS-ALAS by collaboratively drawing on familiar genres: training classes, manuals, online help, and informal phone calls. Various unpredictable innovations will form a genre ecology in which these workers will be able to interpret and use the software.

Sam, Mark, Dan, and Terry dealt with half-familiar hybrid genres, genres that resemble their "parents" in the ALAS activity system. They are experienced with PC-ALAS genres and the ALAS activity system, but unfamiliar with GIS genres or geographic location. The study below turns this situation on its head: it examines the difficulties that students who are familiar with GIS genres and geographic location, but unfamiliar with the ALAS activity system, encounter when using GIS-ALAS.

GIS-ALAS AT SCHOOL

We have looked at how experienced ALAS workers perceived, used, and experienced difficulties with hybrid genres in GIS-ALAS because these genres were doubly oriented toward accident location and geographic location, and static databases and dynamic visualization tools. The workers in the above study were experienced with PC-ALAS genres and the ALAS activity system, but unfamiliar with GIS genres or geographic location. What happens if the situation is reversed—as might happen as new employees, who have learned GISes in school, are hired for ALAS activities such as city engineering? Would users who are familiar with GISes, but unfamiliar with ALAS activities and genres, *also* find these hybrid genres to be epicenters for their discoordinations and breakdowns? How do activities affect use, and what are the implications for how these new users might innovate in the future?

In the following illustrative study, I investigate these questions by examining how thirteen students in a GIS class use a GIS-ALAS prototype to locate and analyze accidents. Along the way, I explore a third contradiction that was formed by bringing students into contact with the ALAS activity system: the contradiction between ALAS work and schoolwork.[3]

Methods

I observed thirteen students enrolled in a class on geographic informa-tion systems at Iowa State University. Students averaged just under half a year experience with GISes in general; four of the thirteen had experience with ArcView, the particular GIS on which GIS-ALAS was based. They said it was very similar to the other GISes they have used.

The class in which the students were enrolled was offered through Community and Regional Planning, a field that bears directly on acci-dent location and analysis, and in fact, the professor had briefly dis-cussed the GIS-ALAS project with the class earlier in the semester. Ten students were Community and Regional Planning majors, who might conceivably become involved with accident location and analysis later in their careers. The other three majored in Landscape Architecture, Public Administration, and Water Resources, fields much less connected with the ALAS activity system. I asked these thirteen students to use a second, more customized prototype of GIS-ALAS (Prototype B).

This investigation allowed me to gain a broader perspective on GIS-ALAS design because it allowed me to compare participants with differ-ent types of expertise using similar artifacts. Participants in the chapter 4 study were familiar with the activity of locating and analyzing accidents, but were unfamiliar with GISes. Participants in the other study in this chapter were familiar with both. In the present study, the thirteen stu-dents were familiar with GISes, but were unfamiliar with accident loca-tion and analysis.

The thirteen students completed questionnaires. I then gave them a set of instructions similar to the workshops they had completed weekly in class and observed them as they used Prototype B. Afterward, I inter-viewed them about their use of Prototype B and the breakdowns they had encountered during the session.

1. *Questionnaires* were distributed and collected before the obser-vation. These provided information similar to the questionnaires from the previous stages, and therefore allowed me to compare the

groups. Using this information, I was better able to account for similarities and differences among the groups of participants.

2. *Observations* involved having the participants respond to a set of instructions that resembled their class assignments. The instructions required them to find and analyze certain accidents. I videotaped observations and recorded them in field notes; I later coded the observations. I gave special attention to breakdowns. These coded observations allowed me to examine the data systematically. In particular, they helped me to find patterns of tool use, identify discoordinations, and observe how participants dealt with the various genres in the ecology.

3. *Stimulated-recall interviews*, conducted immediately after the observations, explored breakdowns that participants had encountered as they used Prototype B. Participants were also asked to compare Prototype B with other GISes they had used. I audiotaped these interviews, then transcribed selected portions to help me interpret video data and analyze breakdowns.

Once I had collected the data for this group, I analyzed them using modified versions of the methods employed in the chapter 4 study.

Participant Profiling   In this study, participant profiling involved the following steps:

1. *Summarizing demographics.*   First, I examined questionnaire and interview data in terms of participants' demographics, including age, gender, years of experience with GISes, and years using various operating systems. These data helped me understand how the students' backgrounds differed from those of the workers in the previous studies.

2. *Transcribing usage comments.*   I reviewed interview data, transcribing portions relating directly to the following issues: how participants perceived and managed Prototype B genres, points at which they had trouble perceiving and managing those genres, and complaints and suggestions the participants had about Prototype B. These transcribed portions served to more fully profile participants.

I then stored these data in a database, where I could easily arrange, sort, and explore them.

Videocoding   Although I used a method for gathering and coding data that was quite similar to that used in the Chapter 4 study, in this study I concentrated on coding very different sorts of breakdowns. Chapter 4, an in situ study of experienced participants at work, allowed me to use detailed breakdown categories based on participants' interaction with the system. That study assumed that the participants were to some degree familiar with the system. But this study does not make that assumption. *None* of the student participants were familiar with Prototype B, so they naturally encountered what were considered mild breakdowns under the old system: hesitations, lingering over menu choices, and so forth. These were to be expected from new participants.

For this study, I was more interested in breakdowns that halted or seriously impeded participants' sessions. To identify such breakdowns, I invited participants to voice questions during the session. Then I coded their questions as breakdowns. I associated these breakdowns with the actions students were performing as they asked the questions; like the videocoding in chapter 4, this videocoding thus allowed me to compare successful and unsuccessful actions.

I tested interrater reliability to determine whether the coding scheme was systematized enough to be teachable to other raters. One rater was trained during an hour-long session by viewing and coding one observation, then comparing the result with my coding. After the training, the rater coded three sessions, each of which was randomly selected from one of three groups: male native English speakers, female native English speakers, and nonnative English speakers of both genders. The rater coded 24.2 percent of the total video data. Table 5.7 indicates that the rater reliably applied the coding scheme.

Chronological Accounts   After conducting the macroscopic and microscopic analyses, I compared them with the videotapes to construct chronological accounts of all participants' sessions.

Table 5.7
Cohen's kappa for the four categories

Artifact	Action	Operation	Breakdown
0.943	0.945	0.929	0.824
(94.3%)	(94.5%)	(92.9%)	(82.4%)

1. *Tracing breakdowns to discoordinations.* Once I had coded breakdowns, I investigated them by examining the video data where the breakdowns occurred, as well as stimulated-recall interviews discussing these or similar breakdowns. These data gave me evidence to determine which breakdowns could be associated with specific discoordinations.

2. *Tracing discoordinations to contradictions.* Finally, I compared the identified discoordinations with the contradictions I identified in chapter 3. These data allowed me to associate discoordinations with specific contradictions, and consequently make connections among the microscopic, mesoscopic, and macroscopic analyses. These connections were elaborated through the heuristic of the contradiction-discoordination-breakdown (CDB) table.

After concluding this study, I was able to draw conclusions about the implications of pulling existing genres into the computer interface.

Results and Analysis

Although students encountered breakdowns using various genres in GIS-ALAS, students' breakdowns tended to cluster around the map window, the Identify Results window, and the Report Table window. Here, we will focus on the first two. The results suggest that the first contradiction, among representational systems, was associated with multiple breakdowns for the students. The second contradiction, between static databases and dynamic visualization tools, does not manifest itself visibly—probably because students were accustomed to using dynamic visualization tools, not static databases, in the activity system of the class. That is, the second contradiction did not exist for the students.

By the same token, though, a third contradiction manifested between the ALAS activity and the students' class activity. This contradiction should not be surprising—in fact, the differences between school and workplace are often discussed (e.g., Freedman, Adam, and Smart 1994; Breuch 2001)—but its presence points once again to the sociocultural embeddedness of design.

Below, I examine the map window and the Identify Results window, connecting the associated breakdowns with the discoordinations and contradictions that coconstitute them (tables 5.8 and 5.9).

Table 5.8
Breakdown categories

Breakdown	Description	Example
Assistance needed in interpretation	Participant has trouble interpreting an interface feature.	"From—so these are like the records of the accidents and stuff?"
Procedural question	Participant indicates confusion about the procedure outlined in the instruction sheet.	"Is this what you're talking about the layers? Listed on the left side of the map? You just turn them on and off?"
Question about artifact's properties	Participant wants to know whether an artifact has certain properties.	"Can this move out?"
Requests clarification	Participant requests clarification of researcher's previous comment.	CS: "And find one of these dots and click squarely on it." Participant: "Find one of the dots?"
Unexpected behavior	Participant indicates that the software is behaving unexpectedly.	"Something's not working here? Just trying to get back out?"

Map Window

The map window was associated with seventeen breakdowns that students encountered—25.4 percent of all breakdowns. Six of the thirteen participants (46%) encountered breakdowns when using this window. Participants' breakdowns had to do with *themes*, the layers of map data that participants could show or hide. These breakdowns were associated with the contradiction between accident location and geographic location, but also with the contradiction between the complex GIS-ALAS themes, oriented toward accident location, and the simpler themes used in school activities, oriented toward learning. Since the breakdowns alert us to these differences, they can help us to find hard-to-learn aspects of the genre (that is, aspects difficult to reconcile with traditional learning activities) and give us a starting point for redesigning those aspects.

Table 5.9
Number of breakdowns by genre for student group

Genre	Breakdown categories				
	Procedural question	Assistance needed in interpreting	Unexpected behavior	Requests clarification	Question about properties	Total
Identify Results window	9	8	1	2	0	20
Report Table window	6	7	3	0	1	17
Map window	9	5	1	1	1	17
Dialog box	0	2	1	0	0	3
Message window	1	1	1	0	0	3
Vertical menu	1	0	2	0	0	3
Control window	1	0	1	0	0	2
Button bar	1	0	0	0	0	1
Horizontal menu	1	0	0	0	0	1
Total	29	23	10	3	2	67

Students' school activities involved learning to use GISes through relatively simple applications. Thus they were used to dealing with perhaps half a dozen themes with simple names such as "hydrology" and "rail." The GIS assigned a distinct color to each theme so that students could easily differentiate the themes in the map window.

But the activity of accident location and analysis involved far more complicated data, data that required participants to learn different coordination strategies if they were to make sense of the data. In the task I gave the students (a simple task, in ALAS terms), they had to deal with twenty-one to thirty-six themes. Because these themes were so numerous, coordination became far more complex. Themes could not all be listed in the themes pane at once; they required longer, more complicated names to distinguish between them; and they were often assigned similar color shades because the themes outnumbered the distinct colors the computer could display. The sheer number of themes led to breakdowns: students could not tell how many themes there were, what each theme represented, or which themes were associated with which map features (table 5.10).

The themes were numerous partly because of how designers implemented the underlying data structure, using fragmented rather than

Table 5.10
Contradictions, discoordinations, and breakdowns related to numbers of themes

Contradiction	Between students' activities and ALAS activities: *Students' activities.* Schoolwork and test taking—activities that involve simplified GISes. *ALAS activities.* Finding accidents through reducing complexity—an activity that requires a complex GIS.
Discoordinations	Between familiar themes panes and the GIS-ALAS theme pane. Between familiar theme names and GIS-ALAS' theme names. Between familiar easy-to-distinguish color assignments and GIS-ALAS' difficult-to-distinguish color assignments.
Breakdowns	Students could not tell how many themes there were, what each theme represented, or which themes were associated with which features on the map.

Table 5.11
Contradictions, discoordinations, and breakdowns related to theme labels

Contradiction	Between representations of the roadway system.
Discoordinations	Between representations of county designations.
Breakdowns	Students were unsure how to interpret theme names; they selected inappropriate themes; they had trouble distinguishing themes.

unified representations of accidents (as I discussed earlier). These fragmented representations reflected the contradiction between accident location and geographic location. But they had repercussions for learning GIS-ALAS as well, since they involved a contradiction between accident location and students' activities.

Students also encountered breakdowns and discoordinations associated with the contradiction between roadway representations arising from different activities. They were familiar with the coordinate representation of roadways used by GISes, including the simple theme labels I mentioned above. But the GIS-ALAS map window also drew from the node-link system, which made its way into the themes' names. Each accident theme began with the number of the county in which the accidents took place. (For example, the 1994 B records in Story County were stored in the theme named "Co. 85 Yr. 94 B Records.") Consequently, students had difficulty coordinating theme labels with the themes that show up on the map; they were not sure what each map feature represented. They thus encountered breakdowns when trying to interpret theme names, select themes, and distinguish among different themes on the map. (See table 5.11.)

Students did not have a frame of reference for examining roadway system representations. We can imagine that, given time, they might adapt genres (such as cheat sheets) to deal with problems. Such genres could help mitigate contradictions—but we are back where we started, since the contradiction still exists.

Identify Results Window

The students' breakdowns, like those of the experienced workers, also clustered around the Identify Results window: eight of the thirteen students (61.5%) encountered a total of twenty breakdowns (30% of all breakdowns) associated with this window. This clustering points to an embedded contradiction in this hybrid genre, the contradiction between accident location and geographic location. The clustering indicates learning difficulties. Below, I explore the breakdowns, discoordinations, and contradictions encountered by the students.

Students experienced breakdowns interpreting the differences among A, B, and C (accident, property damage, and injury) records, so they were often unable to find the data that I asked them to find in the protocol. And even when participants were able to select the proper records from the Identify Results window, they were often unable to interpret data identifiers within each record. These identifiers are often cryptic, as are the data they hold. For example, during the interview, one student discussed difficulties with interpreting various identifiers:

> Well, I guess "int class" [int_class], that's something that looking at it I wouldn't know. "ref underscore node" [ref_node], that, I mean, "dir underscore node" [dir_node]—But things like "total killed" [total_kill], "total injury" [total_inju], "total vehicle" [total_vehi], those for the most part you can look at them and figure out.

Like the workers in the previous study, these students experienced breakdowns when interpreting records and the identifiers within the records. These breakdowns indicate two discoordinations. In terms of genre perception, even students who were familiar with GIS programs were not equipped to interpret the cryptic identifiers and the categorical data associated with them. In terms of genre management, students could not view A, B, and C records side by side—something that would have helped the student I just quoted as she struggled to make sense of the record types. These discoordinations were associated with a contradiction between the complex underlying data structure (representing ALAS data) and the GIS data representations with which students were familiar (table 5.12).

Again, the Identify Results window is a hybrid genre around which destabilizations cluster. We might expect that if students were to use GIS-ALAS consistently in their school assignments, they might eventually learn to interpret records and identifiers, perhaps by examining PC-ALAS reports. Doing so might help to mitigate the destabilizations clustered around this genre. Yet destabilizations remain at each level, and

Table 5.12
Contradictions, discoordinations, and breakdowns related to data identifiers

Contradiction	Between the activities of accident location and geographic location: *Accident location.* The data representations in the ALAS activity system. *Geographic location.* GIS data representations with which students are familiar.
Discoordinations	Between different genres representing data: *GIS data.* Involves conventional terms and categories. *GIS-ALAS data.* Involves cryptic labels and category numbers. Between different ways of arranging data: *GIS data.* Conventional, spatial arrangement (one record represents one data point). *GIS-ALAS data.* A more complex, layered arrangement of data (several records represent a compound data point).
Breakdowns	Students encountered eight breakdowns that kept them from interpreting records and identifiers well enough to make sense of the data.

any one of these might exacerbate others. A microscopic breakdown in interpreting an identifier, for instance, can highlight the macroscopic differences between work and school.

Summary: Contradictions, Discoordinations, and Breakdowns Encountered by GIS Students

Like the previous study of ALAS workers, this study of GIS students suggests that GIS-ALAS' hybrid genres were sites of contradiction. Each hybrid genre was the union of genres that developed separately to support quite different, even contradictory activities; the hybrid genre retained that double orientation toward the activities. So students had more knowledge about GISes than the ALAS workers, but they still encountered breakdowns when using these hybrid genres. Although these breakdowns were sometimes so different from the workers' breakdowns as to appear unconnected, we can trace many of them to one of the two contradictions that underlay the worker's breakdowns: the contradiction between accident location and geographic location. In addition, we can trace some of the students' breakdowns to a third contradiction: between accident location and students' school activities. These contradictions can manifest themselves in discoordinations and breakdowns, but they can also lead to innovation and learning.

The study has implications for pulling genres into the computer interface. As we saw in chapter 4, genres are interconnected and animated through their users' interpretations and practices. One might expect that by pulling an entire genre ecology into an interface and automating the connections between genres, designers could fix and regulate the activity. Apparently that was the goal of GIS-ALAS' designers. Yet this centripetal approach did not yield a smoother running system *or* a system that could encapsulate the activity. Furthermore, in pulling genres together, designers brought those genres' activities into contradictory tension.

CONCLUSION

What do these two studies teach us about pulling genres into computer interfaces? If nothing else, they teach us to approach the task cautiously.

Genre ecologies, as we saw in chapter 3, grow and develop over time as groups of workers use them to mediate their work activities. Workers' shared interpretations of their tools and their work depend on the relatively stable ways in which they interpret the genres in a given ecology—including not just the official genres but also the unofficial, subversive innovations. But when CTRE's designers developed GIS-ALAS, they developed it centripetally: they pulled in only the official genres and linked those genres via automation,[4] meaning that some of the interactions among genres could happen only in official ways. They assumed that the genres, their connections, and their automated practices—in a sense, the context itself—would be pulled in as well. But the new design left behind the web of unofficial, centrifugal genres and practices that held the activity together.

When this web of genres and practices was left behind, the familiar official genres—the map, the report—were made strange in their union with GIS interface genres. For the ALAS workers, this strangeness meant that when they used these hybrid genres, they often experienced a pull between familiar activities (locating accidents, using static databases) and the activities in which the interface genres were developed (locating geographic features, visualizing data dynamically). These tensions manifested themselves as macroscopic, mesoscopic, and microscopic destabilizations as workers tried to use the hybrid genres. Workers immediately began inventing innovations. On the flip side, the students found that the familiar GIS interface genres acted differently, became harder to interpret, and required explanations. The context of the activity was not pulled into the interface; the interface, as faithfully as it represented familiar genres such as the map, was not intuitive. Like the workers, the students experienced a pull between activities—here, between their familiar school activities and ALAS work—and that pull manifested as destabilizations at various levels as the students worked with the hybrid genres.

These tensions between activities became visible not only in the destabilizations, but in workers' and students' attempts to reintegrate GIS-ALAS into their activities. For the workers, these attempts involved relating GIS-ALAS to other genres with overlapping functions (Sam, Terry) and imagining innovations that might work in conjunction with GIS-ALAS genres (Mark, Dan). For the students, these attempts involved situating GIS-ALAS as a school assignment, drawing on spoken genres such as procedural questions and patterning their interaction with me after the workshops with which they were familiar. In both studies, participants were not bounded by the interface and actively made connections to other genres outside it. GIS-ALAS, a centripetal solution, immediately became entangled in centrifugal innovations.

The studies in this chapter, then, suggest that the centripetal act of pulling genres into an interface cannot in itself preserve the context of an activity, regulate workers' behavior, or solve workers' problems with the software. In fact, a centripetal solution can have the opposite effect, embedding new contradictions into hybrid genres and removing some of the ecological connections that make information systems successful. For a new information system such as GIS-ALAS to be successful, workers must continue to develop the ecology through their own centrifugal innovations. And as we have seen, workers typically get started on the new ecology immediately.

It is worth noting that many of the problems encountered in these studies have since been dealt with. For instance, the cryptic names and county numbers have been linked with metadata (Schuman et al. 1998, 189) and aliases (p. 190). A three-dimensional stacking display now shows all accidents at a given location, circumventing the problem that Sam and others had with interpreting a stack of dots as a single accident. Finally, police officers are now able to enter precise accident coordinates by clicking on a map and pinpoint the accidents with handheld global positioning systems (Schuman et al. 1998, 190). These fixes, as useful as they are, still allow quite a bit of room for improvement. In the last chapter, I discuss how ALAS might further be improved—by the workers themselves.

6

Designing Open Systems: Possible Trajectories for ALAS Genres

In one possible future, a few years from now: *At a police station in Waterloo, a police officer named Marta starts up Open-ALAS, the database and visualization system that she will use for locating and analyzing traffic accidents in a particular area. Since she often runs this query, she has written a macro to select the area and pull up only the accidents that have happened within a 100-foot perimeter in the past year. She is particularly proud that her macro displays both the mapped location of the accidents and a table summarizing the accidents by behavioral type.*

She learned the macro language a few months ago, through looking at the reference manual and examples on the official ALAS website. Some other Open-ALAS users on the message board were always there to coach her through the tough parts, and in fact she still posts to the board to get help on problems and to help less experienced users with their *problems. Not only does helping make her feel useful, it rewards her in other ways: when someone finds her help useful, they award her points. The five people with the most points at the end of the quarter are recognized in the DOT newsletter; Marta thinks that if she is one of those five people, she might be able to improve her promotion chances.*

Marta logs into the ALAS website and reads the message board. Someone in Muscatine is having trouble figuring out how to set up a query basically similar to hers. She posts her macro, and after some thought, also enters it into the knowledge base of Open-ALAS solutions along with a brief set of instructions. Who knows, she thinks, it might help other workers who are just getting used to Open-ALAS—and if they rate it highly, that means more points too.

In the headnote in chapter 1, Barbara subverted PC-ALAS by creating her own unofficial genre on a sticky note, using it to cut several steps from the official procedure. She had to subvert the official information system because PC-ALAS was rigidly fixed: it did not allow her to adapt it to her needs, but rather was hard-coded into what the designers had decided was the optimal configuration.

In the fictional scenario above, however, Marta is in a very different position. Her version of ALAS (a fictional system I have called Open-ALAS) is open to all sorts of changes. It provides a simple visual macrolanguage to facilitate end-user programming, meaning that even relatively inexperienced workers can write simple macros to customize routines. It has a simplified data structure so that workers can easily understand and customize data readouts. It is paired with a web application where workers can contribute to a knowledge base and post questions and answers on a message board. Open-ALAS also has facilities for reporting bugs and providing development guidance for designers. In addition, Open-ALAS is not predicated on the assumption that all work takes place on the computer screen—the forum and knowledge base can accommodate even the most idiosyncratic solutions, so if Marta decides something is best done with a sticky note, she can tell the other developers about her solution and even display examples she has scanned in. At this point Open-ALAS is a fantasy, and some might think it is a rather utopian fantasy. But it could be constructed from existing software tools and its components have been tested in a variety of contexts (discussed below).

Throughout this book, I have argued that the trope of worker-as-victim, dominant in many user-centered design approaches, does not do justice to the ways people like Barbara and Marta actually interact with designed information. Such approaches assume that a properly designed system will provide all of the guidance users need; it can be perfectly fit to their work world if it is designed by a principled, capable designer. But as I have illustrated in the ALAS studies, workers chafe against these official, centrally designed systems because these systems in themselves cannot encompass all the workers' needs and are not dynamic enough to support their ever-changing activities. That is, whereas these approaches assume a relatively static, bounded work structure, genre tracing presumes a dynamic, social, expansive work activity in which communities interpret, use, and shape the genres that collectively mediate their work. Rather than allowing their work to grind to a halt because it is not adequately supported, workers assert their own agency by adding new innovations to their genre ecologies to fill ecological niches. Sometimes these innovations supplant the official systems, leading to an outright rejection of official solutions. At other times, as in the ALAS studies, workers' innovations supplement, subvert, and reshape the official systems, leading to dynamic and growing genre ecologies that adapt to the workers' changing activities. These genre ecologies tend to grow in unexpected ways and in various directions to support the interrelated activities in which workers are engaged. So how can we build information systems that accommodate rather than resist workers' innovations? How can we cultivate the dynamic social interactions that make workers' innovations sustainable? How can we encourage consensual innovations within communities?

The point of the previous chapters has been to outline genre tracing as a methodology for *investigating* how workers interact with designed information, one that avoids the trope of worker-as-victim and that puts workers' innovations at center stage. In this chapter, I consider the implications of genre tracing for *designing* information systems like Open-ALAS.

To discuss how to apply genre tracing to information design, I will briefly leave the ALAS activity system that I have been using as an extended example, and instead turn to three projects that take a decidedly different approach to design. Mark Zachry and I (Spinuzzi and Zachry 2000) have characterized this approach as an *open-systems* approach. Later in this chapter I return to Open-ALAS, describing in more detail how it could be developed and maintained.

OPEN SYSTEMS: A DEFINITION AND THREE EXAMPLES

Zachry and I argued that "computer documentation is traditionally assumed to function in a *closed system* in which workers use only the documentation shipped with the product, rather than drawing on more diverse resources" (p. 170). The term *closed system* can be applied to more than just documentation, of course: in chapter 1, we saw that some user-centered design approaches tend to lead to systems that are centripetal and centrally controlled. These closed systems are predicated on the assumptions "that document sets [or other designed information] are centrally designed, officially produced, and authoritatively controlled sets of artifacts, and that improving user documentation [or other designed information] involves consolidating a tight and rational control over these closed sets" (p. 170). These user-centered design approaches, although they are less rigid and constraining than system-centered design approaches, seek to rescue workers by consolidating their innovations in a closed system that the designers can centrally control and fine-tune. In other words, they are an attempt to build an artificial ecology, one planned from the top down rather than allowed to grow organically.

The ALAS studies have demonstrated the difficulties with the closed-system perspective. In attempting to regulate workers' activities, closed systems often inhibit the many intersecting activities in which workers must function. To get their jobs done, workers often must adapt additional genres, reinterpret parts of the closed system in light of their own activities, and sometimes even abandon the closed system altogether. That is, they often find that they must subvert the system, open it up, and find ways to build in support for activities that it excludes.

Zachry and I suggested that writers of computer documentation (and other information designers) need to recognize and design for workers' tendency to adapt artifacts. "An *open systems* approach," we argued, "entails recognizing that human interactions with complex technologies are inevitably mediated by dynamic and unpredictable clusters of communication artifacts and activities ... best described as *genre ecologies*" (pp. 170–171). This awareness of compound mediation leads us to try heuristics such as genre ecology diagrams, but it also leads us to explore design approaches that make it possible for workers to consensually modify the system's genres and add their own genres to the system (pp. 178–179). That is, an open system can consist of an officially designed core that provides openings for workers' contributions. The point is not to rescue workers with a better designed system, but to provide a base for workers to build on.

In ecological terms, an open system should be like an artificial starter reef that, once placed, serves as a site around which a genuine ecology can grow. An open system is a centrally designed artifact, of course, but it exists as a nexus for workers' innovations, just as an artificial reef functions as a nexus for a developing underwater ecology. The open system, like an artificial reef, might help to shape the ecology that grows around it, but it is not designed to maintain control over the ecology or constrain the ecology. Rather, it ideally works in harmony with the ecology, providing just enough stability to allow the ecology to flourish.

In the remainder of this section, I describe three types of information systems that exhibit characteristics of open systems: spreadsheets, knowledge bases, and online civic forums.

Example 1: Spreadsheets

As Bonnie Nardi argues in *A Small Matter of Programming* (1993), spreadsheets are end-user programming systems—that is, systems that allow users to create useful applications in a short time without prior programming instruction. Nardi describes an ethnographic study of spreadsheet use that she and James Miller conducted (see also Nardi and Miller 1991), in which end users created and shared a variety of applications. Nardi (1993, 110) notes that spreadsheets are well suited for end-user programming because they provide both a basic formula language and an advanced macrolanguage; they are *"modular*, keeping apart components that are primarily for the use of end users from those that can be learned and used separately by more advanced users." "Communities of users," she explains, "span a *continuum* of programming skill ranging from end users to local developers to programmers" (p. 104). The modular system means that end users (those who "tend not to use computers strictly for their own sake" (p. 104)) can undertake basic programming tasks through an easy-to-learn and task-specific formula language. More advanced local developers ("domain experts who happen to have an intrinsic interest in computers and have more advanced knowledge of a particular program" (p. 104)) can use a more flexible, more complex macrolanguage. Whereas these two groups can alter the behavior of the spreadsheet, programmers (who are trained in programming and involved with the actual source code of the spreadsheet) can alter the spreadsheet itself. Since the spreadsheet accommodates programming by various skill levels, all three groups can program to some degree. Furthermore, the spreadsheet's design "provides a growth path for individual users" (p. 114), allowing inexperienced end users to develop expertise and become more advanced local developers.

For instance, Nardi reports that some end users never learn to use macros (p. 113). But they can define some specific functionality in a spreadsheet, then ask a local developer or programmer to create macros that they can add to their own programs. In other words, even end users who never learn advanced programming can know enough to specify programmatic needs for advanced programmers.

Other end users may learn enough to be considered local developers. One local developer that Nardi interviewed, for instance, was never formally trained in programming. In fact, when he began macro programming, he did not initially realize that he *was* programming. He thought he had invented something new (pp. 112–113).

End users did not simply train themselves. Nardi found that end users formed communities in which more experienced local developers collaborated with less experienced users to develop spreadsheet applications. For instance, "many end users never learn to use macros, but they ask local developers or programmers to create macros that they then add to their projects" (p. 113). Similarly, end users "share spreadsheets in the form of templates, and often the assumptions underlying a template are unclear and must be communicated to the person attempting to use the template" (p. 120), meaning that users' programmatic innovations could make the rounds and were accompanied by increased communication. Furthermore, Nardi reports that end users took pride and pleasure in their programming activities as they customized spreadsheets for their particular domains: they saw their contributions as accomplishments that they could share with other workers (p. 36).

A spreadsheet, then, can be considered an open system because it provides openings for workers to contribute their own innovations, and it offers several ways to connect those innovations. For instance, workers in Nardi's studies shared spreadsheet templates with examples of end-user programming; printed spreadsheets so they could mark them up with a pencil, an important part of debugging;[1] called each other for help in understanding programs or for codeveloping programs; looked at manuals; and drew on a variety of other official and unofficial genres.

Example 2: Design Assistant

Most organizations have what Nardi calls "gardeners": people who have particular technical expertise and who are willing to share it with others (p. 108; see also Nardi and O'Day 1999). Yet often these gardeners are overwhelmed by requests for help. Moreover, they are often hard to find: workers must rely on informal networks to find out which gardener can help them. Finally, when gardeners leave an organization, their expertise is often lost. In the context of software development, these three problems led Terveen, Selfridge, and Long (1995) to develop Design Assistant. Design Assistant was a database of software design knowledge[2] that the authors characterize as *"community-specific folklore—* information that is relevant to the local design practice and that 'you don't learn in school' " (p. 5). The authors characterize Design Assistant as an instantiation of "living design memory," a user-maintained organizational memory of folklore that traditionally had been unwritten and informally disseminated.

Terveen and colleagues argue that since this folklore—the tips, tricks, and tacit procedures of a community—had traditionally been disseminated in informal, ephemeral ways, the experts (Nardi's "gardeners") often found themselves so swamped with requests that they "spend more time disseminating knowledge than applying their expertise to developing software—laboring under a sort of expertise tax" (p. 6). In response, Terveen, Selfridge, and Long developed Design Assistant. Design Assistant supported two ways developers could contribute knowledge: *knowledge addition*, in which users enter new knowledge into the database, and *knowledge update*, in which later users elaborate and evolve the existing knowledge base.

Knowledge addition entailed "the addition of new knowledge generated during development activities and as new domains mature" (p. 8). Terveen and associates identify several points at which new knowledge is generated and articulated, including expert initiative (when an expert articulates knowledge that has been tacit in the organization) and customer impact (when a customer identifies negative impacts that the software design has had on their work). In Design Assistant, this knowledge is added by either a software developer or a specially designated knowledge engineer. In either case, Design Assistant associates each entry with the contributor's name, phone number, and e-mail address so that users can contact contributors with follow-up questions—a feature that distributes the vital networking knowledge traditionally so hard to come by (pp. 8–9).

As Terveen, Selfridge, and Long note, however, "The ownership relationship is in itself knowledge that must evolve over time as people leave the organization or their responsibilities shift" (p. 9)—and in any case, some contributions are better articulated and qualified than others. Thus, Design Assistant also provides for *knowledge update*, in which knowledge engineers solicit evaluations and suggestions from users, then periodically change or update the knowledge base according to those suggestions. "This process," Terveen and colleagues tell us, "institutionalizes knowledge engineering as an ongoing activity in the design process" (p. 9). The process is partially automated: at the end of each session with Design Assistant, users are automatically asked to rate and comment on the advice they have received, and the path they have taken through the knowledge base is recorded for later analysis. Thus users collaboratively update as well as add knowledge.

Like the spreadsheet, Design Assistant can be considered an open system, although one with very different capabilities. Design Assistant provides a space in which users can make their tacit knowledge explicit through familiar genres such as definitions, instructions, and process descriptions. And it provides openings for less official genres that have traditionally been key to circulating tacit knowledge, such as help calls, e-mailed requests for help, hallway conversations, and (we might imagine) other sorts of informal genres used by software developers such as pseudocode, code examples, and flow diagrams. Design Assistant became a sort of collaborative documentation project, but its designers recognized that even collaboratively written documentation is not enough: other genres must be allowed to grow and flourish.

Example 3: A Departmental Website

Knowledge systems such as the one described by Terveen, Selfridge, and Long are designed primarily for retaining and rating information about how to handle various situations. Database-driven systems with similar architectures have also been used for functions such as community building. For instance, in 2000–2001, Jennifer Bowie, Xiangyi Li, Ida Rodgers, and I developed a web application meant to function as a forum for an academic department's civic discourse (Spinuzzi 2002b; Spinuzzi, Bowie, Rodgers, and Li, in preparation).

Our team redesigned the Texas Tech University Department of English website. The old site, which was maintained by a computer support staffer and some technologically experienced department members, was what the web design industry calls *brochureware*: it primarily provided information about a service and offered few channels for feedback or contributions. Although brochureware sites are serviceable, they are also monologic (Bakhtin 1981). Consequently, sharp power differences arise among citizens with different standings, different experiences, and different types of expertise. Some of the fallout from these power differences is political: some members cannot contribute to the site, while others do not see such contributions as their duty, and still others begin to feel disenfranchised. There are also practical ramifications. Websites are already hard to maintain, and the job becomes harder when people do not feel empowered to enact changes themselves.

Although the situation at the Department of English was not dire, the old website did introduce inequities among departmental members (hereafter "citizens"). These inequities mirrored academic divisions within the department. Technologically experienced citizens tended to include faculty and graduate students in technical communication and in composition and rhetoric. Technologically inexperienced citizens tended to be faculty and graduate students in literature and in creative writing, as well as staff. Whereas technologically experienced citizens tended to maintain their own portions of the site, technologically inexperienced citizens had to work through the intermediary of the computer support staffer. Consequently, the site grew asymmetrically, with well-developed technical communication and rhetoric and composition pages but underdeveloped literature and creative writing pages. Furthermore, the site tended to get out of date quickly. Announcements were left on the home page long after the event they announced had passed; new faculty members were not immediately given directory listings; curriculum changes were not reflected in the site.

Our design team believed that one answer to these related problems would be to construct a truly dialogic site, one that was designed using a conversational metaphor and that would consequently support the epideictic, deliberative, and forensic activities of the department. In short, we developed a *civic forum* to which all citizens could contribute despite variations in their technological expertise. In this forum, citizens were able to submit (and own) their own contributions through a variety of channels. Furthermore, the site functioned as a forum for a geophysical community.[3] It coexisted with rather than replacing the other genres that citizens used to get things done.

The redesigned site used webforms (special web pages with blanks for citizens to fill in information) that allowed citizens to simply type in the information they wanted to include. For instance, a citizen who wanted to make an announcement could bring up the announcement form, fill in the date of the event, title, and brief description, then submit the announcement (see figure 6.1). The site then automatically displayed the announcement on the home page until the day after the event. Since the form did not involve actually building a page or coding HTML, citizens found the task of making announcements much easier. And since the website automatically removed expired events, it did not become cluttered with out-of-date information. Similarly, citizens could control their own profiles in the directory, suggest Internet resources for other citizens, and perform a variety of other tasks.

The redesigned website was an open system, composed of a centrally designed core (the visual design, site architecture, database architecture, and code) to which citizens could add their own contributions (announcements, self-descriptions, and so on). However, the site faced challenges in terms of sustainability: although it was technically operative at the time of writing, it is not yet clear whether it has been fully adopted by the community.

Like spreadsheets and Design Assistant, the Texas Tech University Department of English website is an open system. It has formalized cer-

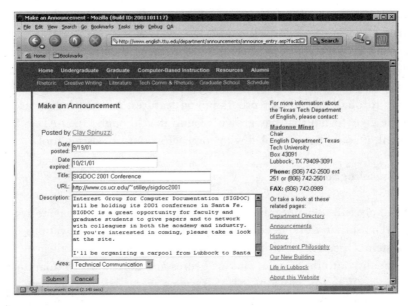

Figure 6.1
A webform for making an announcement. The citizen fills out and submits the form without having to code HTML, gain FTP access to the server, or go through a technologically knowledgeable intermediary. The citizen's name and e-mail address are automatically appended to the resulting announcement so that other citizens can contact him or her in a variety of ways.

tain genres (such as announcements, directory profiles, and descriptions of organizations). But at the same time, these genres are flexible enough that citizens can write in their chosen textual genres (for instance, a citizen might choose to write her self-description in iambic pentameter), add links, include graphics, and integrate with existing and improvised offline genres. In addition, rather than attempting to supplant existing genres, this site supplements them and provides ways for citizens to link to them.

REDESIGNING ALAS AS AN OPEN SYSTEM

These three examples demonstrate different approaches that can be used to design open systems. Each allows workers to modify, extend, and customize a centrally designed core in ways they deem important; their innovations become important parts of the system. In designing open systems, we can apply each approach—and others—separately or in tandem.

To further illustrate open systems, let's return to the fictional example of Open-ALAS that I described Marta using at the beginning of the chapter. Open-ALAS consists of a centrally designed core that workers modify through its end-user programming features, its knowledge base, and the civic forum that has grown around it. Although Open-ALAS is fictional, it could be assembled with some effort out of existing tools.

End-User Programming

If we apply end-user programming to Open-ALAS, we can imagine several avenues that workers could use to embed their own innovations in the system. Open-ALAS includes ways for workers to program their own functionality into the system, altering genres and developing or adapting new ones. Whereas previous ALAS systems were strictly read-only—workers could only run queries and select data, not change the system—Open-ALAS is configurable in a variety of ways. Like the spreadsheet that Nardi describes, Open-ALAS provides modular opportunities for programming, including both a basic visual query system (perhaps expressed in a formula language, perhaps in a "wizard" or series of dialog boxes) and an advanced macrolanguage for more ambitious workers.

Basic Programming   As Nardi suggests, basic programming includes things that workers routinely do in a variety of programs—customizing reports (cf. Mirel 1996), developing formulas, and using wizards. Indeed, PC-ALAS and GIS-ALAS both include some of these tools. Open-ALAS could greatly expand those capabilities for workers. For instance, a modified print wizard could allow workers to develop and save report formats that are customized for very specific types of queries. A wizard for complex searches might introduce workers to Boolean logic and a complex query language such as SQL, a step toward advanced programming.

Such openings could lead workers to link their own customized innovations with other innovations and other genres, both inside and outside the interface. For example, if workers could highly customize reports, a county engineer might format all of her reports to provide information that county engineers find important for record-keeping, such as a title, print date, print time, and short description at the top. She might include only the information relevant to her particular project, since regrading roads, raising bridges, and erecting traffic lights are after all very different projects requiring very different sorts of information. In fact, she might come up with a color scheme to distinguish these different projects, and that color scheme might correspond to, say, the color of the folders that hold the printed records. She might even include a graphic of the map for the location, or perhaps a reference to a map that has already been printed. And her entire office might eventually standardize on her customized report, making it a widely used genre that has been adapted by an entire community to fill an important ecological niche.

Advanced Programming   Beyond the basic programming features I describe above, Open-ALAS could also include advanced programming capabilities through a macrolanguage. With this end-user programming capability, workers could begin to contribute functionality as well as information. They could assert more control over the interface genres in place, invent their own genres, and establish and articulate their own automated connections among genres. In other words, they could all become codesigners of the system and the ecology in which it is embedded, not in the way that most user-centered design approaches typically envision, but in a much more direct and democratically empowering way.

In the headnote at the beginning of this chapter, Marta has developed a macro that adds exactly the sort of functionality she needs to do her job as a law enforcement officer. Not everyone will find this innovation useful because they might not do the sorts of things that law enforcement officers do. But some workers will find it tremendously useful. And end-user programmers who are more experienced than Marta might be able to take her code, improve it, and use it as a base for adding even more functionality. Furthermore, parts of her code might be useful for still other end-user programmers working on their own innovations. Eventually, Open-ALAS' developers might find that some of these innovations are exceptionally useful, so they might include the macros in the next release.

It is worth noting here that ALAS products already offer some advanced programming capabilities. For instance, GIS-ALAS is essentially the ArcView GIS customized using FORTRAN code, and a sufficiently motivated worker can examine and modify this code. VB-ALAS, based on Visual Basic, is under development and may be open to complex macro-based end-user programming. Despite these macro capabilities, however, at this point workers have not been invited to use them and the architecture of the software actually discourages macro use by anyone but developers. The fictional Open-ALAS would instead encourage and scaffold workers so that they could become development partners.

The Open-Source Model Beyond the technical capabilities, Open-ALAS could profit from the lessons of the open-source movement. Yamauchi et al. (2000, 329) suggest that open-source development represents "a model of dispersed collaboration" in which spontaneous work is later coordinated and supported by collaboration over various communication media. Open-source programmers take the initiative to frame and develop a project, then share their work with others who critique, revise, and extend their work.[4]

This model could work well with the sort of local development supported by end-user programming. For instance, suppose that in response to her own needs, Marta develops the macro described at the beginning of this chapter. She recognizes that this macro could be useful to other law enforcement officers, since they do the same sort of work that she does, and that they might be able to make further suggestions, so she posts the source code to a message board at the ALAS site. Sure enough, other officers are intrigued by the project and pool their expertise to improve and extend the code. If the project is important enough to the community, Marta might find herself becoming a team leader for organizing the project.

This vision of end-user programming may strike some as utopian. But as Nardi shows, workers already program spreadsheets and other software—not every worker, but enough workers to make a difference.

Knowledge Base

As chapter 4 illustrates, when workers are isolated, they find it difficult to share their knowledge about the system or their workarounds. Innovations such as Barbara's use of sticky notes and Rod's habit of clicking on field labels rarely spread to other workers, and consequently they rarely became refined. Similarly, when workers have trouble interpreting a PC-ALAS feature such as the search function, as Mike and Sherry did, they cannot warn others about such problems. These workers could not share their community-specific folklore because few ways existed to identify and communicate with other PC-ALAS users.

Knowledge bases such as Design Assistant are designed to deal with exactly this sort of situation. We can imagine how a knowledge base could let Open-ALAS workers share their innovations, skills, and common problems, and in the process how it could anchor collaborations and foster networks that have historically been all but impossible in the ALAS activity system.

Historically, knowledge in the ALAS activity system has been shared through official genres such as software manuals, online help, and occasional training sessions. A few workers occasionally phone each other. A commonly accessible knowledge base can expand this genre ecology, not (necessarily) replacing existing genres, but augmenting them with other genres that have been developed and shared by the workers. As Joanna Wolfe and Christine Neuwirth (2001) have pointed out, textual annotations have traditionally been used to share knowledge, create networks, and provide insight into texts' readers. Wolfe and Neuwirth confidently predict that "digital technologies promise to revive [annotation] practices and create new ones" (p. 335). But these genres need not be limited to the textual.

A knowledge base could provide collaborative, evolving documentation that workers themselves write. (Examples include many websites maintained by the open-source community: ⟨www.everything2.com⟩, ⟨www.faqts.com/knowledge_base⟩, ⟨www.mandrakeuser.org/mub⟩.) This knowledge base could be a clearinghouse for workers' local innovations. These innovations could encompass programming innovations such as Marta's macro, of course, including code and perhaps executable

Table 6.1
A multimedia knowledge base could open the door to a proliferation of genres, some perhaps more desirable than others

Type of medium	Examples
Textual	Procedural description, instructions, macro code and explanations, poems, short stories illustrating a procedure
Visual	Screen shots, scans of Post-Its, flowcharts, streaming video demonstration
Aural	Narration, jingles

files. But they could also include less conventional innovations such as how to coordinate work activities using sticky notes—and even a scanned image showing a sample sticky note. In other words, the content of the knowledge base could be quite unconventional, broad, and in a variety of media, allowing workers to describe all sorts of localized innovations. Consequently, the "folklore" of the physically dispersed ALAS community can spread. Workers could choose the genres in which they want to work. If Marta has discovered that Open-ALAS allows her to develop a macro for selecting certain traffic accidents, she could write a procedural description, provide screen shots demonstrating the procedure, put together a streaming video demonstration with narration, or even (if sufficiently motivated) record her own catchy jingle that describes the procedure (table 6.1).

One can imagine that some of these contributions may be more useful to Open-ALAS workers than others. As Bowker and Star (1999, 257) point out, organizational *forgetting* is just as necessary as organizational *remembering*.[5] Perhaps Marta's jingle is on everyone's lips, while her written procedures remain unread. Design Assistant handles this problem by letting users evaluate the knowledge-base entries. If workers consistently rate an entry poorly or read it less often than competing entries, that entry could eventually drop out, while highly rated entries could be made more prominent. In Open-ALAS, such a rating system would allow the community of workers to collaboratively prune less useful entries from a knowledge base that might very well expand rapidly.

In addition to making knowledge available, the knowledge base can help workers identify experts. Currently ALAS workers tend to meet experts in rare training sessions and typically do not cultivate relationships with them. A knowledge base is one way to cultivate such relationships, meaning other genres such as the help call become available in the ecology. If Marta's procedure, video demonstration, or catchy jingle is not clear enough, workers could call or e-mail her with questions.

Furthermore, workers could post their contributions under categories that they themselves nominate. Workers could thus find answers within their own domains rather than combing through answers that might not fit their activities. For instance, Marta's approach of repeatedly finding accidents at a specific intersection is rarely used by traffic safety workers, as we saw in chapter 4, so it might be categorized differently from statewide or countywide searches. Knowledge bases could serve subgroups or special interest groups as well as the larger general community of ALAS workers.

Community Building

The previous two sections discussed end-user programming and a collaboratively developed knowledge base. Both presume a community of workers. And a community implies more than simply information swapping. In a community, people deliberate, praise, and judge. Communities do grow around programming groups and knowledge bases (such as ⟨www.everything2.com⟩), but such communities often lack the sort of infrastructure necessary to do more than swap information and discuss its applications. Compare the relatively impoverished set of online communication mechanisms typically used in software development (Yamauchi et al. 2000) and online university courses (Zachry 2000) with the wide range of civic mechanisms (including genres) that geophysical communities use to carry out their forensic, epideictic, and deliberative activities: voting, award ceremonies, legislation, juries, and hundreds of others. Without such civic mechanisms and a rich ecology of genres to support them (from ballots to legal briefs to award speeches), workers can swap solutions, but those solutions will tend to be reactionary rather than proactive and forward looking. In other words, there is a world of difference between the folklore that shows up in knowledge bases and the sort of long-term collaborative planning done in civic life.

Indeed, this difference shows up in the studies described in this book. One problem that marks the unofficial solutions devised by ALAS workers is that these solutions tend to be reactionary. When Barbara uses a sticky note to avoid the unwieldy map in chapter 4, for instance, she is not planning for the future or consciously finding ways to improve the software; she is just trying to improve her own work. Indeed, Beyer and Holtzblatt (1998, 370–371) object to the idea of workers literally designing their own systems precisely because workers' solutions tend to be reactionary.[6] Thus, Beyer and Holtzblatt (and many other user-centered designers) say, trained designers must step in to develop lasting solutions.

Yet workers do not have to be reactionary. They can be proactive, develop projects, and devise long-term plans, and in fact they do these sorts of things constantly in their work. (For one example, see Haas and Witte's (2001) study of a collaborative project involving a city government and a consulting engineering firm.) The question is how to foster and support these sorts of activities in terms of Open-ALAS development. One possible way is to provide a civic forum, a space in which workers can organize themselves, discuss their goals as a community, and collaboratively chart a course for the software.

I have suggested that Open-ALAS is utopian, and this suggestion may be the most utopian of all. But it has perhaps the most promise because it breaks down the distinction between the official and the unofficial that I have been discussing throughout the book. Rather than cleanly separating the worker-victims from the designer-heroes, it provides a more formal mechanism for workers to fully engage in collaborative problem solving—and to subsequently guide designers in meeting their needs as a community. And beyond its potential for providing workers with more control over the software's development, such a civic forum allows end-user programming and knowledge bases to be more useful and open parts of the system.

The civic forum represents the recognition that workers should have a way not just to *promulgate* innovative solutions such as programs and folklore (in the knowledge base), but also to *investigate* and *judge* past efforts and solutions, *praise* or *condemn* each others' actions, and *deliberate* future lines of development.[7]

Judging the Past   To learn from their past actions, communities must be able to investigate, judge, and evaluate what has happened in the past. In the Open-ALAS activity system, this sort of interaction may begin as simply as workers evaluating each others' contributions to the knowledge base. But as workers organize, they will find themselves engaging in other types of forensic interactions. For instance, they may find themselves examining the results of development projects, evaluating candidates for committees, or even questioning the past decisions of software developers. These forensic discussions may lead to thoughtful collaborative criticisms of the way things have been done. Unlike the isolated, reactionary subversions that workers have traditionally employed, these discussions could lead to reflection and underpin deliberations about how to proceed in the future.

To take an extended example, suppose that the ALAS community decides to start an end-user programming project for developing a particular type of accident summary. Marta leads this group. Before they begin programming, the group asks questions such as these:

- Why is the software this way? Why does it currently summarize accidents in this way?
- Are there good reasons for this arrangement? Have similar development projects been started in the past, only to fail for technical reasons?
- We asked the software developers to implement a similar change in the past. Why was it not implemented?

Such investigations can extend beyond technical constraints. For instance, if Marta's team is thinking about bringing a new team member on board to work on this ongoing project, they might ask questions such as these:

- How is this person's track record as a colleague? Does she work well in a team? Does she pitch in?
- How well has this person taken direction in previous projects?

- Has this person shown herself to be inventive?
- Has this person mastered the basics of the macrolanguage?

If the ALAS community eventually decides to move toward a more formal organizational structure—for instance, a parliamentarian structure with elected committees and offices—ALAS workers might find themselves engaging in their own forensic investigations as they compare and vote for candidates.

Evaluating the Present   Communities must look to the present as well. They must be able to praise and blame individuals who particularly help or harm the community. In the Open-ALAS activity system, the community may begin by praising meritorious contributions on message boards. But as workers organize, they may find other occasions for evaluating people and their actions. For example, they may find themselves presenting formal awards to workers who have been especially helpful in providing answers to the knowledge base or developing particularly useful macros, or on the flip side they might find themselves voting to condemn the actions of a particular member of the community. Such interactions can cement and organize the community of workers as well as improve individual workers' opportunities for advancement.

To take an extended example, suppose that Marta's team develops the new accident summary. The summary becomes so useful that 85 percent of registered workers download it within a year, and surveys indicate that 81 percent of workers are still using it six months later. What's more, it cuts half an hour from a common analysis task. To recognize this extremely useful macro, the ALAS community votes to award Marta and her team the prize for Best New Macro in the annual ALAS Awards.

Since the macro has proven so useful, ALAS' software developers decide to rewrite it in FORTRAN and introduce it into the next release of the software. Doing so will make the functionality much faster, they reason. But some members of the ALAS community condemn this action, since it will also take the control over this functionality away from the end users. They assert that control is more important than speed. Others praise the decision, characterizing it as a blow for worker empowerment since the software developers are taking their contributions seriously.

In this scenario, ALAS workers both praise and condemn actions. In doing so, they reinforce and clarify what they value as a community, and they may expose contradictions in the community—such as the contradiction between two different sorts of worker empowerment in the example above—which can then be addressed and deliberatively worked through as a community.

Deliberating the Future   Finally, communities must be able to deliberate on and commit to future action, both publicly and privately. In the Open-ALAS activity system, such deliberations may begin as simply as using e-mail or message boards to discuss the sorts of features workers would like to see in the next release. But deliberative interactions can also make their way into various aspects of the activity system, from determining the date of the next training session to planning an end-user programming project to debating whether a macro should be taken over by developers. Deliberative discussions can lead to organizational changes for accommodating them—such as parliamentary procedures and committees—and to thoughtful, long-term action.

For instance, as end-user programming projects increase, workers may find themselves organizing programming committees, voting on officers to head those committees, and examining proposals for future development, documentation, and training. Indeed, Open-ALAS workers might find themselves drawing on familiar organizational structures and genres as models for organizing their efforts, just as users' groups around the world have done. Such genres might include parliamentary bylaws, motions, bills, and ballots, all of which can be shared electronically.

Deliberative discussions can also determine the future direction of the community itself. For instance, suppose that the software developers decide to rewrite a popular macro in FORTRAN. Some ALAS workers condemn the software developers' plan, while others praise it. The resulting discussion may lead to a decision about the developers' plan, but it may also lead to a decision about how to handle such incidents in the future.

The sort of civic forum that I have outlined here is certainly *technically* feasible, and one can find forums that share some of these characteristics in both e-commerce (see Zachry 2001b) and web-based pedagogical environments (Zachry 2000). Based on the online communities that regularly form around certain popular websites, I believe that it is also *socially* feasible—that is, workers quite possibly would contact each other to investigate past actions, praise or condemn present actions, and deliberate about future actions. This forum would not necessarily evolve into an egalitarian one—certainly the workers' current social arrangements are not egalitarian (see also Haas and Witte 2001, 446)—but it would provide workers with a way to communicate with each other, coordinate their work, and develop new social arrangements.

CONCLUSION

Throughout this book, I have argued that workers are not victims awaiting a qualified designer to rescue them from poor information design. Rather, workers continually draw on existing genres to develop local, ad hoc solutions to recurrent problems in their particular workplace. They take official genres that were designed for broad situations and modify them with unofficial genres to produce solutions tailor-made for their own local situations. In doing so, they build genre ecologies that collectively mediate their complex activities.

These genres work at many different levels, sometimes in surprisingly complex ways. The impulse of user-centered design approaches is to catalog them, select the most important ones, redesign those genres, and make them official. But this task is Sisyphean, since workers' activities change constantly and since officially designed information must meet the needs of different workers, each potentially in a very different set of activities. As I argued in chapter 2, many user-centered design approaches tackle this Sisyphean task by assuming that design problems have a single crux that can be addressed. If no such crux exists—and I have argued that none does—then a centralized approach to information design faces significant hurdles. What unofficial genres should be made official? How often do designers have to identify and officialize such genres?

In this chapter, I have suggested that a design approach based on genre tracing would take a very different tack. This design approach would be decentralized; would invite workers to be true codesigners rather than clients or informants; would break down the official-unofficial distinction by providing workers with the means to develop, promulgate, reflect on, and collectively stabilize their own genres; and would encourage workers to develop stable communities and civic structures along with the genres used to support their activities. This design approach would still value the contributions of trained information designers, but their contributions would provide an environment for workers' innovations rather than replacing them with official structures. I have illustrated this approach by speculating about possible trajectories that ALAS genres might take. Using the insights from genre tracing studies, I have speculatively outlined an open system that breaks down the official-unofficial distinction by presenting multiple avenues for workers to contribute.

The genre tracing methodology encourages us to explore the various intersecting activities and the ways genres have developed—and continue to develop—to support them. It provides a cultural-historical perspective of design. Most important, it gives us an opportunity to explore workers' innovations that are usually rendered invisible by other approaches. These workers are inventive, wily, devious, sly, cunning, and crafty. And they deserve to be heard.

Notes

Chapter 1

1. Bravo provides some really horrific anecdotes about poor information design in which workers are invariably victimized by shortsighted managers.

2. In Johnson's view, writers must be properly trained or enlightened to be authoritative. Sadly, writers "are often forced to be part of the system-centered approach because it is mandated (consciously or unconsciously) by the institution or organization they work within" (Johnson 1998, 124). System-centered design is portrayed as a product of ignorance on the part of a faceless and oppressive bureaucracy; user-centered design comes from the enlightened struggle of heroes.

Chapter 2

Parts of this chapter are based on Spinuzzi 2002c.

1. I use the term *destabilization* rather than the more common *disruption* here and throughout because I want to emphasize that each time a worker encounters such a problem, his or her entire activity is affected. When such problems become numerous or severe, the repercussions are felt through the entire activity, which at some point must be reconstructed (reorganized, reconstrued) or collapse (cease to function).

2. By "sociocultural theory" I mean the range of non-Cartesian, materialist social-cultural-historical approaches that Barbara Mirel (1998a) has labeled "constructivist": the sociology of knowledge, activity theory, the politics of technology, distributed cognition, situated learning, cognitive complexity theory, genre theory, and pragmatic philosophy. I avoid the label "constructivist" because elsewhere constructivism has been characterized as individualist, structuralist, and rule-bound (Nystrand, Greene, and Wiemelt 1993), and such a characterization is at odds with this body of sociocultural thought.

3. For instance, suppose that a worker loses a forefinger and finds it more difficult to click a mouse. The microlevel breakdowns she encounters might inspire

her to advocate mesolevel changes in work practices to better accommodate workers with disabilities. Those changes could help to transform the overall work activity.

4. I identify genre tracing here as a methodology rather than a method. What makes it unique is not a set of *methods*, but its *methodological* orientation.

5. Other analytic frameworks exist for exploring compound mediation. See Spinuzzi 2001c for a comparison of three of these frameworks.

6. The agencies I deal with here have begun to call traffic accidents *crashes*, since the term *accident* implies assumptions about circumstances and intentionality that might not always obtain. I use *accident* throughout because it is a more familiar term for most readers, it is still understood by these workers, and it is embedded in the names of some of the software tools (e.g., PC-ALAS).

Chapter 3

1. Such studies of computer systems are not unknown (Bødker 1993; Bødker and Gronbæk 1996; Haas 1996; Orlikowski and Yates 1994; Zuboff 1988), but they tend to be narrower in detail or scope.

2. "Data" should not be understood as objective and value-neutral. The data stored in ALAS are the results of many, many discrete narratives—sometimes even conflicting narratives—that have been monologized and transformed multiple times in ways that render them amenable to quantitative analysis. The data are systematically transformed by ALAS workers into solutions, solutions that take the form of new legislation, grant proposals, law enforcement activities, and roadway structures.

3. Later, the damage threshold went up to $400, then $500. In 1998, it was changed to $1,000.

4. That is, one genre is translated into another. These transformations make it possible to analyze accident data quantitatively, but at the price of losing or compressing the individual narratives. In this case, the heteroglossic (multivoiced) reports are monologized (compressed into one voice) as they are quantified and categorized for the database. For instance, one DOT worker who entered data from accident reports into the database told me that when two reports from the same accident conflict, she used her own judgment to reconcile them.

5. WSA's wholesale quantification of the roadway system had precedence in the control sections established in the previous eras. These control sections coexisted with other representations up through the end of my studies in 1998, although they do not figure prominently in the rest of this account.

6. "Users" were considered to be those *making* the requests, not those who actually operated the machine (Wilbur Smith and Associates, 1974a).

7. By 1998, the jobs of locating and entering data were consolidated. At this later date, locators would pull up scanned versions of the reports, convert the

locations to the node-link system via node maps and scratch paper, and enter the data directly into a computerized form.

8. The results of standardization are reflected in the activity system diagrams for this and later eras: unlike the diagrams in the pre-ALAS era, these diagrams are not split into local and state levels.

9. Some might characterize these formats as "system-centered," but I argue that they were admirably adapted to the activities of a particular group of workers: systems analysts. The problem is that they had to be used by workers engaged in very different activities.

10. Such workarounds helped users get by for a while. Again, we see a mounting number of genres being coordinated in more complex ways, an indicator of worsening contradictions.

Chapter 4

1. Of course, as is shown by the 2000–2001 controversy over Ford Explorer accidents involving Firestone tires, sometimes information normally deemed irrelevant can indeed be linked to accidents. That information has not been *historically* deemed relevant, so in Iowa, there is no easy way to link tire brand to particular types of accidents; the distinction simply disappears at the point that the driver's report is filled out. One can imagine how ALAS genres might be changed to address the controversy. For more on how classification schemes are based in cultural-historical milieus, see Bowker and Star 1999.

2. One participant took part in the round of questionnaires and interviews, then later took part in the round of questionnaires, observations, and interviews. All other participants took part in only one round of research.

3. It also bears some resemblance to GOMS (Card, Moran, and Newell 1983).

4. PC-ALAS allows workers to run statewide requests by specifying County 00 in the City/County Request dialog box. But Rod and Sherry, who both had to run such requests, were apparently unaware of this capability. Sherry in particular could have saved considerable time and avoided many problems had she known about this capability.

Chapter 5

These studies were analyzed in a somewhat different way in Spinuzzi 2001b.

1. As Souleyrette and Strauss (1999, 119) point out, when developing transportation GISes, "early decisions about scale and accuracy can have long-lasting effects."

2. The workers actually used prototypes of GIS-ALAS and Explorer-ALAS, a stripped-down version that only allowed workers to view, not affect, the mapped data. The functionality of the two systems was nearly identical at this stage.

3. For more on differences between work and school, see Breuch 2001; Freedman, Adam, and Smart 1994; Spinuzzi 1996.

4. In Suchman's (1987) terms, developers tried to build *plans* into the automated genres, rather than leaving room for the workers' *situated actions*.

Chapter 6

1. These marked-up spreadsheets are similar to the pseudocode used by professional programmers, which often involves informally drawn flowcharts, arrows, and conceptual diagrams (Bellamy 1994).

2. For want of a better term, I use *knowledge* here because the authors do. As Brown and Duguid (2000) point out, the terms *knowledge* and *information* are often conflated. Brown and Duguid suggest that *information* is treated as a substance, "something that people pick up, possess, put in a database, lose, find, write down, accumulate, count, compare, and so forth," whereas "knowledge is something we digest rather than merely hold" (p. 120). "Focusing on knowledge ... turns attention towards knowers," and "knowledge lies less in [an organization's] databases than in its people" (p. 121). I will elide this discussion except to point out that Design Assistant technically traffics in both knowledge and information: it stores information in the database, but it also supports knowledge by enabling workers to develop social networks.

3. That is, citizens all occupy the same building and interact offline as well as online. See Doheny-Farina 1996.

4. The open-source model can be applied to other community activities besides software development. For instance, Erik Berglund and Michael Priestly (2001) suggest cultivating open-source software documentation that would be maintained by a community and managed by a company.

5. See Ackerman 1994 for an extended discussion of organizational memory and how workers perceive it.

6. Not surprisingly, Beyer and Holtzblatt's (1998) Contextual Design approach tends to extract these sorts of reactionary responses from individual users; see Hackos, Hammar, and Elser 1997 for a corrective.

7. These three sorts of interactions reflect the branches of forensic, epideictic, and deliberative rhetoric discussed in Aristotle (1932, 17). These three branches of rhetoric were developed to meet the oratory needs of the Athenian democracy in which Aristotle lived. Not coincidentally, these branches correspond to the three branches of government in most representative democracies: the judicial, executive, and legislative branches.

References

Ackerman, M. S. 1994. Definitional and contextual issues in organizational and group memory. Paper presented at the Twenty-Seventh Annual Hawaii International Conference on System Sciences, Honolulu.

Ackerman, M. S., and Halverson, C. 1998. Considering an organization's memory. *CSCW '98 conference proceedings*, 39–48. New York: ACM.

Aristotle. 1932. *The rhetoric of Aristotle*. Trans. Lane Cooper. New York: Appleton-Century-Crofts.

Artemeva, N., and Freedman, A. 2001. "Just the boys playing on computers": An activity theory analysis of differences in the cultures of two engineering firms. *Journal of Business and Technical Communication, 15*(2), 164–194.

Bakhtin, M. M. 1981. *The dialogic imagination: Four essays*. Austin: University of Texas Press.

Bakhtin, M. M. 1984. *Problems of Dostoevsky's poetics*. Minneapolis: University of Minnesota Press.

Bakhtin, M. M. 1986. *Speech genres and other late essays*. Austin: University of Texas Press.

Bannon, L. 1995. The politics of design: Representing work. *Communications of the ACM, 38*(9), 66–68.

Barton, B. F., and Barton, M. 1993. Ideology and the map: Toward a postmodern visual design practice. In N. Blyler and C. Thralls, eds., *Professional communication: The social perspective*, 49–78. Newbury Park, CA: Sage.

Bazerman, C. 1988. *Shaping written knowledge: The genre and activity of the experimental article in science*. Madison: University of Wisconsin Press.

Bazerman, C. 1994. Systems of genre and the enactment of social intentions. In A. Freedman and P. Medway, eds., *Genre and the new rhetoric*, 79–99. London: Taylor and Francis.

Bazerman, C. 1997. Discursively structured activities. *Mind, Culture, and Activity, 4*(4), 296–308.

Beabes, M. A., and Flanders, A. 1995. Experiences with using contextual inquiry to design information. *Technical Communication, 42*(3), 409–420.

Bellamy, R. K. E. 1994. What does pseudo-code do? A psychological analysis of the use of pseudo-code by experienced programmers. *Human-Computer Interaction, 9,* 225–246.

Berglund, E., and Priestly, M. 2001. Open-source documentation: In search of user-driven, just-in-time writing. *ACM SIGDOC 2001 conference proceedings,* 132–141. New York: ACM.

Berkenkotter, C., and Huckin, T. N. 1995. *Genre knowledge in disciplinary communication: Cognition/culture/power.* Hillsdale, NJ: Erlbaum.

Beyer, H., and Holtzblatt, K. 1998. *Contextual Design: Defining customer-centered systems.* San Francisco: Morgan Kaufmann.

Bisantz, A. M., and Ockerman, J. J. 2002. Informing the evaluation and design of technology in intentional work environments through a focus on artefacts and implicit theories. *International Journal of Human-Computer Studies, 56,* 247–265.

Bjerknes, G., and Bratteteig, T. 1995. User participation and democracy: A discussion of Scandinavian research on system development. *Scandinavian Journal of Information Systems, 7*(1), 73–98.

Blomberg, J., Suchman, L., and Trigg, R. 1997. Back to work: Renewing old agendas for cooperative design. In M. Kyng and L. Mathiassen, eds., *Computers and design in context,* 267–288. Cambridge, MA: MIT Press.

Bødker, S. 1991. *Through the interface: A human activity approach to user interface design.* Hillsdale, NJ: Erlbaum.

Bødker, S. 1993. Historical analysis and conflicting perspectives—contextualizing HCI. Paper presented at EWCHI'93, East-West Human Computer Interaction, Moscow.

Bødker, S. 1996. Applying activity theory to video analysis: How to make sense of video data in human-computer interaction. In B. Nardi, ed., *Context and consciousness,* 147–174. Cambridge, MA: MIT Press.

Bødker, S. 1997. Computers in mediated human activity. *Mind, Culture, and Activity, 4*(3), 149–158.

Bødker, S., and Gronbæk, K. 1996. Users and designers in mutual activity: An analysis of cooperative activities in systems design. In Y. Engeström and D. Middleton, eds., *Cognition and communication at work,* 130–158. New York: Cambridge University Press.

Bowker, G., and Star, S. L. 1999. *Sorting things out: Classification and its consequences.* Cambridge, MA: MIT Press.

Bravo, E. 1993. The hazards of leaving out the users. In D. Schuler and A. Namioka, eds., *Participatory design: Principles and practices,* 3–12. Hillsdale, NJ: Erlbaum.

Breuch, L.-A. M. K. 2001. The overruled dust mite: Preparing technical communication students to interact with clients. *Technical Communication Quarterly, 10*(2), 193–210.

Brown, B. A. T. 2001. Unpacking a timesheet: Formalisation and representation. *Computer Supported Cooperative Work*, *10*, 293–315.

Brown, J. S., and Duguid, P. 1994. Borderline issues: Social and material aspects of design. *Human-Computer Interaction*, *9*, 3–36.

Brown, J. S., and Duguid, P. 2000. *The social life of information*. Boston: Harvard Business School Press.

Button, G., and Dourish, P. 1996. Technomethodology: Paradoxes and possibilities. In M. J. Tauber, V. Bellotti, R. Jeffries, J. D. MacKinlay, and J. Nielsen, eds., *Human factors in computing systems: CHI '96 conference proceedings*, 19–26. New York: ACM.

Card, S. K., Moran, T. P., and Newell, A. 1983. *The psychology of human-computer interaction*. Hillsdale, NJ: Erlbaum.

Carroll, J., and Campbell, R. L. 1989. Artifacts as psychological theories: The case of human-computer interactions. *Behavioral and Information Technology*, *8*(4), 247–256.

Clement, A. 1994. Computing at work: Empowering action by "low-level" users. *Communications of the ACM*, *37*(1), 52–63.

Clement, A., and Van den Besselaar, P. 1993. A retrospective look at PD projects. *Communications of the ACM*, *36*(4), 29–37.

Coble, J. M., Maffitt, J. S., Orland, M. J., and Kahn, M. G. 1996. Using contextual inquiry to discover physicians' true needs. In D. Wixon and J. Ramey, eds., *Field methods casebook for software design*, 229–248. New York: Wiley.

Cole, M. 1996. *Cultural psychology: A once and future discipline*. Cambridge, MA: Belknap Press of Harvard University Press.

Cooper, G., and Bowers, J. 1995. Representing the user: Notes on the disciplinary rhetoric of human-computer interaction. In P. J. Thomas, ed., *The social and interactional dimensions of human-computer interfaces*, 48–66. New York: Cambridge University Press.

Cooper, G., Hine, C., Rachel, J., and Woolgar, S. 1995. Ethnography and human-computer interaction. In P. J. Thomas, ed., *The social and interactional dimensions of human-computer interfaces*, 11–36. New York: Cambridge University Press.

Doheny-Farina, S. 1996. *The wired neighborhood*. New Haven: Yale University Press.

Dumas, J. S., and Redish, J. 1993. *A practical guide to usability testing*. Norwood, NJ: Ablex.

Ehn, P. 1989. *Work-oriented design of computer artifacts*. Hillsdale, NJ: Erlbaum.

Ehn, P. 1993. Scandinavian design: On participation and skill. In D. Schuler and A. Namioka, eds., *Participatory design: Principles and practices*, 41–78. Hillsdale, NJ: Erlbaum.

Engeström, R. 1995. Voice as communicative action. *Mind, Culture, and Activity*, *2*(3), 192–214.

Engeström, Y. 1990. *Learning, working, and imagining: Twelve studies in activity theory.* Helsinki: Orienta-Konsultit Oy.

Engeström, Y. 1992. *Interactive expertise: Studies in distributed working intelligence.* Helsinki: University of Helsinki.

Engeström, Y. 1999a. Activity theory and individual and social transformation. In Y. Engeström, R. Miettinen, and R.-L. Punamäki, eds., *Perspectives on activity theory*, 19–38. New York: Cambridge University Press.

Engeström, Y. 1999b. Expansive visibilization of work: An activity-theoretical perspective. *Computer Supported Cooperative Work*, *8*, 63–93.

Engeström, Y., and Escalante, V. 1996. Mundane tool or object of affection? The rise and fall of the Postal Buddy. In B. A. Nardi, ed., *Context and consciousness: Activity theory and human-computer interaction.* Cambridge, MA: MIT Press.

Erickson, T. D. 1990. Working with interface metaphors. In B. Laurel and S. J. Mountford, eds., *The art of human-computer interface design*, 65–74. Reading, MA: Addison-Wesley.

Forsythe, D. E. 1999. "It's just a matter of common sense": Ethnography as invisible work. *Computer Supported Cooperative Work*, *8*, 127–145.

Freedman, A., Adam, C., and Smart, G. 1994. Wearing suits to class: Simulating genres and simulations as genre. *Written Communication*, *11*(2), 193–226.

Freedman, A., and Smart, G. 1997. Navigating the current of economic policy: Written genres and the distribution of cognitive work at a financial institution. *Mind, Culture, and Activity*, *4*(4), 238–255.

Geisler, C. 2001. Textual objects: Accounting for the role of texts in the everyday life of complex organizations. *Written Communication*, *18*(3), 296–325.

Geisler, C., Bazerman, C., Doheny-Farina, S., Gurak, L., Haas, C., Johnson-Eilola, J., Kaufer, D. S., Lunsford, A., Miller, C. R., Winsor, D., and Yates, J. 2001. IText: Further directions for research on the relationship between information technology and writing. *Journal of Business and Technical Communication*, *15*(3), 269–308.

Greatbatch, D., Heath, C., Luff, P., and Campion, P. 1995. Conversation analysis: Human-computer interaction and the general practice consultation. In A. F. Monk and G. N. Gilbert, eds., *Perspectives on HCI: Diverse approaches*, 199–222. New York: Academic Press.

Gronbæk, K., Grudin, J., Bødker, S., and Bannon, L. 1993. Achieving cooperative system design: Shifting from a product to a process focus. In D. Schuler and A. Namioka, eds., *Participatory design: Principles and practices*, 79–98. Hillsdale, NJ: Erlbaum.

Gronbæk, K., Kyng, M., and Mogensen, P. 1993. CSCW challenges: Cooperative design in engineering projects. *Communications of the ACM*, *36*(4), 67–77.

Haas, C. 1996. *Writing technology: Studies on the materiality of literacy*. Mahwah, NJ: Erlbaum.

Haas, C., and Witte, S. 2001. Writing as embodied practice: The case of engineering standards. *Journal of Business and Technical Communication, 15*(4), 413–457.

Hackos, J. T., Hammar, M., and Elser, A. 1997. Customer partnering: Data gathering for complex on-line documentation. *IEEE Transactions on Professional Communication, 40*(2), 102–110.

Hackos, J. T., and Redish, J. C. 1998. *User and task analysis for interface design*. New York: Wiley.

Hackos, J. T., Winstead, J. S., Gill, S., and Hartmann, M. 1995. Finding out what users need and giving it to them: A case-study at Federal Express. *Technical Communication, 42*(2), 322–327.

Hart-Davidson, W. 2001. On writing, technical communication, and information technology: The core competencies of technical communication. *Technical Communication, 48*(2), 145–155.

Hasu, M., and Engeström, Y. 2000. Measurement in action: An activity-theoretical perspective on producer-user interaction. *International Journal of Human-Computer Studies, 53*, 61–89.

Heath, C., and Luff, P. 1991. Collaborative activity and technical design: Task coordination in London underground control rooms. *Proceedings of the European Conference on Computer-Supported Cooperative Work: ECSCW '91*, 65–80. Amsterdam: Kluver Academic.

Heath, C., and Luff, P. 1996. Documents and professional practice: 'Bad' organizational reasons for 'good' clinical records. *CSCW '96 conference proceedings*, 354–363. New York: ACM.

Heath, C., and Luff, P. 2000. *Technology in action*. Cambridge: Cambridge University Press.

Henry, P. 1998. *User-centered information design for improved software usability*. Boston: Artech House.

Herzog, M. T. 1999. GIS technology and implementation. In S. Easa and Y. Chan, eds., *Urban planning and development applications of GIS*, 9–32. Reston, VA: American Society of Civil Engineers.

Holtzblatt, K., and Beyer, H. 1993. Making customer-centered design work for teams. *Communications of the ACM, 36*(10), 93–103.

Holtzblatt, K., and Beyer, H. 1996. Contextual design: Principles and practices. In D. Wixon and J. Ramey, eds., *Field methods casebook for software design*, 301–334. New York: Wiley.

Hovde, M. R. 2000. Tactics for building images of audience in organizational contexts. *Journal of Business and Technical Communication, 14*(4), 395–444.

Hutchins, E. 1995. *Cognition in the wild*. Cambridge, MA: MIT Press.

Hutchins, E. 1997. Mediation and automatization. In M. Cole, Y. Engeström, and O. Vasquez, eds., *Mind, culture, and activity: Seminal papers from the Laboratory of Comparative Human Cognition*, 338–353. New York: Cambridge University Press.

Iowa Department of Transportation. 1990. The DOT's shining STARS. *INSIDE* (December) 2.

Johnson, R. R. 1998. *User-centered technology: A rhetorical theory for computers and other mundane artifacts*. New York: SUNY Press.

Johnson-Eilola, J. 1997. Wild technologies: Computer use and social possibility. In S. A. Selber, ed., *Computers and technical communication: Pedagogical and programmatic perspectives*, 97–128. Greenwich, CT: Ablex.

Johnson-Eilola, J. 2001. Datacloud: Expanding the roles and locations of information. *SIGDOC 2001 conference proceedings*, 47–54. New York: ACM.

Kaptelinin, V., Nardi, B. A., and Macaulay, C. 1999. The activity checklist: A tool for representing the "space" of context. *interactions*, 6(4), 27–39.

Korpela, M., Mursu, A., and Soriyan, H. A. 2002. Information systems development as an activity. *Computer Supported Cooperative Work*, *11*, 111–128.

Kuutti, K. 1995. Work processes: Scenarios as a preliminary vocabulary. In J. M. Carroll, ed., *Scenario-based design: Envisioning work and technology in system development*, 19–36. New York: Wiley.

Kuutti, K. 1996. Activity theory as a potential framework for human-computer interaction research. In B. Nardi, ed., *Context and consciousness: Activity theory and human-computer interaction*, 17–44. Cambridge, MA: MIT Press.

Kuutti, K., and Bannon, L. 1991. Some confusions at the interface: Re-conceptualising the "interface" problem. In M. I. Nurminen and G. R. S. Weir, eds., *Human jobs and computer interfaces*, 3–19. Amsterdam: Elsevier/North-Holland.

Kuutti, K., and Bannon, L. 1993. Searching for unity among diversity: Exploring the "interface" concept. In S. Ashlund, K. Mullet, A. Henderson, E. Hollnagel, and T. White, eds., *Human factors in computing systems: CHI '93 conference proceedings*, 263–268. New York: ACM.

Kyng, M., and Mathiassen, L. 1997. *Computers and design in context*. Cambridge, MA: MIT Press.

Lave, J. 1988. *Cognition in practice: Mind, mathematics, and culture in everyday life*. New York: Cambridge University Press.

Lee, B. 1985. Intellectual origins of Vygotsky's semiotic analysis. In J. V. Wertsch, ed., *Culture, communication, and cognition: Vygotskian perspectives*, 66–93. New York: Cambridge University Press.

Leont'ev, A. N. 1978. *Activity, consciousness, and personality*. Englewood Cliffs, NJ: Prentice-Hall.

Leont'ev, A. N. 1981. *Problems of the development of mind*. Moscow: Progress.

Luff, P., and Heath, C. 1998. Mobility in collaboration. *CSCW '98 conference proceedings*, 305–314. New York: ACM.

Macaulay, C., Benyon, D., and Crerar, A. 2000. Ethnography, theory and systems design: From intuition to insight. *International Journal of Human-Computer Studies, 53*, 35–60.

McCarthy, J. 2000. The paradox of understanding work for design. *International Journal of Human-Computer Studies, 53*, 197–219.

Medvedev, P. N., and Bakhtin, M. M. 1978. *The formal method in literary scholarship: A critical introduction to sociological poetics.* Baltimore: Johns Hopkins University Press.

Miettinen, R. 1999. The riddle of things: Activity theory and actor-network theory as approaches to studying innovations. *Mind, Culture, and Activity, 6*(3), 170–195.

Millen, D. R. 2000. Rapid ethnography: Time deepening strategies for HCI field research, *DIS '00 conference proceedings*, 280–286. New York: ACM.

Miller, C. R. 1984. Genre as social action. *Quarterly Journal of Speech, 70*, 157–178.

Mirel, B. 1988. The politics of usability: The organizational functions of an in-house manual. In S. Doheny-Farina, ed., *Effective documentation: What we have learned from research*, 277–298. Cambridge, MA: MIT Press.

Mirel, B. 1996. Writing and database technology: Extending the definition of writing in the workplace. In P. Sullivan and J. Dautermann, eds., *Electronic literacies in the workplace: Technologies of writing*, 91–112. Urbana, IL: National Council of Teachers of English.

Mirel, B. 1998a. "Applied constructivism" for user documentation. *Journal of Business and Technical Communication, 12*(1), 7–49.

Mirel, B. 1998b. Visualizations for data exploration and analysis: A critical review of usability research. *Technical Communication, 45*(4), 491–509.

Moreland, S. 1992. An accident data nightmare relieved with PC-ALAS. *pc-trans* (Fall) 19–20.

Morson, G. S., and Emerson, C. 1990. *Mikhail Bakhtin: Creation of a prosaics.* Stanford, CA: Stanford University Press.

Muller, M. 1993. PICTIVE: Democratizing the dynamics of the design session. In D. Schuler and A. Namioka, eds., *Participatory design: Principles and practices*, 211–237. Hillsdale, NJ: Erlbaum.

Muller, M. J., Tudor, L. G., Wildman, D. M., White, E. A., Root, R. W., Dayton, T., Carr, R., Diekmann, B., and Dykstra-Erickson, E. A. 1995. Bifocal tools for scenarios and representations in participatory activities with users. In J. Carroll, ed., *Scenario-based design for human-computer interaction.* New York: Wiley.

Myers, G. 1990. *Writing biology: Texts in the social construction of scientific knowledge.* Madison: University of Wisconsin Press.

Nardi, B. A. 1993. *A small matter of programming: Perspectives on end user computing*. Cambridge, MA: MIT Press.

Nardi, B. A., ed. 1996. *Context and consciousness: Activity theory and human-computer interaction*. Cambridge, MA: MIT Press.

Nardi, B. A., and Engeström, Y. 1999. A web on the wind: The structure of invisible work. *Computer-Supported Cooperative Work, 8*, 1–8.

Nardi, B. A., and Miller, J. 1991. Twinkling lights and nested loops: Distributed problem solving and spreadsheet development. *International Journal of Man-Machine Studies, 34*, 161–184.

Nardi, B. A., and O'Day, V. L. 1999. *Information ecologies: Using technology with heart*. Cambridge, MA: MIT Press.

Nyce, J. M., and Lowgren, J. 1995. Toward foundational analysis in human-computer interaction. In P. J. Thomas, ed., *The social and interactional dimensions of human-computer interfaces*, 37–47. New York: Cambridge University Press.

Nystrand, M., Greene, S., and Wiemelt, J. 1993. Where did composition studies come from? An intellectual inquiry. *Written Communication, 10*, 267–333.

Orlikowski, W. J., and Yates, J. 1994. Genre repertoire: The structuring of communicative practices in organizations. *Administrative Science Quarterly, 39*, 541–574.

Pawlovich, M. D. 1996. *A geographic information system–based accident location and analysis system (GIS-ALAS)*. Unpublished master's thesis, Iowa State University, Ames.

Pawlovich, M. D., and Souleyrette, R. R. 1996, May. A GIS-based accident location and analysis system. Paper presented at the TRB semisesquicentennial transportation conference, Ames, IA.

Prior, P., and Shipka, J. 2002. Chronotopic lamination: Tracing the contours of literate activity. In C. Bazerman and D. R. Russell, eds., *Writing selves/Writing society*. Fort Collins, CO: The WAC Clearinghouse and Mind, Culture, and Activity. Available: ⟨http://wac.colostate.edu/books/selves_society/⟩.

Raeithel, A., and Velichkovsky, B. M. 1996. Joint attention and co-construction of tasks: New ways to foster user-designer collaboration. In B. A. Nardi, ed., *Context and consciousness: Activity theory and human-computer interaction*, 199–233. Cambridge, MA: MIT Press.

Ramey, J., Rowberg, A. H., and Robinson, C. 1996. Adaption of an ethnographic method for investigation of the task domain in diagnostic radiology. In D. Wixon and J. Ramey, eds., *Field methods casebook for software design*, 1–16. New York: Wiley.

Raven, M. E., and Flanders, A. 1996. Using contextual inquiry to learn about your audiences. *Journal of Computer Documentation, 20*(1), 1–13.

Rubin, J. 1994. *Handbook of usability testing*. New York: Wiley.

Rude, C. 1995. The report for decision making: Genre and inquiry. *Journal of Business and Technical Communication, 9*(2), 170–205.

Russell, D. 1995. Activity theory and its implications for writing instruction. In J. Petraglia, ed., *Reconceiving writing, rethinking writing instruction*, 51–77. Mahwah, NJ: Lawrence Erlbaum Associates.

Russell, D. R. 1997a. Rethinking genre in school and society: An activity theory analysis. *Written Communication, 14*(4), 504–554.

Russell, D. R. 1997b. Writing and genre in higher education and workplaces: A review of studies that use cultural-historical activity theory. *Mind, Culture, and Activity, 4*(4), 224–237.

Sachs, P. 1995. Transforming work: Collaboration, learning, and design. *Communications of the ACM, 38*(9), 36–44.

Salomon, G., ed. 1993. *Distributed cognitions: Psychological and educational implications*. Cambridge: Cambridge University Press.

Salvo, M. J. 2001. Ethics of engagement: User-centered design and rhetorical methodology. *Technical Communication Quarterly, 10*(3), 273–290.

Schmandt-Besserat, D. 1986. The origins of writing: An archaeologist's perspective. *Written Communication, 3*(1), 31–45.

Schriver, K. 1997. *Dynamics in document design: Creating texts for readers*. New York: Wiley.

Schryer, C. F. 1993. Records as genre. *Written Communication, 10*(2), 200–234.

Schryer, C. F. 2000. Walking a fine line: Writing negative letters in an insurance company. *Journal of Business and Technical Communication, 14*(4), 445–497.

Schuler, D., and Namioka, A., eds. 1993. *Participatory design: Principles and practices*. Hillsdale, NJ: Erlbaum.

Schuman, W. G., Strauss, T., Gieseman, D., and Souleyrette, R. R. 1998, August 19–20. Iowa Department of Transportation statewide coordinated GIS. Paper presented at the Crossroads 2000 Conference, Ames, IA.

Selfe, C., and Selfe, R. 1994. The politics of the interface: Power and its exercise in electronic contact zones. *College Composition and Communication, 45*, (480–504).

Sless, D. 1994. The Telecom bill: Redesigning a computer generated report. In R. Penman and D. Sless, eds., *Designing information for people: Proceedings from the symposium*, 2nd ed., 77–97. Fyshwick, Australia: Goanna Print.

Sless, D. 1998. Building the bridge across the years and disciplines. *Information Design Journal, 9*(1), 3–10.

Smart, G. 2002. A central bank's combined use of written/oral genres and technology to orchestrate its "communications strategy" in the arena of public policy. In C. Bazerman and D. R. Russell, eds., *Writing selves, writing society*. Available: ⟨http://wac.colostate.edu/books/writing_selves/⟩.

Smart, K. L., and Whiting, M. E. 2002. Using customer data to drive documentation design decisions. *Journal of Business and Technical Communication*, 16(2), 115–169.

Smart, K. L., Whiting, M. E., and DeTienne, K. B. 2002. Assessing the need for printed and online documentation: A study of customer preference and use. *Journal of Business Communication*, 38(3), 285–314.

Souleyrette, R. R., and Strauss, T. 1999. Transportation. In S. Easa and Y. Chan, eds., *Urban planning and development applications of GIS*, 117–132. Reston, VA: American Society of Civil Engineers.

Spinuzzi, C. 1996. Pseudotransactionality, activity theory, and professional writing instruction. *Technical Communication Quarterly*, 5(3), 295–308.

Spinuzzi, C. 2000. Exploring the blind spot: Audience, purpose, and context in "Product, process, and profit." *Journal of Computer Documentation*, 24(4), 213–219.

Spinuzzi, C. 2001a. Grappling with distributed usability: A cultural-historical examination of documentation genres over four decades. *Journal of Technical Writing and Communication*, 31(1), 41–59.

Spinuzzi, C. 2001b. "Light green doesn't mean hydrology!": Towards a visual-rhetorical framework for interface design. *Computers and Composition*, 18, 39–53.

Spinuzzi, C. 2001c. Software development as mediated activity: Applying three analytical frameworks for studying compound mediation. *SIGDOC 2001 conference proceedings*, 58–67. New York: ACM.

Spinuzzi, C. 2002a. Compound mediation in software development: Using genre ecologies to study textual artifacts. In C. Bazerman and D. R. Russell, eds, *Writing selves/Writing society*. Fort Collins, CO: The WAC Clearinghouse and Mind, Culture, and Activity. Available: ⟨http://wac.colostate.edu/books/selves_society/⟩.

Spinuzzi, C. 2002b. Documentation, participatory citizenship, and the web: The potential of open systems. *ACM SIGDOC 2002 Conference Proceedings*, 194–199. New York: ACM.

Spinuzzi, C. 2002c. Toward integrating our research scope: A sociocultural field methodology. *Journal of Business and Technical Communication*, 16(1), 3–32.

Spinuzzi, C. 2002d. Modeling genre ecologies. *ACM SIGDOC 2002 Conference Proceedings*, 200–207. New York: ACM.

Spinuzzi, C. 2002e. A Scandinavian challenge, a US response: Methodological assumptions in Scandinavian and US prototyping approaches, *ACM SIGDOC 2002 Conference Proceedings* (208–215). New York: ACM.

Spinuzzi, C., Bowie, J., Rogers, I., and Li, X. In preparation. Open systems and citizenship: Developing a departmental website as a civic forum. Unpublished manuscript.

Spinuzzi, C., and Zachry, M. 2000. Genre ecologies: An open-system approach to understanding and constructing documentation. *Journal of Computer Documentation, 24*(3), 169–181.

Star, S. L. 1995. The politics of formal representations: Wizards, gurus, and organizational complexity. In S. L. Star, ed., *Ecologies of knowledge: Work and politics in science and technology,* 88–118. Albany: SUNY Press.

Stowell, F., and West, D. 1994. *Client-Led Design: A systemic approach to information system design.* London: McGraw-Hill.

Suchman, L. A. 1987. *Plans and situated actions: The problem of human-machine communication.* New York: Cambridge University Press.

Suchman, L. A. 1995. Making work visible. *Communications of the ACM, 38*(9), 56–64.

Sullivan, P., and Porter, J. E. 1997. *Opening spaces: Writing technologies and critical research practices.* Greenwich, CT: Ablex.

Syverson, M. 1999. *The wealth of reality: An ecology of composition.* Carbondale: Southern Illinois University Press.

Terveen, L. G., Selfridge, P. G., and Long, M. D. 1995. Living design memory: Framework, implementation, lessons learned. *Human-Computer Interaction, 10,* 1–37.

Traffic and Highway Planning Department. 1961. *Analysis of fatal accidents in Iowa, 1961.* Ames, IA: Traffic and Highway Planning Department.

Traffic and Highway Planning Department. 1963. *Analysis of accidents involving fatalities in Iowa, 1963.* Ames, IA: Traffic and Highway Planning Department.

Tufte, E. R. 1983. *The visual display of quantitative information.* Cheshire, CT: Graphics Press.

Turner, P., Turner, S., and Horton, J. 1999. From description to requirements: An activity theoretic perspective. *GROUP 99 conference proceedings,* 286–295. New York: ACM.

Tyre, M. J., and Orlikowski, W. J. 1994, July. The myth of continuous improvement. *Chemtech,* 12–19.

Viller, S., and Sommerville, I. 2000. Ethnographically informed analysis for software engineers. *International Journal of Human-Computer Studies, 53,* 169–196.

Vygotsky, L. S. 1978. *Mind in society: The development of higher psychological processes.* Cambridge, MA: Harvard University Press.

Wertsch, J. V. 1998. *Mind as action.* New York: Oxford University Press.

Wilbur Smith and Associates. 1972. *Development phase: Accident location and accident analysis systems.* Houston: Wilbur Smith and Associates.

Wilbur Smith and Associates. 1974a. *Accident location and analysis system user's manual.* Houston: Wilbur Smith and Associates.

Wilbur Smith and Associates. 1974b. *Phase I implementation: Accident location and analysis system.* Houston: Wilbur Smith and Associates.

Winograd, T., and Flores, F. 1986. *Understanding computers and cognition: A new foundation for design.* Norwood, NJ: Ablex.

Winsor, D. A. 1996. *Writing like an engineer: A rhetorical education.* Mahwah, NJ: Erlbaum.

Winsor, D. A. 1999. Genre and activity systems: The role of documentation in maintaining and changing engineering activity systems. *Written Communication,* 16(2), 200–224.

Winsor, D. A. 2001. Learning to do knowledge work in systems of distributed cognition. *Journal of Business and Technical Communication,* 15(1), 5–28.

Wixon, D., and Ramey, J, eds. 1996. *Field methods casebook for software design.* New York: Wiley.

Wolfe, J. L., and Neuwirth, C. M. 2001. From the margins to the center: The future of annotation. *Journal of Business and Technical Communication,* 15(3), 333–371.

Wood, J., and Silver, D. 1995. *Joint application development.* 2nd ed. New York: Wiley.

Yamauchi, Y., Yokozawa, M., Shinohara, T., and Ishida, T. 2000. Collaboration with lean media: How open-source software succeeds. *CSCW '00 conference proceedings,* 329–338. Philadelphia: ACM.

Yates, J. 1989. *Control through communication: The rise of system in American management.* Baltimore: Johns Hopkins University Press.

Yates, J., and Orlikowski, W. 2002. Genre systems: Structuring interaction through communicative norms. *Journal of Business Communication,* 39(1), 13–35.

Zachry, M. 2000. The ecology of an online education site in professional communication. In T. J. Malkinson, ed., *SIGDOC 2000 conference proceedings,* 433–442. New York: ACM.

Zachry, M. 2001a. Constructing usable documentation: A study of communicative practices and the early uses of mainframe computing in industry. *Journal of Technical Writing and Communication,* 31(1), 61–76.

Zachry, M. 2001b. User-centered design: Promise and peril for next generation technical communicators. Paper presented at SIGDOC 2001, Santa Fe, NM.

Zuboff, S. 1988. *In the age of the smart machine: The future of work and power.* New York: Basic Books.

Index